CROSSING OVER

An Oral History of Refugees from Hitler's Reich

TWAYNE'S
ORAL HISTORY SERIES

Donald A. Ritchie, Series Editor

PREVIOUSLY PUBLISHED

Rosie the Riveter Revisited: Women, the War, and Social Change
Sherna Berger Gluck

Witnesses to the Holocaust: An Oral History
Rhoda Lewin

Hill Country Teacher: Oral Histories from the One-Room School and Beyond
Diane Manning

The Unknown Internment: An Oral History of the Relocation of Italian Americans
during World War II
Stephen Fox

Peacework: Oral Histories of Women Peace Activists
Judith Porter Adams

Grandmothers, Mothers, and Daughters: Oral Histories of Three Generations of
Ethnic American Women
Corinne Azen Krause

Homesteading Women: An Oral History of Colorado, 1890–1950
Julie Jones-Eddy

The Hispanic-American Entrepreneur: An Oral History of the American Dream
Beatrice Rodriguez Owsley

Infantry: An Oral History of a World War II American Infantry Battalion
Richard M. Stannard

Between Management and Labor: Oral Histories of Arbitration
Clara H. Friedman

Building Hoover Dam: An Oral History of the Great Depression
Andrew J. Dunar and Dennis McBride

From the Old Country: An Oral History of European Migration to America
Bruce M. Stave and John F. Sutherland with Aldo Salerno

Married to the Foreign Service: An Oral History of the American Diplomatic Spouse
Jewell Fenzi with Carl L. Nelson

Her Excellency: An Oral History of American Women Ambassadors
Ann Miller Morin

Doing Oral History
Donald A. Ritchie

Head of the Class: An Oral History of African-American Achievement in Higher
Education and Beyond
Gabrielle Morris

Children of Los Alamos: An Oral History of the Town Where the Atomic Age Began
Katrina R. Mason

A Stranger's Supper: An Oral History of Centenarian Women from Montenegro
Zorka Milich

RUTH E. WOLMAN

CROSSING OVER

An Oral History of
Refugees from
Hitler's Reich

T W A Y N E   P U B L I S H E R S
An Imprint of Simon & Schuster Macmillan
New York

PRENTICE HALL INTERNATIONAL
London   Mexico City   New Delhi   Singapore   Sydney   Toronto

Twayne's Oral History Series No. 21

Crossing Over: An Oral History of Refugees from Hitler's Reich
Ruth E. Wolman

Twayne Publishers
An Imprint of Simon & Schuster Macmillan
1633 Broadway
New York, New York 10019

Library of Congress Cataloging-in-Publication Data

Crossing over : an oral history of refugees from Hitler's Reich / Ruth E.
Wolman
    p.   cm.—(Twayne's oral history series; no. 21)
    Includes bibliographical references (p.) and index.
    ISBN 0-8057-4584-X (alk. paper)
    1. Jews, German—California—Los Angeles—Interviews. 2. Jews, Austrian—
California—Los Angeles—Interviews. 3. Refugees, Jewish—California—Los
Angeles—Interviews. 4. Holocaust, Jewish (1939–1945)—Germany—Personal
narratives. 5. Holocaust, Jewish (1939–1945)—Austria—Personal narratives. 6.
Oral history. 7. Los Angeles (Calif.)—Ethnic relations.
    I. Wolman, Ruth E. II. Series.
    F869.L89J534 1995
    979.4'94004924—dc20   95-22021
                                                                CIP

The paper used in this publication meets the minimum requirements of American
National Standard for Information Sciences—Permanence of Paper for Printed
Library Materials. ANSI Z39.48–1984.∞ ™

10 9 8 7 6 5 4 3 2 1

Printed in the United States of America

In memory of

Marianne Wolman, my mother,
who took many opportunities
to share stories of her life

and of the millions who were never able to do so

Jews waiting for exit visas at a police station in Vienna, Austria, March 1938.

Contents

Foreword   ix
Preface   xi
Acknowledgments   xv
Photographs and Credits   xvii
Introduction   xix

The Interviews   1
    Marianne Wolman   3
    Otto Wolman   25
    Gerty Frankel   51
    Fritz Frankel   77
    Ann "Annchen" Ikenberg   93
    Irene and Paul Dreyfuss   115
    Eva and Rudy Brook   123
    Theja Sommer   129
    Ernie Sommer   147
    Frank Bauer   169
    Martha Schwarz   185
    John Lesser   201
    Annie and Joseph "Sepp" Lampl   213
    Hedy Wolf   231
    Ernest Wolf   243

Epilogue   253
Appendix A: Timeline of Some Key Events during the Third Reich   257
Appendix B: European Landmarks of the Gruppe   259
Appendix C: Immigration Routes of the Gruppe   261
Appendix D: Gruppe Connections   263
Glossary   265
Selected Bibliography   267
Index   269

Foreword

The interviews in *Crossing Over* operate on two levels. First, they compose a study of the *Gruppe,* a circle of Jewish couples who settled in Los Angeles after emigrating from Germany and Austria to escape Nazi rule. Only a few members of the *Gruppe* had known one another before crossing over; they came together in their new community for mutual support. Second, the interviews are family histories, told by an older generation to their children. For some of these first-generation Americans, assimilated into the culture themselves, this would be the first time they would hear a complete account of their parents' transition to the New World. These oral histories recall family, friends, schools, jobs, and courtships from the *Gruppe* members' earlier lives in Europe; the shock of a new, anti-Semitic political regime; the decision to make an escape; and the difficulty of becoming established in a society so different from that left behind. The *Gruppe* provided these immigrants with a network of support as they entered new occupations, raised families, and persevered. The interviews speak both to the experiences of the many Jews who abandoned Europe for America during Hitler's rise to power and to the experiences of those people who continue to migrate to the United States for political reasons.

Oral history may well be the twentieth century's substitute for the written memoir. In exchange for the immediacy of diaries or correspondence, the retrospective interview offers a dialogue between the participant and the informed interviewer. Having prepared sufficient preliminary research, interviewers can direct the discussion into areas long since "forgotten" or no longer considered of consequence. "I haven't thought about that in years" is a common response, uttered just before an interviewee commences with a surprisingly detailed description of some past incident. The quality of the interview, its candidness and depth, generally will depend as much on the interviewer as the interviewee, and the confidence and rapport between the two adds a special dimension to the spoken memoir.

Interviewers represent a variety of disciplines and work either as part of a collective effort or individually. Regardless of their different interests or the variety of their subjects, all interviewers share a common imperative: to collect memories while they are still available. Most oral historians feel an additional responsibility to make their interviews accessible for use beyond their own research needs. Still, important collections of vital, vibrant interviews lie scattered in archives throughout every state, undiscovered or simply not used.

Twayne's Oral History Series seeks to identify those resources and to publish selections of the best materials. The series lets people speak for themselves, from their own unique perspectives on people, places, and events. But to be more than a babble of voices, each volume organizes its interviews around particular situations and events and ties them together with interpretive essays that place individuals into a larger historical context. The styles and format of individual volumes vary with the material from which they are drawn, demonstrating again the diversity of oral history and its methodology.

Whenever oral historians gather in conference, they enjoy retelling experiences about the inspiring individuals they have met, the unexpected information they have elicited, and the unforgettable reminiscences that would otherwise have never been recorded. The result invariably reminds listeners of others who deserve to be interviewed, provides them with models of interviewing techniques, and inspires them to make their own contribution to the field. I trust that the oral historians in this series—as interviewers, editors, and interpreters—will have a similar effect on their readers.

DONALD A. RITCHIE
Series Editor, Senate Historical Office

Preface

It was lunch break outside a Los Angeles furniture factory in the fall of 1942. One manual laborer noticed the leather attaché case from which another worker took his sandwiches. Recognizing such a case to be that of a fellow European, he walked across the yard to greet the other man. So began the friendship of two refugees, a former Austrian lawyer and a former German judge. The two men began to talk. Excited by this camaraderie, they met outside work with their wives. Shortly after, three immigrant couples got together, then five. The *Gruppe* began to meet regularly and to grow in size.

Participants in the *Gruppe* were Austrian and German Jews who had fled Europe at the brink of the Holocaust, between the years 1938 and 1941. They were not "survivors" in the strictest sense, if that term requires extensive confinement in a Nazi concentration camp. More precisely, they were Hitler refugees. While most Jews who came to the United States at that time settled in New York, these were among the few who chose to settle in Los Angeles. Fifty years later, the voices of 18 of these immigrants are recorded in this collection of oral histories gathered either through direct interview or by report from their children. All focus on their lives during the years of transition, from the rise of Hitler in 1933 to the end of the war in 1945.

The *Gruppe* did not coalesce simply by virtue of prior friendship and/or common national origin. Although a few members had been close friends in Europe and some had been casually acquainted, most met for the first time in Los Angeles. In its heyday, the *Gruppe* included about 36 people. Membership was selective, and to be invited, as one woman noted, "you had to be intelligent and able to discuss cultural, economic, and political issues." The *Gruppe* met initially to keep their "intellectual knives sharp" and to find relief from the drudgery and mental dulling of physical work. The members were, for the most part, very well educated. Some had just completed their professional studies, while others had not quite, before university doors were closed to Jews. They were in their late 20s or early 30s. Most had been well assimilated into the daily life of their predominantly Christian European communities. Almost all were liberal or socialist in their political outlook. Some were ardent Zionists; a few were anti-Zionists. All identified strongly with the cultural richness of their heritage.

The *Gruppe* met monthly, always with a topic for discussion. Either a member or an occasional guest gave a speech and then led the ensuing exchange. The gatherings culminated in a social hour for dessert and casual conversation. Members began to socialize outside scheduled meetings. Some lived in the same neighborhood, even within walking distance. As friendships developed and children were born, the *Gruppe* became an extended family for these immigrants who had lost members of their own families in the ravages of emigration and the Holocaust. Some shared holidays, birthdays, and even vacations.

By the end of the 1940s, discussion evenings became less regular. Families had moved farther apart, although almost all remained in the Los Angeles area. But the friendships continued and many grew stronger. Some of the children became friends and two even married each other. To this day, members of both generations (and also some in the third) provide support for one another in times of joy and sorrow. As the *Gruppe,* they celebrated their fiftieth anniversary and continue to get together annually for New Year's Eve.

My interest in gathering histories of the *Gruppe* members is traceable to a song I heard in an oral history workshop. "Tell me your story . . . " began the song, which continued with themes of immigration, rootlessness, and the value of sharing one's life story. As a participant in the workshop, I was asked to note my thoughts while listening to the song. I wrote, "It reminds me of the years when I tried so hard to assimilate, to be just like the kids around me. I did not like being the only child in class whose parents were immigrants, Jews, Democrats, nonsmokers, nondrinkers, both working, etc. My parents encouraged me to be like other children, while no doubt they tried to be more like the American adults whom they met. Many years passed before I began to feel comfortable with the ways in which I was different. That happened when I observed that people could really be interested in hearing about these differences." Certainly issues of being a first-generation American are central to any story I now tell of myself.

Given the impetus of this workshop experience, I wanted to learn more about my heritage. I decided to interview my parents, to record what they would tell about their lives. Immigration years were of particular interest to me, and I had not heard much about this period. I wondered if other children of the *Gruppe* had the same interest. In the summer of 1989, I arranged a meeting with several of them. It was immediately evident that as children of Hitler refugees we shared some disquieting "baggage" and that we were eager for a forum in which to discuss it. Also, we each felt deprived of a portion of personal history. My unfamiliarity with my parents' past was not unique. We made a list of questions with which to structure interviews with our parents. I edited these questions and added others—some that interested me as a psychologist and a few that I borrowed from the oral history workshop.

Each interview would begin with an open-ended question: "What was your life like during the few years before immigration?" And later, "What was your life like during the first years in Los Angeles?" We wanted to understand how our parents had experienced those years in practical and emotional terms. Beyond addressing these transition years, questions extended to other issues: feelings of "being at home" in the world, use of German language, sense of identity (European, American, Jewish, enemy alien), ability to adapt, role of the *Gruppe,* experiences of anti-Semitism in the United States, return to city or town of childhood, awareness of destruction of European Jewry during the war, and inclination to talk about the immigration period.

Although the plan was for each person to interview his or her own parents (or grandparents), I conducted most of the interviews in their entirety and completed those begun by others. Fourteen members of the *Gruppe* were alive and all were willing to participate. The histories of two couples who had died were written by their children, relying on memory and whatever they could find in writing by their parents.

A benefit of doing so much of the interviewing myself was that it gave me the opportunity to know the older generation of the *Gruppe* in a new way. As an adult, I could now talk individually and at length with exceptional people whom I had known all my life and taken for granted. I also enjoyed an intimacy with them as I transcribed the interviews. Sometimes long into the night, I listened to their taped voices telling me about adjustments to uncertain and often threatening conditions, adventures, fears, loneliness, pain, and sadness; also about hope, optimism, and excitement. It was fascinating to hear how a similar set of circumstances could affect people so differently. Personality and style were reflected in what each person remembered and in how they reported their experiences, choices, and feelings. Not surprisingly, the histories told by husbands and wives often included discrepant, sometimes even conflicting, details.

The process of editing the transcripts was a challenging one. Each participant took a first and generally cursory pass at this. Then I had to decide how much to include, how polished it should be, and how to make it most coherent to other readers. I wanted the written words to reflect each speaker's style, but still be certain they flowed smoothly. Although I did make many changes, the contributors clearly remain the authors of their histories. The reader may feel that the interviewer's questions often redirected the conversation rather abruptly. Indeed that *was* frequently the case. The effect is exaggerated here because, in the interest of space, I have omitted many connecting phrases. In other cases, it is because questions and answers have been excluded.

Throughout the book, wherever one contributor refers to another (except to the spouse), the name of the latter appears in boldface type. This should help the reader to follow the interplay between *Gruppe* members. Also, when an interviewer is someone other than myself, that interviewer's name is designated. I encourage the reader to examine the appendixes prior to reading the interviews. They include a timeline of key events during the Third Reich, maps that illustrate geographical landmarks in Europe and immigration routes cited in personal histories, and a diagram depicting the initial social connections of *Gruppe* members.

What cannot be simply illustrated is the severing, if not obliteration, of family ties that each of these people experienced because of the Nazi scourge. Individual family trees, however, do provide powerful graphic documentation of the carnage wrought by the Holocaust. With each contributor to this book, I drafted family trees that portray the generations beginning with their grandparents. The truncated limbs of these trees convey with a visceral impact what words and statistics cannot. . . . As I recorded the names of family members who perished during those years and placed the *Magen David* (Jewish star) next to their names, tears welled up inside me. So very many snuffed-out lives. So many untold stories. I feel gratified that I have been instrumental in recording a few histories, in words that will not be lost to the families and friends of the contributors or to others who may be interested.

In the following pages, a select group of refugees tell how they persevered through extreme personal and national trauma, relocation, and adaptation. They speak of persecution, the threat of annihilation, the decision to flee, the search for refuge, and then the struggle to adjust to an often bewildering new country and the pain and joy of putting down new roots. Among the "fortunate" of Hitler's victims, those who got out "in time," they are a tiny fragment of the vast Jewish community that Hitler sought to destroy.

Acknowledgments

Deep and heartfelt thanks to all members of the *Gruppe* for giving so generously of themselves by sharing their stories with me and their children and for doing the initial editing of the transcripts. Thank you to Miriam Rogson, Judy Navon, Vincent Brook, Debbie Kirshbaum, Sybil Goldenblank, and Lanny Lampl for contributions of interviewing and writing. Thanks also to India Koopman, my Twayne editor, whose facility to turn a phrase has gracefully enhanced the original manuscript.

Photographs and Credits

Jews waiting for exit visas at a police station in Vienna, Austria, March 1938. Photo: Österreichisches Institut für Zeitgeschichte, Wien, Bildarchiv, courtesy of the United States Holocaust Memorial Museum. Page vi.

Marianne Wolman. Photo by Kenneth Rabiroff. Page 3.

Otto Wolman. Photo by Ruth E. Wolman. Page 25.

Otto and Marianne Wolman, London, 1939. Page 48.

Otto and Marianne Wolman, Pasadena, 1992. Page 49.

Gerty Frankel. Photo by Ruth E. Wolman. Page 51.

Fritz Frankel. Photo by Ruth E. Wolman. Page 77.

Fritz and Gerty Frankel, Los Angeles, 1940. Page 84.

Ann Ikenberg. Photo by Ruth E. Wolman. Page 93.

Ann Ikenberg with her husband, Fred, Los Angeles, 1939. Page 102.

Irene and Paul Dreyfuss, Switzerland, 1974. Photo by Michael Dreyfuss. Page 115.

Irene and Paul Dreyfuss, Catania, Italy, 1936. Page 122.

Eva and Rudy Brook, Los Angeles, 1982. Page 123.

Eva and Rudy Brook, Los Angeles, 1942. Page 126.

Theja Sommer. Photo by Ruth E. Wolman. Page 129.

Theja and Ernie Sommer, Dresden, Germany, 1935. Page 133.

Ernie Sommer. Photo by Ruth E. Wolman. Page 147.

Theja and Ernie Sommer, Los Angeles, 1987. Page 166.

Frank Bauer. Photo by Ruth E. Wolman. Page 169.

Frank Bauer and his wife, Magda, Los Angeles, 1940. Page 175.

Magda and Frank Bauer, Los Angeles, 1987. Page 183.

Martha Schwarz. Photo by Ruth E. Wolman. Page 185.

Martha Schwarz and her husband, Kurt, Shanghai, China, 1943. Page 192.

Martha and Kurt Schwarz, Los Angeles, 1984. Page 198.

John Lesser. Photo by Ruth E. Wolman. Page 201.

John Lesser and his wife, Ruth, on their wedding day, Vienna, 1934. Page 202.

John and Ruth Lesser, Los Angeles, 1983. Page 210.

Annie and "Sepp" Lampl. Photo by Ruth E. Wolman. Los Angeles, 1995. Page 213.

Annie and "Sepp" Lampl, Los Angeles, 1940. Page 228.

Hedy Wolf. Photo by Ruth E. Wolman. Page 231.

Ernest Wolf, 1991. Page 243.

Ernest and Hedy Wolf, Sweden, 1940. Page 245.

Introduction

"No other immigration in American history has given us such a tremendous proportion of talent as the German-Austrian immigration of 1938."[1] An extravagant statement indeed, but one that is supported by Anthony Heibut's *Exiled in Paradise*, in which he documents the many well-known artists, scientists, psychoanalysts, Hollywood figures, and other luminaries who came to the United States and prospered.[2] A more modest claim would assert that the refugees fleeing Hitler's Reich during the 1930s were unlike any previous immigrant group. They tended to be middle and upper class, highly educated, cultured, and cosmopolitan. The number of professionals among them was unprecedented; likewise the many independent proprietors, government officials, and other white-collar workers. The men and women of the *Gruppe* represent a microcosm of that immigration, albeit not of its "illustrious." As in the larger group, the skills and talents of these people, intended for expression in their homeland, were diverted to the United States.

These Jews had been living in the golden age of European Jewish history. Although Jews had resided in Europe for 2,000 years, the six decades prior to Hitler's assumption of power had been the first in which Jews of Germany and Austria enjoyed the official "privilege" of civil and political equality. During that interlude, they expressed long-restrained energy and skill in every sphere of activity. Jewish life seemed almost inextricably interwoven with the cultural, intellectual, economic, scientific, and even political mainstream. Intermarriage was widespread (estimated at 25 percent of Jews marrying in Germany in 1930); so was conversion.[3] Jewish artists, writers, scholars, scientists, and other professionals thrived in a new climate of openness. They were recipients of a remarkable number of Nobel Prizes. Jews became the dominating force in the powering of the lagging Austrian economy as they developed industries, transportation systems, banking, and international trade. And when World War I enveloped the two countries, Jews participated and died in disproportionate numbers, despite propaganda claiming the opposite.[4]

The aftermath of that war proved to be disastrous for the Jews. Germany was in the grip of economic depression, massive unemployment, social unrest, and national bitterness from both military defeat and the demands imposed by the Versailles Treaty. The climate was ripe for a charismatic leader who promised guidance out of despair, who preached the racial superiority of the Germans, and who played upon the increasing anti-Semitic sentiment that blamed Jews for economic calamity. Through seduction and intimidation, Hitler was appointed chancellor of the German Reich in early 1933. Within a few months, the Nazis (National Socialist Party) were well on the path to total dictatorship. This period was marked by mass arrests of trade-unionists; suppression of free speech and all political opposition; opening of the first concentration camps, where those arrested were held without trial; purging of opponents of the regime from civil service positions (including teachers); gutting of the judicial system and establishment of a People's Court answerable only to Hitler; and, of course, the first steps of an orchestrated policy of persecution against German Jews.[5] Within 12 years, Jewish life in Europe would be virtually destroyed.

Prior to that time, acts of violence against Jews had been isolated and sporadic. Official persecution began in April 1933 with the first of 400 separate pieces of legislation enacted between then and 1939 that defined, isolated, excluded, and impoverished German Jews.[6] Jewish businesses and shops were to be boycotted throughout the country. Jews were dismissed from civil service positions. In the following month, Jews were dismissed from universities and the press. Jewish books and books written by opponents of Nazism were destroyed in huge public bonfires. The Nuremberg Race Laws of 1935 stripped German Jews of citizenship. Only those who were Aryan by race were entitled to civil and political rights. (This was the first time in history that Jews were persecuted for so-called racial identity rather than religious belief.[7]) Jewish physicians were forbidden to treat non-Jews. Jewish lawyers were forbidden to practice at all. In the fall of 1938, the regime took another step to deprive Jews of any means of livelihood. Jewish businesses still in existence were taken over by Aryans, bought for a pittance, the Jewish workers and managers dismissed. Most Jews no longer had economic means of existing, having been expelled from the professions, businesses, the arts, schools, and unions. Additionally, legal contracts between Jew and non-Jew were no longer binding.[8]

The neighboring country of Austria had also been also decimated by economic crisis and political turmoil after World War I. There were doubts about the country's ability to survive as an independent nation. Although Nazism was officially outlawed in Austria, Nazi sentiment there rapidly increased as Hitler's power escalated in Germany; Nazis in Austria became bolder in expressing their beliefs and in conducting military training exercises.

Uncertain of his control, in part because the previous chancellor had been assassinated by Nazi storm troopers, Chancellor Kurt von Schuschnigg met with Hitler in February 1938 to strike a bargain: Hitler would guarantee Austria's independence, provided Austria's Nazis could operate legally. Just one month later Hitler's troops were at the border with an ultimatum—allow Nazis already in the cabinet to take over, or go to war.

As Schuschnigg was resigning via radio broadcast, the streets filled with rampaging Nazis, shouting and attacking Jewish-looking people. With stunning alacrity, Hitler's troops occupied the country. **Marianne Wolman** describes this event, the *Anschluss:* "One evening, I think it was March 12, 1938, Hitler marched into Austria. I was teaching, preparing my students for the high school equivalency exam. The windows were open and all of a sudden we heard shouting: 'Down with the Jews! Kill the Jews!' And we heard steps going in a long parade. When I went downstairs to go home, there were many people in the street. All those that I saw wore a swastika and I wondered, 'How had they done this so quickly?' "

Already on that first night, all Jews entering railway stations and airports were arrested. By the next morning, flags with swastikas were flying from the rooftops as storm troopers "patrolled" the streets. Violence and harassment ran riot throughout Vienna. Homes, businesses, and shops were looted, their owners mistreated and arrested. It was not safe to be in the streets, at work, or at home.

Hitler was received warmly by the native Austrian population. After declaring the absorption of Austria into the Third Reich, he visited Vienna and was cheered along the streets by a half-million supporters, nearly one third of the city's population.[9] These were surely not all Nazis, but, as Benno Weiser Varon writes in his autobiography, "the collapse of the Empire and the depression-induced poverty had produced a national inferiority complex, and the idea of exchanging the has-been Austrian nationality for that of Germany, which under the vigorous Nazi leadership had emerged as one of Europe's greatest powers, did not lack attraction."[10]

Virtually overnight, the Austrian Jews were driven out of the professions, from all public and most private employment. Jewish children were expelled from public schools. Persecution was not the only thing on the Nazis' mind; plunder was an even greater priority, for the German economy was being strained in preparation for war. Rich and prominent Jews were prime targets of Nazi wrath. They were subjected to all sorts of taxes, ransoms, and confiscations. Jewish-owned businesses were ransacked. The outer districts of Vienna were made *judenrein* (free of Jews) by mass evictions. By the end of that first year of occupation, 60 percent of all Jewish homes and apartments in Vienna had been taken over for use by Aryans.[11] Following the pattern established in Germany, Jewish businesses were Aryanized (that is, ownership was transferred to non-Jews). The dismantling of the Jewish community, which had taken place over the previous six years in Germany, took only one year in Austria.

Given the degree of wrath executed upon the Jews of Germany and Austria, one would think they must have been a great threat in terms of number and power. The reality was that when Hitler came to power, Jews in Germany numbered less than 1 percent of the population, in Austria, 3 percent. In early 1938, of Germany's 65 million residents, 500,000 were Jews; of Austria's 7 million, 185,000 were Jews. The vast majority of Austrian Jews lived in Vienna, where they comprised 10 percent of the population.[12] Many there were visible, well positioned and accomplished, but certainly not endangering the well-being of others. It is interesting to note that various sources report significant differences in population. This may be due to difficulties in documenting "Jewishness," given that intermarriage was so widespread.

In the fall of 1938, Hitler stepped up operations to expand the Reich and to expel Jews. By threatening invasion of Czechoslovakia, he was able to annex the Sudetenland, that portion of the country that had German-speaking citizens, albeit a minority in the territory. In the same month, all Polish citizens living in Germany were summarily expelled. Polish guards denied them entry at the border, and German police wouldn't allow them back into Germany. A makeshift camp was thrown together at the border until the situation could be resolved. The parents of a 17-year-old Polish student living in Paris were among the first group to be rounded up and deported to this no-man's-land. In desperation, Herschel Grynszpan went to the German Embassy to seek revenge. He intended to kill the ambassador. Instead, on November 7, he shot a minor embassy official. Ernst vom Rath's death was just the excuse needed for "retaliative" acts of vengeance to be inflicted on the Jews of the Reich. Mob violence was officially sanctioned as all hell broke loose.

Kristallnacht (night of broken glass), November 9–10, 1938, was a full-scale pogrom unleashed across the cities and towns of Germany and in annexed Austria. The destruction was staggering: more than 1,000 synagogues burned; more than 7,000 Jewish businesses trashed and looted; many Jewish schools, cemeteries, hospitals, and homes destroyed or Aryanized; nearly 100 Jews killed and thousands subjected to wanton and sadistic torments. The attackers were often neighbors. At the same time, 30,000–35,000 men were arrested and incarcerated in three concentration camps—Buchenwald, Dachau, and Sachsenhausen—recently expanded to accommodate such an influx of prisoners.[13]

Ernie Sommer was returning home that fateful night, after an unsuccessful attempt in Hamburg to procure a visa to Cuba.

> I took the train back to Dresden. People got on at Leipzig and said, "The Jewish synagogue is in flames. They are plundering the Schoken warehouse." I did not know then that it was an organized action throughout the country.

When I got to Dresden and took the streetcar home, I came by the place where the synagogue was. But there was no synagogue anymore. There were just burnt-out walls. I got out and mixed with hundreds of celebrating people. They didn't recognize that I was Jewish. Standing in front of the shell of that burnt-out synagogue, I saw one of the most terrifying views I ever have encountered. The elders of the temple, dressed in *talleisim* [shawl-like garments] and high silk hats, each carrying a half-burnt Torah, were forced to parade back and forth. The howling masses were making fun of them and shouting insults against Jews. I was standing there and my insides were screaming. It was too dangerous to open my mouth.

Ann Ikenberg and her husband, Fred, lived in Düsseldorf, next door to the chief rabbi.

Arrests began at the rabbi's house. We were prepared. We had our identification papers, all papers for America, affidavits, and some money in our attaché case. We walked right by the Nazis on the front steps. They ignored us, not realizing we were Jews. We walked the whole night through the city! I'll never forget the sight of fire burning through the *Magen David* on top of the synagogue. I had a feeling I can't describe to you. As we walked, people started plundering stores and said to me, "*Fräulein, warum nehmen Sie sich denn nichts?*" [Young girl, why don't you take anything for yourself?] People took whatever was in the stores. . . . After walking all night, I went back to our apartment. Fred wouldn't go back (and never did). The apartment was in shambles. When the Nazis had come to our door and nobody answered, they were so mad that they kicked in the door. They had smashed all our silver and crystal. I quickly packed two suitcases of our belongings, and we left for the village of Fred's parents.

In the aftermath of *Kristallnacht,* the Nazi leadership imposed a fine of 1 billion reichsmarks (equivalent to $400 million) on the remaining Jewish population for the assassination of vom Rath and an additional 250 million reichsmarks for "cleanup" expenses.[14]

Needless to say, the horror of this event dramatically illustrated that survival was contingent on emigration and provided additional impetus in that direction. Jewish exodus from Germany had already begun in 1933 as a flight of panic in reaction to the Nazi accession to power. Thirty-seven thousand had left that first year, primarily to neighboring European countries, hoping to eventually return home. Fewer emigrated in each of the subsequent four years.[15] But in 1938, as the Nazis tightened their grip, the pace increased greatly, such that by year's end half of the 1933 Jewish population had left Germany.[16] By the time war broke out in September 1939, three-fifths of the population had emigrated.[17] In Austria, emigration began immediately after the *Anschluss* in early 1938. By the end of the year, 66,000 of the

185,000 Jews had left; by the end of 1939, two-thirds of Austria's Jews had fled.[18]

It is important to keep in mind that escape from Germany or Austria did not guarantee survival. Many people simply delayed their demise by going legally or illegally to nearby countries that subsequently fell to the Nazis. But for the fortunate, that emigration led to a new home or at least a temporary safe haven while waiting for a visa to another country. At least half the people in the *Gruppe* immigrated first to countries that were more accessible than the United States, hoping these would be stepping stones to America.

The numbers tell nothing of the personal agony and bureaucratic maze that each individual experienced while contemplating whether and how to emigrate and while going through the subsequent process of trying to do so. "Emigration was a traditional Jewish response to persecution, but in 1933 in Germany, emigration—or flight—was an individual decision, not communal policy."[19] Nazi accession to power was a profound shock to the acculturated German Jews. Most were fiercely patriotic and felt more deeply German than Jewish. So long as they experienced no significant physical mistreatment and were still able to earn a livelihood, most were determined to remain in their homeland, whose future was their own.[20] It was inconceivable that a legal government could destroy them. Others reasoned that because they (or their fathers) had fought for their country in World War I, they would be given preferential treatment. (This *was* the case, but only temporarily.) For most, a decision to wrench oneself away from all that was loved and familiar was too much to consider—until the conditions became so bad that fear of the consequences of remaining became overwhelming.

The Nazi regime wanted Jews out of the country and initially did not inhibit departure beyond imposing a 25 percent flight tax on all money and goods the refugees took with them (shipped, transferred out of the country, or hand carried). In fact, with documentation that supported imminent emigration, concentration camp inmates were sometimes released. But by 1938–39, for those who made the decision to leave—or rather, to try to leave—the obstacles were formidable. Bureaucratic barriers were extraordinary, insurmountable for many.

To leave Germany or Austria during that later period, Jews had to obtain a variety of clearances and documents, in addition to paying the tax (which was steadily increased) on articles they wished to ship or carry with them. The process was designed "to harass and humiliate us," as **Ann Ikenberg** recalls, and also to extract as much money as possible. Also required were documents stating that all taxes and debts had been paid and that any police record had been cleared. **Gerty Frankel** describes the experience of procuring documents:

> It wasn't that you just went and asked for the papers. They had to make an
> investigation about you. First you needed to apply and then they made the

investigation, and finally you had to appear at the proper time and place to find out if you were eligible to get the papers! Some were contingent on getting a paper from another authority; you could only get a tax confirmation if you could prove there was no police activity against you. The investigations took a long time. There were thousands of people applying for them. It could happen that you got one paper and used it to file for paper B, but by the time paper B was ready, paper A had expired! Furthermore, to apply, you couldn't just walk into an office and present yourself. Again, you were one of thousands. You started lining up in front of the offices the evening before. If I say a hassle, it's an understatement!

She goes on to describe the procedure for sending or taking out personal property:

You had to prepare an exact list of what you were going to send or take, go to an office where somebody looked the list over and gave you a document that said you had permission to take the specified articles out. If you planned to take a typewriter along, as I did, you had to have it appraised. The appraiser issued a document that confirmed that you are the owner of that article appraised for a certain amount and that you had permission to take it out. You had to pay a percentage of the appraised value. Again, you couldn't just walk into the appraiser's office. You had to make an appointment first and then he would be busy. If you were shipping things out, you had to make an appointment with a moving company and then request an official to supervise the packing to make sure you didn't smuggle anything not on the list. You had to pay a tax on the more valuable items. And you had to pay the supervisor!

By the time they were ready to emigrate, many Jews had little money left. And at final departure, it was with no more than the allowable sum of 10 marks (equivalent to $4 at that time).

Yet another affront in the preparation for departure was what **Marianne Wolman** recalled as the most painful. She was required to sign a document declaring that she would never again set foot in her homeland, Austria.

But the problems of emigrating were trifling compared with those of immigrating. Where was a Jew to go? Invitations were not forthcoming. No mass schemes ever emerged. It became increasingly difficult to gain entry to *any* country, near or far. Those who found their way out did so primarily through family connections, resourcefulness, luck, and enormous perseverance. Each potential immigrant had to pursue a visa (permission to enter a specific country) and, if going to the United States, an affidavit (guarantee by a citizen to be financially responsible for the newcomer). With the singular exception of China, all countries had strict and limited quotas for immigration. Refugee policies did not exist. Nevertheless, approximately 400,000 immigrants from the Greater Reich (Germany, Austria, and Czechoslovakia) were absorbed by nations around the world between 1933 and 1941. The majority went to the United States (112,000), Latin America (85,000), and Great Britain (72,000); most others to Palestine (56,000), France (30,000), Shanghai, China (17,000), and Australia (6,500).[21]

Jews were preoccupied with staying alive and finding a way to emigrate. As they lost means for making a living, securing shelter and food became increasingly difficult. It wasn't safe to be at home or in the street. As **John Lesser** states matter of factly: "It was dangerous to walk on the streets because they picked up Jewish boys. They closed off the street and took the Jews away. Nobody in their families knew what had happened or where they were." **Frank Bauer** was arrested while standing in line at the American Consulate, waiting to register for a visa. "Many of us were rounded up and taken to the police station. The next three days and nights were terrible. We were standing up most of the time like sardines. We couldn't sleep and didn't get anything to eat. Then the Gestapo came and we were asked about our emigration intentions. I did not have a visa or affidavit. I was sent to Dachau."

Desperate that a visa might never become available or unable to procure an affidavit, some people tried to escape. A few dramatic emigrations were made by skiing from Austria to Switzerland via the Alps. **Otto Wolman** made a more modest attempt to flee. "I arranged with a friend of mine that we would go together. We had met somebody who had some connections with people in Aachen, a German town at the border with Belgium. These people were helping Jews to cross the border in a place where they knew there was no border patrol—for a fee of course. We had not much to lose, so we started off from Vienna." In fact, such potential escapees had much to lose. If caught, they risked jail or worse.

Most Jews tried to get out legally. People typically sought visas for countries where they had some connection—through family, friends, or business—or where they thought they might have some means of earning a living. They lined up for hours, even days, in front of consular buildings to begin the process of application. People waiting in lines could number in the thousands. Storm troopers sometimes terrorized them, forcing the Jews to run across the street. Someone who had been in line all night might consequently find himself close to the end.

Eventually, each applicant received a number that indicated his position, as a citizen of a particular nationality, in the lineup for visas to the desired country. A Polish citizen living in Vienna who wanted a visa to the United States applied at the U.S. Consulate in Vienna and would receive a number very different from that received by his Austrian counterpart. Admission quotas varied, based on country of birth. It was not unusual for people to apply for visas to several countries and then take the one that came first.

Until 1938–39, most refugees went to Palestine. The shock of the Nazi takeover had strengthened the Zionist movement, and although few German Jews were Zionists ideologically, Palestine was an appealing destination for people persecuted for being Jewish. Zionists established programs to assist Jews for this emigration; one provided intensive agricultural training to prepare people for kibbutz work. Two *Gruppe* couples were involved in these programs. Unfortunately for those who wanted to go to Palestine, the quota was small, and after 1939 immigration was curtailed severely as the British (Palestine was under British mandate) grew uneasy about antagonizing the Arab population there. All totaled, about 56,000 did get into Palestine by 1941, including 12,000 who did so "illegally."[22]

As a haven of freedom, the favored country for immigration was the United States. Getting a visa for the United States meant obtaining an affidavit signed by a sponsor who lived there. This sponsor had to submit papers guaranteeing the ability to financially support the immigrant if need be and showing payment of all back taxes and fines. Given the post-Depression climate, these requirements could not be met by everyone. Some Jews had family or friends in the United States who, if unable to meet the requirements themselves, might find someone who could do so. Others had to be resourceful in their pursuit of a sponsor. **Annie Lampl**, whose father had been a representative of an international lumber exporting company, explains how she found help: "I looked through my father's hundreds of calling cards that he collected through his extensive travels. I was only interested to find Americans among his many cards and there were quite a few. I wrote to them all. None answered but a woman in Oakland, California, who wrote that she remembered my father very well, that her husband had died in the meantime, but she was very happy to send all the necessary papers to get me over."

Otto Wolman had no connections in the United States.

> I did what many other people did—scrounge around for someone in America who would guarantee for me. I went to the main post office and looked in telephone books of New York for people with the same last name as mine. I found a few Wohlmanns. I wrote letters, telling them my story and asking them to help me immigrate. One good day, I really did receive a letter from a lady who said my letter had been delivered to her neighbors in an apartment building. Those neighbors had moved out. She had taken the liberty of opening the letter and thought this was an opportunity for her to help somebody.

Once a sponsor volunteered or was found, clearances and other papers had to be collected. Not infrequently, these were lost or stolen within the various government offices. But eventually, with the coveted affidavit in hand, a potential émigré began the most difficult wait of all—the wait until his or her number came up for the issuance of a visa to the United States. This might happen days, weeks, or years later or—most likely—not at all. Some people found a way to get to countries that permitted entry if they had sufficient evidence that they would leave when possible. England took in a sizable number of temporary residents for whom work permits had been issued. Women willing to work as domestics gained entry once they were offered positions there. Half of the people in the *Gruppe* were still in Europe when World War II began, several in England, where they lived through the terror of air raids, blackouts, and bombings. Somehow they made do, living marginally and waiting.

Why was it so extraordinarily difficult to get into the United States? In hindsight, the story proves to be a source of moral shame. The official quota was in fact sizable. Quotas had been established by the Immigration Act of 1924, using the 1890 census as its base, and set at 2 percent of the number of individuals of each nationality who resided in the United States.[23] For Germans, the annual quota was a substantial 26,000 as a result of the large German influx at the end of the eighteenth and beginning of the nineteenth centuries.[24] With the exception of 1938 and 1939, however, that quota was never filled.[25] In fact, for the years 1933–37, the *total* number of Germans (and not all were Jews) to enter the United States was between 21,000 and 27,000.[26]

The reason for this dismal record is that the United States, a nation of immigrants, was reluctant to admit Jewish refugees. In part, this was because the Depression had taken a heavy toll. Unemployment was high and Americans feared an influx of penniless foreigners. Anti-alien, isolationist, and anti-Semitic sentiment was widespread and was deeply entrenched in Congress, which dictated immigration policy to the consulates abroad. In 1938, even after *Kristallnacht* had been publicized in the media, four separate polls indicated that 71–85 percent of the American public opposed increasing the quota to help refugees.[27]

Nevertheless, the exposure of Nazi brutality in 1938 did oblige President Roosevelt and even the solidly anti-Semitic State Department to reappraise the situation. After Austria was annexed, its quota was added to Germany's for a total of 27,300.[28] This quota was filled for two years and then cut back severely.

It was during this period with a higher quota that most of the *Gruppe* members were notified that their visas had come through—that glorious moment for which each had waited so long. For most, that moment also brought heartache. It meant leaving behind a partner, parents, or siblings who might never receive a visa; one could delay departure only three months before the visa would expire. For some, the receipt of a visa initiated a mad scramble to obtain transit visas for those countries to be traversed on the way to the port of departure. For those leaving after the war had begun, there was the fear that their boat might be torpedoed in European coastal waters. For still others, it was too late to travel "safely" across the Atlantic Ocean; they went instead overland to the east and caught a ship across the Pacific. (The routes taken by the *Gruppe* members were typical of many; see Appendix C.) But for all, this was the opportunity to escape the inferno that would soon engulf their fellow Jews.

The new immigrants arrived in the New World singly, with a partner, occasionally in families. Some were greeted at the point of disembarkment by family or friends; others were not. It is difficult to imagine the feelings of excitement, relief, and at the same time apprehension that clutched at the hearts of these newcomers. The majority (60 percent) arrived and settled in New York City, most gravitating to Manhattan's Upper West Side, which had cultural and educational facilities reminiscent of home. Others went on to Chicago, Cleveland, Boston, and other eastern cities, and a few to the West Coast. They arrived virtually penniless. Those who went directly to relatives received support temporarily, while others depended on HIAS (Hebrew Immigrant Assistance Society) and other Jewish relief agencies for assistance with the immediate needs of food and lodging. For those without means to purchase tickets for travel to farther destinations, loans were available from the agencies.

The German and Austrian Jews who were to later become the *Gruppe* either came directly by ship to Los Angeles or continued their journey from New York by bus or train. Once there they settled into a city with a history of Jewish life totally different from that of the cities or towns from which they had come. Most significant, Los Angeles was a city in which Jews had lived almost from its inception.

The California Gold Rush brought the first sizable migration to that state; several hundred Jews were among the "forty-niners." At the same time, Jewish immigrants were seeking opportunity farther south in California, in the ranching community of Los Angeles. At its first census, taken in 1850, of the 8,500 inhabitants, eight were German-born Jews—six merchants and two tailors. One of these bachelors (as all were) was elected to the first city council. Slowly, more Jewish merchants settled in, mostly from Germany and Poland, seeking their fortune like everyone else. Most were at least somewhat educated and knew how to keep books; they quickly became prominent members of local society. The first bank in the city was founded by two German-Jewish brothers. In short, early Jewish Angelenos won acceptance in every sector of frontier life—economic, legal, and political. Involved in the evolution of the community, they were not constrained by the rigid historical and cultural patterns of many other communities.[29]

Jews continued to be well accepted as they contributed to the communal and economic life of Los Angeles. Because their education was often superior to that of most immigrants, their skills and knowledge made them not only accepted but valued by society. They were included among the membership of the first social clubs. The last decades of the century saw dramatic growth in the Jewish population, such that by 1900 there were 2,500 Jews living in Los Angeles, then a city of 170,000 (that is, 1.5 percent of the total). The Jewish community continued to grow at a much faster rate than the general population; by 1930, Jews numbered 72,000, making up 3.5 percent of the city's population.[30] By then, Jews were entrenched in all sectors of life, perhaps most visibly in the movie industry; most production executives were Jews and several of the major production companies were at least partly owned by Jews.

Despite the recent Depression, Los Angeles had built up a momentum of growth and opportunity. In the 1930s, the Jewish population of Los Angeles nearly doubled as Jews, primarily from other parts of the country, moved west. Also among the new residents were refugees fleeing Hitler's Reich. Their number was actually small, no more than 2,500 by late 1939.[31] Of these, some perhaps chose Los Angeles because it epitomized a break from the past, a chance to start afresh in a place that embodied the American dream. For those who envisioned work in the film industry, Los Angeles was a known oasis. Generally, however—and as was the case for all *Gruppe* immigrants—they came to Los Angeles because relatives, friends, or their affidavit sponsor lived there. But these refugees did not remain dependent on the support of others for long. As quickly as possible, they found housing—often a rented room in somebody's home—took menial jobs, and courageously carved out new lives for themselves.

They had no choice but to start at the very bottom, and even the most humble positions were difficult to find. **Marianne Wolman** describes her initial search: "Every morning, I walked for an hour from where I was staying to downtown L.A. I went to many garment stores, but what could I offer? I didn't even know how to use a sewing machine. Nobody hired me. Finally I was hired as a dessert baker. That lasted for one whole day. I couldn't even lift the bags of flour, they were so heavy. I was so tired when I left that I simply sat down on the curb and cried."

With "luck," these immigrants earned a few dollars by cleaning windows, running errands, sweeping floors, burning trash, loading furniture, sewing, cleaning, or waitressing. Those who didn't know English when they arrived learned quickly. Although drawn to immigrants with similar backgrounds, most also made efforts to find friends outside the émigré circle. As **Hedy Wolf** says: "After staying with our relatives, we rented a back room and shared a toilet with other people. We met other people from Europe who had the same background and the same future and the same worries and the same thoughts. Getting used to a foreign country is never easy, but we were young and we had our lives ahead of us. So we didn't worry too much and it worked out."

Her husband, **Ernest,** puts it succinctly: "You have to adapt to circumstances. You have to do the best you can in each position you are in. This is part of being alive. If you don't adapt, you die." Adapt they did—every day—with energy, optimism, and self-confidence.

Notes

1. E. Wilder Spaulding, *The First Invaders: The Story of the Austrian Impact upon America* (Vienna: Österreichischer Bundesverlag für Unterricht, Wissenschaft und Kunst, 1968), 95.

2. Anthony Heibut, *Exiled in Paradise: German Refugee Artists and the Intellectuals in America from the 1930s to Present* (New York: Viking Press, 1983).

3. Ruth Gay, *The Jews of Germany: A Historical Portrait* (New Haven: Yale University Press, 1992), 254.

4. Ibid., 243; George E. Berkley, *Vienna and Its Jews: The Tragedy of Success, 1880s–1980s* (Cambridge: Abt Books, 1988), 136.

5. Michael Berenbaum, *The World Must Know: The History of the Holocaust as Told in the United States Holocaust Memorial Museum* (Boston: Little Brown and Co., 1993), 18.

6. Ibid., 22.

7. Ibid., 33.

8. David Cooperman, in Rhoda Lewin, ed., *Witnesses to the Holocaust* (Boston: Twayne Publishers, 1990), xiv–xv.

9. Judith Miller, *One, by One, by One: Facing the Holocaust* (New York: Touchstone, 1990), 62.

10. Benno Weiser Varon, *Professions of a Lucky Jew* (New York: Cornwall Books, 1992), 73.

11. Berenbaum, *The World Must Know*, 46.

12. Ibid., 46; Miller, *One, by One, by One*, 67; Lucy S. Dawidowicz, *The War against the Jews, 1933–1945* (New York: Bantam Books, 1975), 13.

13. Dawidowicz, *The War against the Jews*, 101–2; Berenbaum, *The World Must Know*, 54; Gay, *The Jews of Germany*, 265.

14. Gay, *The Jews of Germany*, 265.

15. Dawidowicz, *The War against the Jews*, 173.

16. Gay, *The Jews of Germany*, 270.

17. Dawidowicz, *The War against the Jews*, 374.

18. Berenbaum, *The World Must Know*, 46.

19. Dawidowicz, *The War against the Jews*, 173–74.

20. Howard M. Sachar, *A History of the Jews in America* (New York: Alfred A. Knopf, 1992), 468.

21. Ibid., 484.

22. Ibid.; Gay, *The Jews of Germany*, 270.

23. Judah Gribetz, *The Timetables of Jewish History* (New York: Touchstone, 1993), 383.

24. Sachar, *A History of the Jews in America*, 485.

25. Berenbaum, *The World Must Know*, 56.

26. Sachar, *A History of the Jews in America*, 475–76; Gay, *The Jews of Germany*, 270.

27. David S. Wyman, *The Abandonment of the Jews: America and the Holocaust, 1941–1945* (New York: Pantheon Books, 1984), 8.

28. Gay, *The Jews of Germany*, 270.

29. Neil C. Sandberg, *Jewish Life in Los Angeles* (Lanham, Md.: University Press of America, 1986), 25.

30. Bruce Phillips, "Los Angeles Jewry: A Demographic Portrait," *American Jewish Yearbook, 1986:* 126–95.

31. Max Vorspan and Lloyd P. Gartner, *History of the Jews of Los Angeles* (Philadelphia: Jewish Publishing Society of America, 1970), 197.

The Interviews

MARIANNE WOLMAN

Marianne Wolman

Decisive and determined, Marianne Wolman was the first of her family and her friends to leave Vienna. From England, where she worked initially as a domestic and then as housemother to orphaned German-Jewish boys, Marianne's efforts facilitated the immigrations to London of her husband, Emil, her husband-to-be, Otto, and several relatives. England was already at war when she left for the United States and, again alone, headed for California. Marianne and Otto had one daughter, Ruth.

One evening, I think it was March 11 or 12, 1938, Hitler marched into Austria. I was teaching at a Maturaschule [private school for people who had not attended Gymnasium, the public college-preparatory high school, and yet wanted to go to college] where people studied before they took the final difficult examination, *die Matura*. The windows were open and all of a sudden we heard shouting, "Down with the Jews! Kill the Jews!" And we heard steps going in a long parade. I was petrified! When the class ended, I didn't know what to do. I was terribly scared to go downstairs, but I had to do it.

There were many people in the street. All those that I saw wore a swastika and I wondered, "How had they done this so quickly?" I got home that night and my only thought was how I could get out of this.

The next morning, the man who owned the school where I was teaching called me and said in a very apologetic way, "I hope you'll forgive me if I ask you not to come back anymore. I think we cannot do this to our students." I agreed. I was too scared to go near there anyway. But he called me the next day and said, "The students have voted that you should come back and teach until they take the examination in June." I went back with a pounding heart. As I walked into the classroom, there were about 30 students, 20 already wearing a swastika. I wasn't quite sure how I would manage to teach anything there because I was so frightened. But it worked out until they passed the examinations.

Did you ever ask the students how they felt about you?

No, but two of them called me over the phone and said, "If I should meet you in the street, I will not greet you, and I want you to understand why not. I do not want to greet a Jewish person." Another man tried to persuade me not to leave Vienna and promised me he would hide me until the horrible time was over. It's strange that you would have such differences among a group of students.

So then you knew that you had to get out. What steps did you take between March and June?

Everyone was writing like crazy to people they knew who lived abroad and who possibly could send affidavits. We went to all the consulates you can possibly think of and registered for visas. But about a week after Hitler marched in, all the frontiers began closing. You couldn't leave Vienna and you couldn't legally get into another country. The single exception was England; you could go there with a transit visa if you had proof of a visa application to some other country, and an affidavit in hand, if you hoped to go to the U.S. I knew I had to get out as fast as possible. I read English newspapers every day and I found an ad which asked for a young woman to come to England as a cook. (English people don't like to be domestics!) Such jobs were open to Jewish refugee women.

One day, my stepmother [Marianne's mother died when Marianne was 16 years old] suggested I write to her brother in Los Angeles, the black sheep of the family, whether he could send me an affidavit. He said that he would, but it took forever. He had not paid his taxes for many years, and without doing so, he couldn't sign an affidavit for me. So, poor man, he had to pay all his taxes for years back. Eventually he sent an affidavit. But it could still take forever to get a visa to the U.S. At this point, because Austria had been overrun, we fell under the German quota for a visa to the U.S. I decided that I'd better wait for the visa in England, rather than wait in Austria.

I was married to Emil during this time, as I had been since 1933. He had registered for a visa at the same time as I, and had written to someone in the U.S. in search of an affidavit. Our life together was difficult, in part because I had met another man, Otto, and was in love with him.

Were you still going to the University of Vienna then?

No, you could not. When Hitler marched in, it was closed to Jewish students. They destroyed our papers. Whatever I had done there was no longer documented.

I received an answer to my letter to that English lady whose ad I had answered. She told me that her family needed a cook and, if I considered coming, they would be happy to get me a permit. I knew that was the only way I could get out. No one else, none of my friends had left yet.

Were they trying to?

Everybody was trying, but it was tremendously difficult unless you had relatives in the United States and had registered for immigration before or immediately after Hitler's invasion.

I remember one Sunday when my dear friend Harry Bauer and I were invited somewhere for lunch and we were walking together, as always with fear because terrible things happened to Jews all the time. An SS man stopped us and asked us where we were going. We told him, and then Harry said, "I am a doctor. I cannot stand here. I have to go to a patient." And so the SS man said, "All right, I will just take the woman." He took me into a place where many SS men lived, and there was a big courtyard. He gave me a big bucket, brush, and soap, and said, "Go and clean the toilets." There were many toilets and he made me kneel down and scrub.

I did that for a long time, and then one after another of the men came in and peed on me instead of into the toilets. I still remember my thoughts at the moment: "I've got to get out of here. I cannot live in this place anymore." I heard shouts and screams of Jews whom they were beating in the courtyard through which I had come. I guess because I did not refuse to do this horrible work, after about two hours, the SS man who had brought me in told me to get up, empty the bucket, and get out. The hatred in me was such that I really didn't know how to go on after that. Harry was waiting for me around the corner. He wanted to know what happened to me and to know where

I was. Otherwise I could have just disappeared. Well, that was the day of absolute decision. I had to get out. But I still had to wait.

I remember when I went to my father to say good-bye. I hadn't seen him in a long time. He considered me absolutely insane and told me that he'd been a good Austrian all his life, as was his father and mother and his grandfather and grandmother, and it was just insanity on my part. I told him I'd have to go in spite of what he thought.

Before leaving Vienna, I had to sign a statement promising never to come back into Austria. That was terribly difficult. But on September 1, 1938, I left Vienna, carrying a German passport, and went to England. On the same train were two young women who had been students of mine when I was student teaching a few years before that. They had both been raised in an orphanage in Vienna, and were now leaving because they were half-Jewish. (Both are still friends and I see them sometimes.) The trip wasn't quite as terrible as I had anticipated because I had them to talk with. I went to London, where Harry Bauer waited for me at the station, and I stayed for two days in London with him. We were permitted to take out of Austria the equivalent of $5. I had spent that immediately getting to London. Harry and I didn't go sightseeing. I think we were too depressed to do that. But we walked for hours in Hyde Park. That you could sit on benches which didn't have a sign, "Forbidden for Jews," was a great, great experience for me. And then came the day when I left for Llanelly in South Wales where I had received the job as a cook.

It was a very long train trip. I was met by a very heavy, very pretty, young woman who turned out to be the niece of the Greene family. She took me to the house. My shock was overwhelming. There were 10 people sitting having Sunday afternoon tea—10 people! How could I ever cook for 10 people? I didn't know how to do that! Although they were very friendly, all of them, I remember my horror when I was supposed to cook fish and chips the first time, or porridge which had to be on the stove all night, and I couldn't believe how I would ever get it served in the morning. One other job I had to do was to kindle fires in eight fireplaces. There were no other sources of heating. I had never done this in my life. It was all very difficult. But they were very kind to me, and eventually they told me that really their purpose in hiring me had been to get a young Jewish woman out of hell. That's what they had done for me. And had I not been there with them, I don't think Otto would ever have gotten out of Vienna.

After a month, maybe two, Mrs. Greene invited me to come with her to a nearby city (Llanelly was a very tiny town) to hear a member of Parliament who had just returned from the Continent, where he had investigated what was going on in Germany and Austria. He was an inspiring speaker, and for the first time in my life I heard a non-Jew talk about the horrors of Nazi

Austria and Germany. He asked the British people to please send permits to as many people as they possibly could to save them. When the lecture was over, I tried to go to him and thank him for what he had said, but there were so many people lined up to talk to him that I thought, "Well, it's more important that they get information than that I thank him—I could do this by mail," and left.

It was a night of pea-soup fog, as it often is in England at that time of the year. We drove for just a very brief time when a car ran into us from the back and we stopped. Somebody came running toward the front of our car. It was the man, James Griffiths, who had given the lecture! He wanted to find out if he had damaged the car—which he hadn't. Mrs. Greene said to him, "The young woman here wanted very much to thank you for your words and also to meet you. She has come from Vienna only a short while ago." He was very friendly, leaned over and talked to me and said, "If I can be of any help at any time, be sure and let me know," and handed me a card with his name on it and a telephone number. Then we drove on. I somehow felt this was an enormous piece of luck that had occurred.

Not very long after that, the *Kristallnacht* happened. What really occurred politically was that a crazy young Jew in Paris killed a Nazi official and that was used as the reason to burn down all the synagogues in Austria and Germany. That was called the *Kristallnacht*. Many men were incarcerated in local jails after that event, some sent on to concentration camps. I called Otto at his home. There was no answer. I called my father. There was no answer. And so I thought, "If Mr. Griffiths really meant what he said, this is the time to call him and ask for help." I called him. I was very shy about it—my God, to ask somebody to help a person he had never seen in his life! I told him that I needed some help now. Did he think he would be able to help me get somebody out of Vienna? He said, "I will try. Give me his name, address, and birth date." Twenty-four hours later, Otto received a permit to go to England! It still took a while until he could get out because there were all kinds of things that were necessary to liquidate, although his family no longer owned their business.

Did Otto call you when the permit arrived?

No, but Mr. Griffiths called me and said, "I just want to tell you, it got through." He knew Otto had received the permit. That was a miracle, an absolute miracle! I had tried so hard before to find a way to get Otto out. You cannot imagine all the steps I tried to take. How does one get somebody out of hell? Money couldn't do it. I didn't know anybody. But, as it turned out, I did. That was an absolute miracle. When Otto really came after about two months, we called Mr. Griffiths and on that day we went to see him and thank him, so at least he could meet the person he had been able to get out.

I was still a cook at Mrs. Greene and family. Otto arrived and had a cold. He came with me to the Greenes' house and went to bed. Mrs. Greene nursed him and took care of him. She liked him immediately. Otto stayed in bed for a few days. That was the beginning. Then we were faced with a new problem. He was not permitted to do any kind of work—zero.

Could one work without earning a salary?

No, it was not permitted. You couldn't work, period. The only thing we could do was to find a family that would invite Otto to live with them. This was one of the things we had never thought about. The Greenes found a family willing to invite him to come and live with them for a while. At that time Otto had an affidavit, but no hope to get a visa into the United States. He had the misfortune to be under the Polish quota. His mother had gone to Poland to be with her own mother for her children's births.

What can I tell you about those days? I had a half-day off every Sunday. I would go into Swansea, the town where Otto lived with that very strange Jewish family. We had no place to go. It rained and rained, as it does in England in the winter. Usually, we would go to a tea house, as it was called, and have tea and crumpets and sit for a while, and then walk either in the rain or in the darkness. Then I went back to Llanelly and Otto went back to the family. It was the weirdest time you can possibly imagine. I don't remember for how many months this strange relationship lasted.

Then I was offered a job in Croydon, in the outskirts of London, to be a matron, what you call a housemother, I guess. A rich Jew had given a house and had it furnished for a group of children that he would bring from Germany and Austria who had no parents anymore. He needed somebody to take care of these children and also someone to teach English to the boys. The job was advertised for a couple. I took the job because it provided the opportunity for Emil, still my husband, to get out of Vienna.

How did this man know about you? Or had you applied for the job?

I don't remember. I didn't apply for it. But I was chosen to be the house-mother for 25 little boys. I interviewed two other women who would help me with most of the cooking and cleaning. Twenty-five little boys, aged between 5 and 13! All of them had lost their parents either by watching how they were taken away or were shot in front of them. All terribly disturbed children. I'll never forget the day when they arrived. I don't know how many times I went to the train station. Most of them just carried a bundle of some clothes, and I can remember one had a teddy bear. It was heartbreaking to see those children. Can you imagine children of that age who had just lost their parents being taken to a foreign country? They couldn't speak English. We settled them into that rather big house. There were large rooms, and many children slept in the same room.

The beginning was very, very difficult. The boys didn't trust me. They didn't want to have anything to do with me. They were violently aggressive. All their anger and hatred and fear came out. We had a big yard in which they played and, honestly, there were times when it looked as if they'd kill each other. I just couldn't cope with that aggression. Often during those first weeks I asked the two ladies who were working with me to relieve me and I went into a different part of the house where I couldn't hear the yelling so well. These ladies were not so troubled by it. It took six or eight weeks until the most horrible aggression subsided and the children began to deal with each other like human beings. It was probably the most interesting and most difficult job I ever held. Can you imagine me, at the age of 27 or 28, as the mother of 25 little boys, and all the responsibilities to help them? They began going to school not very long after their arrival. That too was a very traumatic experience because they couldn't understand a word. They didn't know English at all.

You mean they went to a regular English school?

Yes, and they had many problems, as you can imagine. Not only language-wise. Their behavior was totally unacceptable.

Were you supposed to be teaching English to them?

No, I was just supposed to take care of them, to help them get adjusted to the new country and new life. Emil was supposed to teach them English. Strange things happened then. I read them many stories, at first only in German and then slowly in English. I never gave total attention to any individual child. There was no possibility to do so since there were 25 of them. One night (I never slept through one whole night because there were always some children who cried and needed me), a child was crying bitterly and said he had terrible pains in his tummy. I called the doctor, and he came during the night, examined the little boy, and was sure he had appendicitis. So we took him immediately to the hospital in an ambulance. I had to sign a paper that I allowed the surgeon to perform surgery. It was a very hard thing for me to do. I was not his mother. I was just somebody, a stranger really. Everything went well. I went to see him every day, brought books and candies, sat there and sang to him and talked to him. After a week he came "home." There he tried to keep all my attention with him, not wanting to let go.

Can you imagine—a month later the identical scene happened. A child woke up during the night, cried with terrible pains in his abdomen. The doctor came and diagnosed appendicitis, took him to the hospital. Everything happened exactly as the first time. I was very bewildered. It didn't seem possible. Again, I spent every day for several hours at the boy's bedside in the hospital until he came home. Well, when the third case of appendicitis was diagnosed, I was sure it couldn't be real. Thinking back, I am convinced that the children really needed much more than I was able to give them as a collective. They needed the attention of one person exclusively. This was the only way they knew they could get it! I didn't understand that at the time.

Is there anything you would have done differently?

Of course not. But I could have understood what was happening. This turned out to be a most interesting job. I loved it. I loved the children and they loved me. They began to trust me and believe when I told them that I would never leave them without telling them long ahead of time. I told them that I had an affidavit, which meant at some time I would leave to go to the United States, but I would let them know long before I would go. I never had a day off. I was needed constantly. I think it was four months that I worked steadily seven days a week.

Otto lived in London at that time. One day I finally took a day off, met him there, went to Hampton Court, I believe, and had a wonderful day. In the evening, when I came home, I saw all the windows lit up and I began to run. I knew immediately there was something wrong. Why would all windows be lit up? It was only eight o'clock, the children were not in bed yet. I ran until I got to the house, 2 Woburn Road, Croydon. (It was totally bombed; nothing was left when I went to England many years later.) The boys had packed their bundles or little suitcases because they were sure that I had left them. The two women could not calm them down and tell them I'd never do such a thing, that I had only taken a day off. That they couldn't understand. They didn't believe it. So again I could see that they didn't *really* trust me. How could they? Their parents were taken away from them and killed, so why would they trust that I would not also disappear? It took me two hours to calm them down. I can still see myself making a huge pot of chocolate while each child unpacked his bundle. I kept on asking, "Where did you intend to go?" Of course they had no idea—just away, because I was gone. It was an absolutely incredible experience. It took such a long time to calm them down and get them to bed. It was midnight when I turned out the last lights. It took me many weeks after that to ever leave the house again.

At the end of August, the political situation was more and more strained and the fear that Germans would take over the whole world as they intended to do became clearer and clearer to us. On September 1, 1939, England entered the war. We heard about the horrible, horrible things that the Nazis were doing as they marched into Czechoslovakia, went on into Poland, and into Russia. It was hard to believe that this was possible. It sounded then like a terrible dream, and now it was coming to England as well. We were given gas masks to wear in case of an air raid, and I was very, very uneasy to be in charge of those 25 children.

Two days after the war broke out the children were in school, and just at the time school was over the first air-raid alarm sounded. I knew that they would now be in the street trying to get home. I was desperate. I didn't really know what to do. We didn't have an air-raid shelter. We could only go into the dining room, which was in the lowest part of the house. I started to walk toward the school. There were the children running towards me in terror. When we got home, I sat down and tried to explain to them that war was a terrible thing, but that the air-raid alarm was a false alarm. We took off the gas masks and sat down together for a while and talked. I was convinced that I could no longer really hold that job. The responsibilities were such that I could no longer handle them.

Fortunately, the boys were "billeted," as it was called in England. They were taken to the south of England into different homes, where they would stay throughout the war. It was a dreadful decision to let them go away again, but in a way of course I was glad that I no longer had to have responsibility for all these children. I visited them once or twice and found them in very bad shape, very lonely, having great difficulties in again getting used to new homes with such uncertainties in their lives. As a matter of fact, the south of England was bombed the heaviest and the children were taken away from their places again and brought to another area of England. I lost touch with many of them.

Where and how did you live after that?

Otto and I lived together in Wimbleton, in the outskirts of London. No work was possible. I don't know how we lived with very little money. At the end of September 1939, one year after my arrival in England, I was called to the American Consulate to receive my visa. After a very strict physical examination, I received this piece of paper, which was of greatest value. The first thing I read on it was, "Valid only for three months." If you didn't leave England for the United States within three months, this piece of paper became invalid and you would never receive another immigrant visa. That was a terrible thing to read. How could I leave in three months? The war had broken out. There was Otto. I asked the consul if he could tell me when Otto, a man on the Polish quota, could possibly expect to get entrance to the United States. He just shook his head and said, "Not for many years, if at all." With that I left the American Consulate and went back to Otto. I just couldn't make up my mind to leave him again.

It was an absolutely dreadful time. Blackouts, fear of more bombs, the Germans continuing to invade more countries, and the time went on. I remember particularly one afternoon. It was a very dreary, foggy day. Otto and I went to see a movie that still stands out in my memory. At one point Otto said to me, "I have decided that you have to go to the United States. Absolutely! There is no future here and I will come as soon as I possibly can." Both of us knew that was very unlikely to happen.

Where was Emil at that time?

I think he stayed at the Croydon home after I left and the boys disbanded. Emil had received his American visa the same day as I did, since we had registered at the same time. Ernst Mannheimer, my cousin (I can't remember how I got him out of Vienna), stayed at the home too, as did other refugees. Some refugee men, "enemies" once England was in the war, were sent to the Isle of Man and eventually to Australia; others were sent to Canada. Ernst had the first fate. After living in a refugee camp in central Australia, he lived in Melbourne until he committed suicide.

Now the decision was of when to leave. I didn't want to go, but I knew Otto would urge and urge me until I would say, "Yes." Finally, I agreed to leave England and go to the United States without him. I took the last boat before the three months of my visa's validity were up. I had already paid in Vienna for passage with the shipping company, never knowing that I would ever be able to use the ticket.

Was there always space on these ships?

No, not always. And I made reservations for the last possible moment. I went to Southampton and had to wait two days because the boat that was supposed to pick us up had been bombed off the shore. Mines had been placed around Great Britain. Can you imagine the feeling to sit there and wait for the next boat to come? I called Otto each night and begged him to let me come back. He was very stern and told me there was no other way. We had decided this together, and he would follow me as soon as he could.

Finally, on the third day, the boat arrived that was going to take me to the United States. While I was on the gangplank, my name was called and I was paged to come to the telephone. I knew for sure this was Otto calling me and telling me to come back. (As I learned later, it was.) But I couldn't turn around, and once on the ship I couldn't get back. And then a long, long sea voyage in blackout and bad weather and with terribly depressed people around me. It took 14 days to cross the Atlantic. We heard radio messages about boats that had been torpedoed off the shore of England, but we were already out of that area, so there was less of a chance to get torpedoed by the Germans.

Were you in a convoy?

Yes. Other boats were not terribly close by, but always visible. At night there was total blackout; you couldn't see anything. I remember some very stormy days when people were terribly sick and I was the only one in the dining room. Emil was on the same boat, but in a different class. Boats at that time had different classes, a so-to-speak middle class, where I had my ticket, and a lower class, where his cabin was. He had not paid in Vienna, I believe, for his trip. I saw little of him because he was terribly seasick and was hardly out of his cabin.

How many people were on the boat?

I think about 700. It was terribly full. We had waited so long. And then, after 14 days, we were told that the next morning we would land in New York. I remember I was very excited. I *had* to see the Statue of Liberty before entering America. But of all things, I slept. When I woke up we were already landing in New York. Incredible high buildings! To see skyscrapers for the first time! It was totally overwhelming! I had seen many photographs and pictures of New York before, but that first impression was absolutely something I will never forget. It wasn't real. Houses could not be that tall. And so, we went into the harbor of New York.

As Emil and I got off the boat, there was a wonderful face waiting for us. That was our friend, Kurt Stern, the first familiar face in the New World. He waited with us for hours until our luggage came down. My suitcase was broken, all my clothes were hanging out. It was very embarrassing. Kurt took us home to his wife and we met Florie for the first time. They had a very small apartment, yet invited us to stay with them for the first few days. A letter was waiting for me there. It was a letter from Otto, which said, "I called you and wanted to tell you that I think we made a wrong decision. I wanted you to come back." But when I read the letter, I was already in New York. You can imagine how I felt!

After a few days, Emil went on his own and I stayed with the Loeffler family, other friends from Vienna, for the remainder of my days in New York. These were very unusual days. Many of my friends had come to the United States before me. I began to call several of them and to see some of them in New York. It was the most depressing atmosphere you can possibly imagine. It was the end of the Depression in the United States, and it was terribly difficult to find any kind of work, especially if you never had a job in America before. The question, "What is your local experience?" haunted all of us. Everybody envied me terribly that I would go to sunny southern California, to Los Angeles. It was Christmas Eve when I had arrived. It was snowing and bitter cold. I had never been in such cold weather and I was freezing terribly. I spent *Sylvester* [New Year's Eve] with other Viennese friends, but it was a very sad party. Nobody had work, nobody knew what to do, and only I would leave after a week and go to Los Angeles, where I didn't know a soul. I didn't even know the man who had signed the affidavit for me.

I considered for a while to stay in New York where I had so many friends. But I thought I really needed to start a new life, and Emil was going to stay in New York. He got a job already after our second day and I thought it would not be a good idea for me to stay there. I could have; legally, I did not have to go to the place where my affidavit sponsor lived.

So I went on my trek by bus (that's all I could afford), which took I don't even remember anymore how many nights and days. I did spend one night with my friend Lizy, with whom I went to high school. I was not in the mood for sightseeing. But when I was in Washington, D.C., with her, there were such incredibly interesting sights that I took a morning to visit the big library, the biggest library in the United States. Lizy told me how to get there and I waited for the bus. When it stopped, people got off the bus at two doors, one at the front and one at the rear. I was close to the rear of the bus, so when people stopped coming out, I started to mount the bus at the rear door. I heard lots of shouting but didn't know what had happened. All of a sudden, somebody grabbed me by the coat collar and pulled me down and yelled at me, "Don't you know what you're doing? That door is for the Niggers!" I stood there *totally* horrified. I didn't know anything about the black people who were so mistreated there as in so many places. I was so shocked. It was Nazi Germany all over again. All I could think of was, "I want to go home, I want to go home." But there was no home to go to. That was an experience that I will never forget.

The next day, I continued my bus trip, and for one night I stopped in San Francisco where two other friends were waiting for me, Harry and Hanna Bauer [the same Harry who had greeted her upon arrival in London]. We spent one beautiful day together. When I got to Los Angeles, Bill Links [Marianne's step-uncle and affidavit sponsor] met me at the bus. I was really more dead than alive. I was so tired from experiences and impressions and thinking about Otto in England. Uncle Bill looked like a very kind man, which he turned out to be. He took me to his house, where I shared a bedroom with his youngest daughter, who had just finished high school.

The day after my arrival, I went on a bus to UCLA. I wanted to continue my education, which I had interrupted for a long time. That was a disappointment. When I met a lady who was in charge of foreign students who wanted to study there, I had only a little book that showed that I had attended the University of Vienna for four years and listed all the courses that I had taken. She looked at it and said, "What grades did you get?" I said, "There were no grades at the university." She said, "We don't know whether you really passed all those classes." And although I explained to her that if I hadn't passed, there wouldn't have been classes for the next year in the little book, it didn't do any good. She said to me, "Anyway, you would have to pay five times the regular tuition because you are not a resident of California. I can only tell you, go home and get a job as a domestic." And I said to her, "I've done this in England now for a year and a half. I have had it." She looked at me and said, "Well, if you can, find something better. Good luck."

I knew I had to look for a job. What kind of job? I didn't know, and I did the most idiotic things possible! I walked from the Links' house every morning to look for a job in downtown Los Angeles. I went to many garment stores, but what could I offer? I didn't even know how to use a sewing a machine. I had never seen sewing machines like these before. I was only used to a treadle machine, but these were all electric. When I heard how little a seamstress was paid. . . . Well, nobody hired me. Every day I bought two pounds of bananas for lunch for 5 cents a pound—10 cents for my lunch each day. I did this for at least two weeks. My shoes were worn out and they had to be resoled which probably was much more expensive than if I had taken a streetcar.

I was hired in a restaurant as a dessert baker. That lasted for one whole day. I couldn't even lift the bags of flour, they were so heavy. I was slow because I really didn't know how to get around in the kitchen and how to do things en masse. I had learned in England how to bake for 10 people, but this was a big restaurant. So I lasted one day, and I was so tired when I got out that I simply sat down on the curb and cried. I don't know how I got home that day. Maybe Uncle Bill picked me up.

I didn't find a job until March. Through my interest in graphology, I had been invited to a meeting by some medical doctors who had the same interest. One of them had heard of a job opportunity for a young woman to be the governess to two children who would come from Singapore with their parents. The father was on sabbatical, a professor of pathology, born in London, and his wife, an American. The job would be in Santa Barbara. That was the first job offer I had. I accepted it.

The day before I left for Santa Barbara, Uncle Bill was invited to a distant family member and took me along. I met a lady there, a visitor from Seattle, who told me that she had been in Europe every single year for many years—in Czechoslovakia—visiting her aunt. I looked at her and said (You know I sometimes have premonitions I cannot explain), "Where did your aunt live?" She said, "My aunt lived in Jilena." And I said, "What is her name?" She said, "Her maiden name was Weil." And I said, "She is married to my father!" That lady got very excited and asked, "Where is she? How can I help Aunt Bertha?" And I said, "You can send my father and her an affidavit. That's the greatest help that you could do." She got up immediately, went to the telephone and I heard her call her husband and say, "Moishe, I want you to go to the American Consulate tomorrow and send an affidavit to Aunt Bertha Farber and her husband, Gustav." She came back and said, "It will take two or three days until he gets enough papers together, but he will do it." That was another miracle in my life.

And thanks to this lady, they really got out—by the skin of their teeth. Their visas came through and they left on the very last boat before America entered the war. After that there were no passenger boats coming from Europe to the United States, only boats filled with soldiers. Their boat was to go from Spain, via Japan, to New York. They were to call me when they arrived in New York. As it turned out, that boat was torpedoed. I assumed the obvious when I didn't hear from them. In fact, they had not gotten on that boat because my father's passport had been stolen at the post office and they had waited for a replacement. They got on another boat, unlisted, from Spain and called from New York a week after their anticipated arrival. They remained in New York—Bertha until she came to Los Angeles one week before you were born, and Gustav until the late 50s when he returned to Vienna.

So, in the midst of March, I went to Santa Barbara to meet Brian and Chanty, the two children. Chanty was three and Brian, six. Their very friendly parents really treated me like a daughter. I had now a room and my own bathroom. Imagine that—me, a poor refugee girl. I went to the beach with the children every morning. It was summer, with beautiful, beautiful days. Can you have it any better than to sit at the beach most of the day? Or go for walks with two children? But I was so lonely—terribly lonely.

The war was continuing, and the Germans had occupied part of France. One incredible day after that occupation I got a cable which said, "Received visa, arriving in New York," and the date, which I don't remember anymore. It was about six months after I had arrived that Otto was to arrive in New York. I cannot describe the joy! Was it possible that something like this could happen? What had happened? How did he get the visa? I think that's important to explain because it really changed our lives. After France fell, the American embassies there sent all quota numbers that had been reserved for people hoping to go from France to the United States to their embassies in England. All of a sudden, quotas available in England were greatly increased. Previously, the Polish quota was filled for several years. But with the great number of new quota numbers that were sent from Paris to London, Otto was invited to come to the American Consulate to get a visa.

Otto arrived in New York in early July 1940. Can you imagine? He called me in Santa Barbara from New York and told me he had arrived! That was another miracle!

Then came Otto's arrival day in Santa Barbara. I went down to the bus, of course too early, and kept walking around the block, I don't know how many times. Finally, finally, there was a bus coming and it stopped and I watched people coming out, lots of people, but no Otto. The *last* person descending the stairs was Otto. I just couldn't believe it! He really came. It was like he had followed me around the world, from Vienna to London, from London to New York, and finally to Santa Barbara.

We had a wonderful day together, and we spent the first night in a hotel (I was given two days off so I had another free day). But I could tell that Otto wasn't feeling well. Since I remembered that he never complained, I finally said, "Let's find out what's wrong with you." He admitted, "I don't feel well." My horror was that I didn't have any money for a doctor. What in the world was I going to do? Finally, I remembered that I had heard there was a lady in Santa Barbara who had helped some poor refugees get on their feet. It was difficult to get her number, but in desperation I got hold of her and told her that Otto had arrived the day before from England and I thought he was quite sick. "Could you please help us get a doctor? I have no money to pay." She didn't hesitate and said, "Yes, but where will the doctor treat him?" I said, "Maybe if the doctor diagnoses what's wrong with him, we'll make the decisions after that." A doctor came to the hotel, examined Otto very carefully, and then he said, "There is something very wrong in your lungs. We have to get you into a hospital." Well, that was absolutely impossible. In a hospital, we would have to pay five times as much as anyone else because he was a nonresident. So the lady, I think her name was Akerman, made it possible that Otto went into a nursing home. He had bronchial pneumonia. That was a terribly tough beginning.

He stayed there for at least two weeks. When I talked to the doctor at the end of the two weeks, he said, "This man will not be able to work for at least a year. You must feed him well, get him a lot of milk and eggs. He is undernourished as well as everything else." I promised I'd do that. Now the question arose, "What am I going to do with Otto once he gets out of that nursing home?" I talked to my employer about it, and she said, "Well, we have servant quarters and the cook and chambermaid are there. But there's another room and if he wants to come and stay there, he's welcome." That was another gift from heaven. Otto moved into the domestic quarters of the house. Before, I ate with the family, and now Otto *and* I ate with the family. They were extremely friendly to him. I ordered extra milk, butter, and eggs from the milkman and really tried to feed Otto as much as I could. You know how difficult that is. But he was in very bad physical shape, and so he accepted the food. Getting stronger took a long, long time. It was already the end of August or the beginning of September.

In September, the family disbanded and the Santa Barbara chapter in our lives came to an end. We went to Los Angeles. What did we do when we got to L.A.? Well, right away we went to look for some work.

Did you initially stay with the Links family again?

No. We rented a room in a house on Windsor Street with a family and were permitted to use the kitchen facilities. I still remember the family. They had come from Hungary or Czechoslovakia and had two young boys. The mother ruled the house, and every morning she took the boys to a studio in Hollywood to wait until they could get jobs as extras.

This was a room you found through a newspaper ad?

Right. I do not remember exactly how long we stayed with that family. Too long. When we were able to move away, we got our first apartment. It was on Magnolia and had one room with a foldaway bed, a small bathroom, and a kitchenette. Otto and I could not get married yet because my divorce from Emil had not legally been completed. When I got my divorce at the beginning of March 1941, Otto and I were married by a justice of peace on March 8th. We had no witness of our own. Somebody from the street was brought up to witness our marriage. My wedding band was a brass ring we selected from the sewing department at Woolworth's. Then Otto took me for lunch to Cliftons Cafeteria. I still remember what I ate. I had some fish and ice cream. So did Otto. I love ice cream, and you could get as much of it there as you wished!

The next day, we went on our honeymoon. Mrs. Loeffler, an old friend of mine [the same woman she had stayed with in New York], who had a car, took us for our first time into the Mojave Desert. I had never seen trees like this before, very strange palm trees. We were sort of speechless when we looked around. Was this a desert? A desert with trees? My idea of a desert was of only sand and the sky, but it turned out to be very different in the United States.

I'm trying to remember what my job was then. Oh yes, I remember. I had a very temporary job in a preschool. I was supposed to teach the children French in a very, very strict manner, and I just couldn't possibly do that.

Although I had no other job, I left. Otto went looking for a job as a book-keeper and it took him a good while to find one. I eventually found a job in a beautiful preschool owned by Mrs. Bell. This is where my career work with preschool children began.

Let's go back now to the fall of 1940. You've come to Los Angeles from Santa Barbara and you're living on Magnolia Street. You and Otto each find work and you begin to build some semblance of a social network. What were the beginnings of social contact? How did you meet people?

As long as I worked, I met some very nice people who were teaching preschool children like I did, and once in a while we got together. But really we hadn't made any friends. We were total outsiders. How do you make friends in a new country? Just remember, the war was still going on and we got horrible news through newspapers or radio, and we had the worry about families that were left in Vienna or wherever. We didn't even have much need, I believe, for extensive socializing. However, there were some old friends of ours who had come to New York from Vienna and were incapable or unable to find a job there. We suggested that they move to Los Angeles where the sun was shining longer than in any other part of the country and the air was good (believe it or not). So Herman and Gretl Esslau moved to Los Angeles while we were still living at Magnolia.

Did you find them an apartment in your neighborhood?

In the very same house, another single apartment. Herman got some kind of job as a furniture polisher, where he met a German immigrant by the name of Fred Ikenberg and they decided that because Ikenberg and his wife, **Annchen,** were also lonely, that we should all get together some evening and see if we couldn't get to know each other. We did. I also remember that Mrs. Loeffler told me that she had run into a young man whom I must have known before, when she and her husband gave big parties for their daughters in Vienna. His name was **Frank Bauer.** And indeed I remembered the man with the white gloves at parties in Vienna! A bit ludicrous, but yes, it was Frank Bauer whom she brought to our house one day. It happened that Frank and Magda Bauer lived one block away from us, on Arapaho. So we were already four immigrant couples.

One day I got a note from my friend Lizy in Washington, D.C., that a friend of hers was moving to Los Angeles and she very much wanted me to meet him. I still remember when he called. I met Siegfried Eisgrau on the corner of Detroit and Sunset Boulevard. He truly became a good friend, an interesting and very strange man, very verbal, very angry. We called him, *"der Geist, der stets verneint"* (from Goethe), which means in English something like "the mind that says no to everything." And he certainly did.

I do not remember exactly how we met Bert and Lilo Fischer. But I do know that Bert and **Rudy Brook** were both gardeners in homes of very wealthy movie people. We decided to come together once every month to talk about a topic that was interesting to us, because really and truly we knew very little about America, and we were very much interested in the happenings of the war. We also met **Fritz and Gerty Frankel.** Otto had known of Fritz from high school, where he and Fritz's older brother were in the same grade. Otto and Fritz met somewhere in Los Angeles, I do not know where.

As the *Gruppe* grew, we met regularly once a month and we became friends. That group helped for a long time, to get slowly adjusted to the new land. I remember how critical many of us were about America, about poor taste, about the high buildings, about the lack of culture. There was no opera, no concert hall, and no theater—just movies. Where would we ever hear music again? Now, thinking back, Los Angeles really was a great big village, and almost all of us had grown up in big cities. And then, the difficulty of the language. Except Otto, who had learned English at school, and myself and **Frank Bauer,** I don't think any of the others knew much English to begin with. So, in the beginning, for a number of years when we met, we spoke German. Otto and I had decided never to speak German once we got to this country. An idiotic decision. So Otto and I spoke English even when the others spoke German, which they didn't like. Thinking back, it was really a foolish decision because the language had nothing to do with Hitler. But in that time one did not think very much, one only felt.

What can I tell you about the *Gruppe* in the beginning? I think Frankels were the only ones who had been married in New York before they came to Los Angeles. The others were already married in Europe. By coincidence or design, several of us had children in 1943. So you had friends of the same age. There were Bob Bauer, Danny Ikenberg, Miriam Frankel.

Otto and I had decided to have a child as soon as possible. Now thinking about it, it was an incredible idea. How could people who were so insecure financially think about having a child? But it was the greatest wish of my life. And I was by that time already more than 30 years old.

Returning to the Gruppe, *what do you feel it provided you with in the first three or four years? What was its role in your life?*

I think it was the chance really to be able to talk with a group of people. Most of us had jobs way below our education, and it provided us with an opportunity to think together, to exchange opinions, views, raise questions, or talk about the war and our families about whom we hadn't heard anything—only fears, but no real proof that they were not alive any longer. Certainty came quite a bit later. It was like family, the only family we had; there was none else. And that of course drew us closer and closer together.

What it was like for you to be an enemy alien? What sort of restrictions were imposed? How did people treat you, a foreigner of the same nationality as the enemy?

We Austrians were supposed to be enemy aliens, but we were better treated than the German immigrants. They had a curfew and had to be home at 8 o'clock at night. So, for example, when we had *Gruppe* meetings, we always met in a German's home. Austrians were free to go home at any time, but the Germans had to be in their homes by 8 o'clock.

Did you always meet on weekends?

Yes. Everyone was working during the week. We met in the afternoon and sometimes in the evening. We lived quite close together, most within walking distance. It was like we know about New York, where groups of Jews live in one little area. We were closest to the **Frankels,** not only because they lived nearby, but also, **Gerty** and I really hit it off very well. We became very close friends. And then our children were born within one month of each other.

How were you treated as a foreigner by the general population?

I have no recollection that we were treated in a particular way. I only want to mention one thing that I still recall, my only happening of anti-Semitism in America. When I tried to find an apartment, I found a very nice place and decided to rent the apartment, and the lady asked me for a check as a down payment. As I handed her a check, she looked at my name and said, "We do not accept Jews in our house." That was a terrible shock. That was the only and last time that I have had such an experience.

I'm curious about the use of the German language in our household. You said that you and Otto decided not to speak German. I recall that you did speak German sometimes and I didn't like it and asked you to "stop talking that ugly language." I also remember that you talked about me in German and that because I was curious, I actually learned how to understand. So apparently you did talk German sometimes.

21

You were a very precocious child from the beginning. When you were two years old, you spoke quite fluently in English. We decided that because you were doing so well, that it would be a good idea to let you learn another language. But what would be the other language? It would be German because that was the one we knew best. So we began to speak German to you and probably also to each other for a while. You responded in the most unusual way. At least for me at that time it was unusual. When I asked you a question, you would answer in English. You answered a German question in English, so obviously you understood. This continued for quite a while. We didn't give up until you finally said, "I don't like those words. I don't like *Nase* [nose]. I don't like any of it. I don't like the language." It turned out that this happened among other friends. Somehow or other, not clearly understandable, the negative feelings that we had about Germany and also unfortunately about the German language must have oozed out, so a little child could feel that. I have never really figured this out.

Here you're alluding to feelings about Germany. In those first years, I'd like to know about your attitude toward Germany or, even more important, toward the Austrians who had been your friends and neighbors—the non-Jews. And what were you feelings about Austria, the place from which you were expelled?

I knew I would never return to Vienna because I had signed a paper declaring that I would never, as long as I lived, return to that country. I was eager to become an American citizen, which I did exactly the day both Otto and I were permitted to become naturalized. That means I had to wait a bit for Otto to be here for the required five years. Then we became American citizens together. I had no special feelings about Austria during that time. Remember, our families had been deported and a few had left on their own. I was not in touch with any of them, I did not know where they lived. I think four of my cousins got out. I had no feelings. All the ties had broken off. Eventually we learned that most all of them had died. We were isolated completely as far as family was concerned. I had no feelings about Germany, no feelings about Austria. We hated everything that was German. You know, you are not very rational when you go through an experience like that. For example, Otto wouldn't go to a concert conducted by a German conductor. To me this seemed very foolish, but that was the way he felt and there was nothing one could do. Eventually this wore off.

Did you remain in contact with any non-Jews in Vienna? Or reestablish any contacts?

Yes, a few. I had a gentile friend, Marianne Stern, who lived in the same apartment house as my family. I stayed in touch with her for many, many years. Of course I had non-Jewish friends. I wrote to several of them when I was in England. Some replied, others didn't. Those who replied, I stayed in touch with. Otto asked me many times how come I had non-Jewish friends who still wrote to me. I couldn't understand the question really. But Otto didn't have any non-Jewish friends at all. I think that difference between us continued. I made many friends here too who aren't Jewish, which he did not do.

Do you have any sense of what proportion of your Jewish friends in Vienna survived?

About half of my friends were Jewish. Of my closest friends, three were Jewish and none survived.

Did you and Otto join a synagogue soon after settling in Los Angeles?

I don't remember that we joined one. Otto would go to temple on the High Holidays. I would join him in the evenings. I don't think we joined a synagogue until we moved to Altadena in 1950. There we joined the temple of which we are still members.

Was America or Los Angeles anything like you had expected?

I knew very little about the United States. I did know about the very, very high buildings in New York, but they were very different from what I had expected. New York was completely overwhelming. We didn't go sightseeing, just stood there and looked. It was the strangest experience. I felt like I had come from another planet. On my trip from New York by bus to Los Angeles, I began to feel that it was a country in which I might be able to live. And there was the jubilant feeling that there was a country where I was permitted to live, where there was nobody who would feel I am nothing because I am a Jew. For me it was a great feeling of thankfulness to a place that accepted me as who I was—not a committed Jew (that I never was), but I was a Jew. That's the way my parents had raised me.

At what point did you feel really at home living here in Los Angeles?

I was told when I had the first dream in English, that would be the sign. But I felt at home much sooner than that. I think when you were born I was definitely an American.

When did you return to Vienna, and how did you feel there?

Twenty-five years after we got to this country, we took a trip to Europe, with a few days in Vienna. It was a beautiful city, as it always has been. But it was terrible for me. I felt totally disoriented. I could remember the names of streets, but I couldn't find my way to places I had been hundreds of times. I went to the cemetery and tried to find my parents' grave, but I couldn't find it. I had been to my mother's grave many, many times. In the past I could have found it blindfolded. But now, either the bushes had grown too high or there were new trees or—no, it was me. It was a terrible experience for me, that disorientation. All I wanted was to get out.

Here's a question that may take some thinking. Is there someone or some incident or some object that was of special significance in sustaining you in those immigration years, either before you left or at the beginning here? Sometimes we survive critical times partially because of someone or something or some phrase that was given to us by an important person. I don't know if there are any such for you during those years, but if so, that would be of interest to me.

Perhaps my cousin Ernst, who meant so much in my life. He gave me his best and his worst. I remember one of the best things he did for me was when he told me many years before I left Vienna, "You will succeed wherever you go. You will always be liked because you are a very good, decent human being, and you know how to live with other people." Somehow or other, Ernst's absolute trust in my ability, in my making decisions, in my accepting the world if I possibly could, in accepting changes, all of this traveled with me. I think that stayed with me during all the difficult times. I really knew inside of me—and I cannot explain it—I knew I would make it.

But when you asked what gave me the worth of continuing here, there was Otto, with whom I wanted to live. I was madly in love with him and I never thought of anything else. We were together and that was enough. And we were going to have a child. And I had my absolute knowledge that no matter how hard it would be, I would make it. I have lived with that trust, I think, all my life.

24

OTTO WOLMAN

Fearing a night raid by storm troopers, Otto Wolman chose not to sleep at his parents' apartment. Instead, he spent nights alone in his father's defunct office, upstairs in a wholesale business building. He tried once to slip across the German border into Belgium, but the "escort," paid in advance, did not show. Subject to the Polish quota because of national borders that had been redefined after World War I, Otto would never have gotten out of Austria had his future wife, Marianne, then in England, not been in a minor and life-saving accident.

The period just before and leading to emigration was the beginning of the end. I was fully aware of the difficulty of having a future in Austria, of having a job. In 1927, I completed the normal course of studies at the Hochschule für Welthandel [University of Business Economics]. With my father's help, I got part-time work in the office of a shoe factory and collected unemployment insurance for a few months. Then, through a friend of my parents in a grain import company, I got a better position with Winterstein & Naschitz, an agricultural import/export firm where I used my English and French.

I looked to get out of the country. I wrote letters to various companies abroad. I thought of going to Germany or to Italy, where the company I was employed by in Vienna had connections with an import firm of agricultural products. I would have liked to go to Hamburg, Germany. The idea of political danger didn't appear at that time; it was just that the economic future in Austria seemed nonexistent.

Did that have to do with being Jewish?

Austria was in a generally difficult economic condition and for Jews it was especially difficult. Non-Jews could get government jobs, but these positions were closed to Jews. And it was nearly impossible for Jews to get employment in private enterprises not owned by Jews.

So I studied Italian from a grammar book and dictionary at home and wrote an application to the business connection in Italy. Surprisingly, I was hired by this large, wholesale grain import firm in Milan. With mixed feelings, I left my parents and Vienna and became a foreign language specialist—a writing, translating correspondent. The people there were very friendly and intelligent people. I had some trouble in verbal communication. I lived in a furnished room in an ancient, run-down palazzo, ate frequently in a kosher *pensione* operated by Polish Jews. My life in Milan and the work got tedious. It looked like a dead end. I tried to change jobs but had no official work permit, no satisfactory social backing. After about a year (from 1931 to 1932), I returned to Vienna.

I found a position as export correspondent with a firm making artists' paints for export to the Orient and South America. I also resumed my studies and worked on a dissertation. I obtained the degree of Doctor of Business Economics, which was not really helpful in 1933. During those years, most Jewish people were in business or professional positions. They somehow managed to get by. We knew it was tough, but we were young and hoped for the best.

In 1933, I married a young woman I had known for a long time. We had gone together on many week-end hikes in the Vienna Woods. She was a member of the *Blau-Weiss* youth movement [the Blue White, a Zionist group]. To get married and go to Palestine seemed like an escape into a future—into a Jewish land where we could sing Hebrew songs in the street. We went by train to Trieste, then by boat, the *Martha Washington,* to Jaffa. Hundreds of other Jewish people were on the ship. They too wanted to build a new life in Palestine.

I was too Viennese and felt too old and too soft for trying agriculture or work in a kibbutz. I met fellow immigrants from Vienna with whom I could go into an electrical and radio business, and I had a promising interview at the Banca d'Italia. I bought one dunam of land on Mount Carmel as an investment. There was an atmosphere of growing, building, and adventure.

But to be in Palestine was unreal for me. I was overwhelmed by the struggle for survival in a primitive country. Our packing cases with household goods shipped from Vienna by boat never arrived, were looted en route. The daily contact with the people, mostly poor immigrants from Poland, in this poor backward land was even harder on Regi, my wife. She was used to Viennese theater, music, and coffeehouses. After a few unhappy months, we returned to Vienna, and nothing worked out there either. She studied logotherapy and left for London in 1935, and some years later immigrated to New York. We eventually got divorced by proxy. I stayed on in Vienna with my parents.

During these years before the Nazi occupation of Austria, were Jews harassed by Austrians?

Not on the streets or in their homes. Before March 13, 1938, the Austrian police still functioned. The government was a clerical, fascist government. The socialists had been kicked out during a revolt in 1927. Cannons had been placed in the streets and buildings put up by the City of Vienna were shot at and demolished because it was known that socialists lived in them. Now, prior to the Nazi invasion, law and order was still upheld. There was strong anti-Semitism, but no vicious or violent acts were openly practiced.

So the problems were primarily economic, in that it was very difficult, especially for Jews, to get and keep a job.

Right. While there was discrimination, it was not physically violent. However, there was one exception—at the university itself and at all other schools of higher standing. There were lots of Nazi students and they were violent and yelled at Jews, pushed them around and down from ramps and staircases. For some periods of time, the University was closed because of rioting. Some Jewish students tried to resist but were overwhelmed by the many Nazi students.

I know that prior to the German invasion, some Austrian Jews had already left or were trying to leave Austria. Is that because it was felt to be quite likely that the Germans would invade and take over?

No, it was mostly because of the economic difficulties that existed in Austria for Jews. For some years, too, a number of Jews went to Soviet Russia because they were socialists. Some returned subsequently.

What was happening in Germany to Jews at that time? Were they being shipped off to labor camps?

Yes, but not in great numbers. Jobs and property were taken away from German Jews, so they were indirectly forced to emigrate. The difficulty with emigration was that other countries didn't want to accept them. Jews felt they had to get out of Germany, where they had lost their livelihoods, jobs, and possessions. Even their houses were taken away with all sorts of excuses, or they were compelled to sell their houses at ridiculous prices. At that time there was a strong sentiment for going to Palestine; that was the time for Zionists to gain followers. And whoever had relatives in America or other countries tried to go there. In Austria, too, there was flight, an exodus of Jews and socialists who despaired of their future. I had two friends who got out before the *Anschluss*, went to Paris, and got jobs there.

Let's return to you in Vienna just prior to the Anschluss.

There was more and more Nazi activity and things became more and more difficult. I was working with my father in the wholesale shoe business on Franz Josef Kai, one of the main commercial streets in the inner city. It was upstairs, and our customers were Jewish retail merchants who then sold our shoes on installments. We managed to earn a living until March 13, 1938, the *Anschluss*, when everything came to a sudden end. Our customers, the Jewish dealers, couldn't pay us anymore because their customers couldn't pay them. We declared bankruptcy. There were some court proceedings, but they were a farce. I was called before a judge who urged us not to declare bankruptcy but to provide a settlement plan with our creditors. We were supposed to set a "good example." The business stopped functioning. My father continued to go to the store, I think almost every day. He had no place else to go and nothing else to do. He needed something to do. We lived by selling off the inventory and eating up the proceeds.

The bankruptcy court representative inadvertently became our protector. He was an old-time Austrian who wasn't really a Nazi, and he permitted us to remain on the premises until everything was sold out. He came to check on us once a week or every other week, supposedly to make certain we weren't collecting any money. He said hello, was friendly, and that was all. A sign with a swastika on our store stated our bankruptcy. Storm troopers left us alone. At that time, Nazi storm troopers went from door to door or from store to store. Wherever there were Jewish merchants, the troopers stole whatever they could lay their hands on.

I might mention that the incorporation of Austria was not with the outward appearance of peaceful annexation. The Germans came with hundreds of airplanes flying over Upper Austria and Lower Austria [which includes Vienna], which gave the appearance that if there was any resistance it would be quickly put down. Some Austrian troops put up some semblance of resistance, but not much. Many of the Austrian troops were basically Catholic Fascists, but there were plenty of Nazis among them, too.

Immediately, the war against Jews, Social Democrats, and Communists was carried on in the streets. Jews were captured and forced to do calisthenics and to clean the streets. They were beaten. They were detained at the police jails, some released after they had been beaten up and robbed of their personal belongings. It was a chaotic situation, probably not directed from any central headquarters. Anybody who was not Jewish and had some grudge to take out on Jews or on the world in general could do what he pleased. They were *vogelfrei*. That means "free as a bird." Any non-Jew who walked in the streets could spit on me or hit me in the face or kill me, and there would be no recourse possible. To call a policeman would have been futile, because he probably would have either turned his back or helped the aggressor to hurt me further.

Were they taking people out of their homes at that point?

Yes, although mostly the storm troopers were removing and destroying furniture—like thieves and robbers. People were sometimes taken to police headquarters and disappeared. They were sent to concentration camps. For example, **Fritz Frankel** was picked up and taken to Hotel Metropole (which housed police headquarters) and then was transferred to Dachau concentration camp.

When did it become clear to you that you had to get out?

When the Nazis marched into Austria and Austria became part of Germany, it was clearly impossible to stay any longer. There was a rush of people to the American Consulate and to other embassies to apply for entry visas. Long lines of people waited for days. I applied for immigration into Cuba, Mexico, and the U.S. To get a visa to the U.S. was particularly difficult because of strict quotas. I was on the Polish quota, which was full up for many years. A visa to the U.S. was therefore nearly impossible for me. I don't remember whether I had applied before or only after the Germans took Austria.

We made wild and unrealistic attempts to get out. I got approval to apply for permission to enter Mexico but not to any of the larger cities close to the border or coastlines. They were interested in getting immigrants with good backgrounds and education to settle in the interior of Mexico. Immigration to Shanghai was a possibility. Numerous people from Vienna went there, but that felt to me like going into something completely unknown and absurd somehow. So I waited for the American visa, if there would be one.

Lots of people tried to get out illegally to adjoining countries. Many went to Germany, which was quieter at that time. Others went to Czechoslovakia, Hungary, or Yugoslavia, all subsequently occupied by Germany; so those emigrations were only temporary relief from the final destruction.

"Encouragement" for emigration was speeded up by the police and authorities under German control and guidance, who kept on arresting Jews, throwing them out of their homes. Jews were thrown out of their professions; they could not practice anymore as physicians, certainly not as teachers. Wherever they were employees, they lost their positions and had no means of livelihood. This was the best way of pushing them out of the country. And that was the declared goal of the Nazis. They wanted it, like Germany, to be *judenrein*. But other countries didn't want to accept Jews, especially as poor people. If they had some skills, like doctors or engineers, they were not welcome either because they would be competition. No other country really made it easy for Jewish people to immigrate.

I still lived with my parents. But I didn't feel safe there because gangs of storm troopers were going around looking for Jews and were breaking into stores and apartments. They went from house to house, talked to the porter and the manager and asked if there were any Jewish tenants in the building. The resident manager, of course, was scared himself and often took them to the Jewish tenants. Then the storm troopers (with friends and followers) robbed, looted and destroyed contents of the apartments and stores. They either beat up the people who lived there or took them to headquarters where they would be detained for some limited time like hours or days. But their living quarters then identified, these Jews were earmarked for subsequent deportation. We didn't know of any deportations yet, but we did know that many people were in concentration camps in Austria.

In the building where I lived with my parents, about half the tenants were Jewish. As it turned out, none were attacked, robbed or beaten. We were all bypassed by some oversight. Our business didn't exist anymore. But I could use the store. The store was somehow a safe place. I slept there occasionally because it seemed unlikely that surprise visits by Nazi storm troopers would happen at night, upstairs, in a wholesale business building. The managers of the building knew I was there, but they were friendly people and could be trusted.

Was your sister, Steffy, living with your parents at this time, too?

No, Steffy had married Fred Knee, who had a flourishing furniture store in Vienna. But shortly thereafter, that store was "Nazified"; a former employee, a member of the Nazi Party, said, "I want that store," and was put into the store as manager. Then he took over the business completely. In this frequent procedure, the previous Jewish owner had to sign transfer papers, sometimes receiving some money, sometimes not. If he got something, then he might have subsequently been put in jail or camp. Fred got nothing. Then Fred and Steffy had to give up their apartment and moved in with my parents. Steffy was pregnant and about to deliver her baby. They had to find a Jewish hospital, since others were off limits. I think Tirza was born at the Rothchild Hospital.

They succeeded in 1939 to go to Palestine because Fred had been there before. Also, because they were able to prove that they had $1,000 in a Swiss bank account, they could get a visa. This money had been placed in a family account by an aunt of ours, to be used for extreme circumstances. Because of this $1,000, Steffy got a visa as a "Capitalist." British authorities in Palestine permitted new immigrants to come into the country if they could prove that they had either some special trade that was needed in Palestine or at least $1,000. There was a quota for such people. The $1,000 saved Steffy. That aunt whose $1,000 they used lived in Bielitz, Poland. When Poland was overrun, she and her husband were deported. I think they went first to Lemberg by foot and then into some concentration camp. Nothing was heard of them anymore.

With my friends, I continued our Sunday outings to the Vienna Woods, going there by streetcar. We were anxious about meeting groups of young Nazis there, but nothing ever happened. When we got together, often in homes, we discussed emigration. It was possible for women to get to England because there was a great demand for women as household helpers. You *could* get work permits in England. But for men the chance was very minimal. You had to be some special personality or have some special skills. Couples spoke of emigrating separately, the wife first. Then she would try to help the husband come later. It was a miserable and desperate situation. We felt we were not in this world anymore, but somewhere in-between, between this world and nothing.

It was a time of great stress. We didn't know whether we would survive the day in peace and if we would survive the night without disturbance. And then what would the next days bring? It was a hopeless situation. The political situation in Europe got worse. The Germans put an ultimatum to Czechoslovakia to give up the German part of the country, Sudetenland, which had become the northern part of Czechoslovakia after World War I. They set an October 1938 date for invasion unless the Czechs voluntarily would give up that part of their country. Already in 1936, the Germans had occupied the Rhineland without resistance, in violation of a World War I treaty which had placed that area in the hands of the French. This became again the western section of Germany.

I felt like everybody else, that if that ultimatum would come to pass, and the Czechs wouldn't give in, or maybe even if they did give up that part of the country, the Germans would start a war to incorporate them—as they had previously incorporated Austria without a war.

I thought it would be better to get out of Austria before that happened. On Succoth, while at the synagogue, I told my father that I had to leave Austria. He blessed me and cried. I cried, too. I hugged my mother and we wept. I didn't know whether I'd ever see my parents again. I left before the services ended.

I took a raincoat and my *Aktentasche*—the briefcase carried by all Austrians. And a hat—I had a hat, of course. Money? A minimum of money. We were permitted to take out only 10 or 20 reichsmarks. I had not much of an idea how far I would go with that. I had arranged with a friend of mine, Hermann Esslau, that we would go together. We left from the Westbahnhof. Where did we go to? We had met somebody who had connections with people in Aachen, a German town at the border with Belgium. These people were helping Jewish individuals to cross the border from Germany into Belgium in a place where they knew there was no border patrol—for a fee of course. We had not much to lose, so we started off.

Hermann and I went to Aachen by train. In the train I actually felt very comfortable. We didn't wear a swastika, but some other people didn't either. We were out of Austria and in Germany; things were moving calmly. There was no particular excitement noticeable or visible. We went to Köln, proceeded to Aachen, and waited for a rendezvous with the fellow who was supposed to meet us and take us across. I think there was a streetcar going then from Germany to Belgium. We had legitimate German passports. With these, the Germans theoretically should let us out, but the Belgians wouldn't let us in.

How were you supposed to connect up with your "escort"?

Our contact in Vienna told us to wait for him at a certain spot. We waited and he didn't come. There may have been all kinds of reasons for that. He might have changed his mind, might have been put in jail, captured, or . . . . We didn't know. So we stood there in Aachen and nothing happened. We had to decide what to do next. Should we go alone? We were scared. We knew that first we would be stopped by the German border police, and although we had German passports and proper papers, the police might have detained us and/or put us in jail. Or, if we had managed to get past the German guards, we might have been stopped by the Belgian border patrols and been arrested. Even worse, they might have sent us back to the German border police. That was done very frequently by the Belgians, French, and

Swiss. Jews weren't wanted in these countries, so they were sent back to Germany. The whole thing could have resulted in disaster. Jews who had tried to escape illegally were put into jail or a concentration camp.

In the meantime, news came that [Neville] Chamberlain, the British prime minister, had met with Hitler. He had convinced the Allies to sign the Munich Pact with Germany that consented to Germany's claim to the Sudetenland in exchange for a promise of peace and no further territorial demands. Thereupon, the Germans marched into Czechoslovakia and occupied that part of it. (Six months later, Germany took over the remainder of Czechoslovakia.)

Now there was no urgency anymore, so it seemed, to leave Austria. But I hated the idea of simply going back to Vienna and was certainly not convinced that this pact would hold. I remembered that there was a town on the border to Denmark called Schleswig-Holstein, where it was easy to go from one side of the city to the other (across the border) simply by getting on a streetcar. Hermann gave up and went back to Vienna, and I took a train to Hamburg and on to Kiel, toward the border. But then I got scared to do that crossing without knowing anybody. The urgency to leave wasn't enough to push me onward. In Kiel, I bought a train ticket back to Vienna.

So there I was back in Vienna. I again stayed in the apartment with my parents. This was a shadowy period with no future and no present—it was another in-between period. We didn't know what was going to happen. It was a very depressing period with no hope for anything positive except that we were thinking, dreaming, and doing whatever we could to make arrangements to legally get out of there. I bought an open ticket for a boat trip from Hamburg to New York—just in case.

At that point did you have an affidavit?

I think I did have one by then from a gentleman in Kentucky whom I didn't know. He was a distant relative of Regi, who was still in London trying to make a living as a logotherapist.

In addition to that affidavit I had from Mr. Kornblum, I tried to get another one. I did what many other people did—scrounge around for someone in America who would guarantee for me. I went to the main post office and looked in telephone books of New York for people with the same name as mine. I found a few Wohlmanns. I wrote letters, telling them my story and asking them to help me immigrate. I assumed, of course, they were familiar with the situation in Austria from the newspapers and radio. One good day, I really did receive a letter from a lady by the name of Esther Beegle from New York. She said a letter from me had been delivered to her neighbors in an apartment building. Those neighbors had moved out. She had taken the liberty of opening the letter and thought this was an opportunity for her to help somebody. We corresponded, and she eventually did provide an affidavit that was probably valid. But I never used it. I used the one from the fellow in Kentucky, whom I believe was not alive anymore when I finally was able to use it.

So, that was an in-between period between the past and a possible future, waiting for permits and visas. I met with other people in my situation. In the meantime, the gentile world went on; everything seemed to be normal. But there were a lot of people in uniforms in the streets, and the Jewish stores were either empty or had big signs on them covered with painted graffiti—"Jew."

That's how it was until the famous *Kristallnacht* on the ninth of November. Then, a great increase in Jewish people were ordered to the police headquarters and real mass deportations began.

Did you know ahead of time that Kristallnacht *was going to happen?*

No, but it was during a time of increased night attacks by storm troopers, so I was by myself in the store. The next day I heard that synagogues throughout Germany (which now included Austria) had been burned down and that there had been widespread attacks on Jewish stores during that dreadful night. I was afraid that at any moment something horrible would happen. Fortunately, it didn't. Meanwhile I was in contact with Marianne, who had succeeded after some heart-rending decisions to leave Vienna and was working in South Wales. I don't know what became of her apartment.

Maybe Emil remained there?

No, I think it was taken over by some neighbors and the furniture sold at ridiculous prices. And I? What happened to me? I stayed on until, thanks to Marianne, I got a call to the English Consulate and received a tourist visa to England. Many documents and papers had to be secured and things sent away. Finally, after a couple months, in early 1939, came the day that I was able to go to England. I went by train to London, then to Llanelly. There Marianne waited for me. She had a "wonderful" job as a cook and housekeeper for a large family. What shocked me most there was that she stayed in a garret room just under the roof. It had some windows that were broken and it was bitter cold. She had a miserable bed. There was another member of the family who also slept there. It wasn't that there was some discrimination against Marianne. These were poor people and they were used to living very poorly. They were very friendly and compassionate. I stayed there for some time as a guest. That was the way people who got out of Austria or Germany could survive for some time—to be invited by English Jewish families to be

34

their guest. I got a horrible cold there, maybe some sort of pneumonia. Besides Marianne, the lady of the house, Mrs. Greene, took good care of me. She rubbed my chest with Vicks and she too enjoyed it! I was accepted as a friend of the family for a few weeks.

Then the Greenes found another place for me, with a family in Swansea. That's about an hour and a half by bus away from Llanelly. I stayed there, again as a guest, for one or two months. It was painful. I didn't know what to do with myself. I went to the public library, which was very poorly equipped. I had nothing to do but continue waiting for the unlikely American visa.

I left that situation and went to London, where I was helped by the Jewish Relief Committee. I think I got 20 shillings per week. I paid 10 shillings for a room, a miserable room, and did some work for the Refugee Relief Committee, which was helping people get to the U.S. At Bloomsbury House, the committee headquarters, I filed papers in the archives. The building was filled with refugees from Central Europe and was very busy. Marianne had quit her job in Llanelly to take a position as a matron of a home for refugee children in Croydon, a suburb of London. So there was another period in which we were close, but not together.

In London, I "prepared" myself for immigration. Everyone knew that America didn't have jobs for immigrants who knew about German or English literature or who had a good idea of English grammar. It was also unlikely that I'd have the opportunity to be a merchant or be able to use what I had learned in Vienna of economics. What was possibly available would be jobs to make things. So, with my innocent belief in what the immigration experts advised in Vienna, I took a night course in the making of leather bags and briefcases. I didn't learn very much, but somehow got the idea how to cut the patterns for men's and ladies' purses and how they are then made by gluing the pieces together. I didn't get any chance to sew them.

I remember the outbreak of the war. I was at Bloomsbury House. I had been drafted into the air-raid protection group, so I had a steel helmet and a label or sign. There was a lot of noise, church bells rang, and I think cannons went off or bombs were dropped. That was the beginning of the war. At the moment, we didn't have the slightest idea what it really signified. The blackout in London was ordered, complete blackout at night. The traffic came to a standstill except in the Underground [the subway]. People had to carry newspapers or white clothing to be seen. Flashlights were not permitted. That was before the actual bombing of the city started.

My parents had come to London. It was a wonderful, amazing thing that they could come. England was somehow compassionate, permitted thousands of Jewish refugees from Europe to come in, based on the premise that they would stay in England temporarily and then continue to a final country of destination. My parents had documents to show that their daughter was in Palestine and that they had applied for the certificates which would allow them to join her.

My parents' arrival was a sad one. I met them at Victoria Station. We took the Underground since we had no money for a taxi. I had rented a housekeeping room, as was customary in London, for them. It was near the railroad in a district where lots of Jews lived, very miserable and poor. For cooking they had a gas ring, commonly used in England in such modest quarters as this. I noticed they were sorely disappointed, but after all, they had come from a place from which there was no place to go. Gradually, they began to meet and know some people in the neighborhood, some other Jewish émigrés from Germany and Austria. Before long they even found an apartment that had been deserted by British people. Afraid of the German bombing attacks once war had been declared, a lot of Londoners left the city. The refugees, who were thankful to be there, could move into these vacated apartments. So my parents lived in a pretty nice apartment in a five-story flat. They had two or three bedrooms on the ground floor. There was a little garden behind the building, and my father planted tomatoes there.

Did they pay to live in the apartment?

Yes. A cousin of ours who managed to get from Germany to London shared the apartment. She was a corset maker. She and my mother earned some money by sewing. Also, we all made a regular trip, I think once a week, to the Refugee Committee, where we got very minimal support. And I did some secretarial and bookkeeping work for an Austrian who was in the export business. Then I tried something else. Somebody I knew made drawings or designs of dress models and I tried to peddle them to dress manufacturers. I wasn't very successful with that. Anyway, I did earn a few shillings, not very much, and with the support from Bloomsbury House, managed to have a miserable, poor life. I think I still lived in a single room.

So that was life in London. From the beginning of the war, there had been complete blackout at night. Black paper strips were pasted on the windows and gas masks were prepared. We knew the cellar room where to go to in case of a bombing attack. The balloon barrage was set up and made walking at night in the blacked out city uncomfortable. My expeditions to night school were special experiences. Each trip was an adventure in a dark and mysterious country! One evening I walked in the darkness and almost ran into the ropes that were holding a barrage balloon. It was pitch dark.

These were miserable days, but not desperate, because we were sharing the difficulties and problems of the population around us. We had no solid source of income, but there were thousands of people living like us and there was no threat of being chased out or of being killed because we were Jews.

I don't think we knew about the deportations that were going on in Germany and Poland at that time. But the war was going on in Europe and that was bad enough. We did know about the sinking of ships on the seas around Europe and on the Atlantic between America and Europe. Europe was dependent on supplies and communications from America. The sinking of ships caused serious economic hardships and of course made emigration from England or the Continent a risky business.

When Marianne got her visa for America she had a serious problem. Number one, she was afraid that the ship would be sunk, and number two, she was afraid of leaving me behind with little hope that she would see me again. It was a desperate situation. She could have stayed in London and lost her American visa for life, so to speak. We really didn't know what was going to happen, only that everything was temporary. Marianne left.

I remember hearing that just before her boat was to depart, you tried to contact her? Did you intend to ask her not to leave?

No. Marianne was ambivalent, uncertain whether to go, and until the last minute she thought of calling me and canceling the trip. I think I told her to go ahead. There was no prospect of anything good in the future for our semi-life in England. The Germans were having tremendous success with the war effort in Europe. After Austria and Czechoslovakia, they overran Poland in a few days. Then they conquered Belgium, Holland, and France. There was no stopping the German war machine. It seemed likely that there would be severe bombing of Britain, too, and possibly occupation by the Germans. That would have been the end of the Jews of Great Britain, the same as it was on the European continent. There was no reason to assume that they wouldn't eventually devastate England. They had superior war power and airplanes, and could even shoot across the Channel with their rockets and bombs.

The English were somehow ignorant, or just didn't want to believe in the German war power. I remember once I was even called to the police station because I had mentioned to some people that I had seen German warplanes and they seemed to be so powerful. I was warned not to spread such rumors. The English were just like children. They didn't want to believe that Great Britain could be threatened by Germany.

Marianne took off finally. She gave in somehow to my urgings. Her boat left from Southampton in a convoy—a group of ships accompanied by some warships to protect them against German submarines and airplanes.

After Marianne left there was an all-pervasive feeling of emptiness and senselessness and loneliness. And again, that state of numbness about the present and the future. There was no reason to expect anything good from the future. The hope to see Marianne ever again was unreasonable. I was so unhappy for her and for me. There was only waiting and hoping. I continued learning how to make leather goods and wasted time in public libraries. There is nothing worth remembering about that period except the exchange of letters with Marianne—and hoping, hoping . . . Her words of love made it both easier and harder to be thousands of miles away. And I kept on doing some work at Bloomsbury House. Now, as a messenger, I still earned 20 shillings per week.

We were waiting to be bombed. Germany had already conquered most of Europe and was set to invade England. As countries were conquered and Jews could no longer get out, their positions on the list for visas were forfeited. American visa numbers were transferred from consulates in these countries to London. Soon after France fell, I got a notice to go to the American Consulate and get papers that would permit me to leave for the U.S.A. This was fireworks! To get out—and to be with Marianne, who had become the center of my life!

Leaving my parents behind was horrible. I took a train to the ship in Southampton. A terrible feeling of loneliness overcame me. I was going to leave Europe, everything really, my past life, and hopefully going to America into nothing except the one bright light, to meet Marianne.

The trip as such was uneventful. We did not see any submarines, and submarines didn't see us. There were hardly any normal passengers. In fact, the ship was three-quarters empty, mostly occupied by Jewish émigrés from Europe on their last leg of emigration to the United States. It seemed tragic that not more refugees in England had visas and could be on the ship. For me, it was sort of a pleasure trip. It was a pleasure to eat, and it was comfortable to have no worries except about submarines which you could do nothing about. The trip took seven days.

I finally got to New York. I think I saw the Statue of Liberty, or was it foggy? We landed at the Hudson River embankment in the morning. And when permitted to disembark, I saw somebody waiting for me—my old friend Herman Esslau from Vienna. I was really moved because I felt I was not on a foreign continent at all, but a new world that was just a way station in my life. After customs and formalities, Herman and I picked up my two suitcases and walked to his apartment, which was nearby. That was an unusual situation—a new immigrant arriving in New York with a couple of suitcases and walking directly to the place where he was going to stay! Herman looked pretty well. He had no job, but that was nothing new. We shared stories of miseries of all immigrants. Those were the regular stories making the rounds at that time. We walked 10 blocks, quite an exhausting drag, and came to his apartment on 96th Street. That was where most new immigrants lived, in old brownstone buildings, in single rooms. Herman shared his room with Emil, an old friend from Vienna and very fine man. They did some cooking on a ring or perhaps a primitive gas stove, and I remember having some cocoa there.

Excuse me, but how could you stay even briefly with Herman if Emil was living there? And how could he tolerate having you there? Didn't he know that you were on your way to Santa Barbara to be with Marianne, still his wife at that time?

I assume he knew. Emil and Marianne were in divorce proceedings.

It strikes me as a rather extraordinary living arrangement!

The whole situation was very extraordinary, suspended between hell and who knew what next.

Yes, but . . . Anyway, so there you were, the three of you in New York City.

We didn't spend much time together. Each of us went his own way, looking for some connections and work possibilities. Where was Herman's wife at that time? She wasn't in New York, was at a job somewhere else. Family relationships were mixed up; life was temporary. The thing that kept me afloat there was the connection with Marianne. I prepared for the bus trip to California—the goal of my immigration. Everybody envied me for going to California because the situation in New York was very, very difficult for newcomers. I took the trip through the country, which was not very interesting, to put it mildly. It was only long and tiring. I had some trouble understanding the American English. I went first to Los Angeles and was met by the Links, Marianne's step-uncle and aunt. They were very friendly, I guess mostly because they knew I would be leaving the next day. It was wonderful not to be lost in the desert and completely alone.

I took a bus to Santa Barbara. The trip was pretty nice, not very long. Marianne was there, at the final bus stop, a hotel off Main Street. It was like a meeting of the lovers or the couple in a Mozart opera! Did we sing? Maybe not loud and audible, but within us. It was a reunion as we had been dreaming about for years, for eternity. That was the beginning of a new life—in California.

It was like having arrived in a fairy-tale country of luscious gardens and oak forests. Montecito [a most luxurious part of Santa Barbara] was like nothing I had ever seen before except in pictures. The house where Marianne lived and worked was fabulous. I was dazzled by tropical, strange, and amazing impressions. Of course, the most intense and greatest impression of all was Marianne, who looked very well and was there standing, figuratively and emotionally, with wide-open arms. We had a wonderful reunion.

We were together in the same city, but Marianne had a job. I really didn't know what I would to do with myself or where I would live. Fortunately, something happened that we had not anticipated, and we were able to stay close together. I got a very bad cold that developed into bronchial pneumonia. We didn't know what to do. Marianne worked very hard on obtaining some help, and she got it. She has always been a very competent girl when she wants to achieve something! She made it possible for me to stay in the servants' quarters of the house where she had the job as a governess/helper of two little children. Food and anything else was brought to me by Marianne with the best care, attention, and love. I had really a good time there. But for her, it was a double burden or more to put up with me after she spent the day with two rather difficult children. She went with them to the beach almost every day. As I regained my health, I went there too, by bus, and visited with her and wandered around the beach. It was another interim period between yesterday and tomorrow, but it was easy to take because Marianne was so close. We actually had a wonderful time. As I'm now talking to the recording machine many years later, 50 years almost, I'm thinking back of that time in Santa Barbara as one of the highlights of my life.

That period came to an end because the household disbanded. Marianne and I had to get going making our own plans. Marianne had some vague ideas and I had even less. The only thing we knew was that we wanted to go to Los Angeles. We arrived in L.A. by bus. We got a room with a small family in Hollywood. Marianne looked frantically for a job for herself and I contacted a Jewish group that helped new immigrants. They sent me to several places, but the first question I usually encountered was, "What local experience have you had?" It's difficult to get local experience if one begins to look for a job in a strange place, especially in a strange country! Marianne found it a little easier because she had connections with the Psychoanalytic Society. She met several ladies there who referred her to a variety of places. Of course we also looked at all the classified ads in the *Los Angeles Times* and made some calls.

I was referred to a place on Broadway, a sweatshop on the fifth floor. There was a Mr. Cohen from Iraq, who was head of this factory that manufactured brassieres. The place was named Gay Paris. That factory was anything but gay and certainly didn't invite any comparison with Paris! There were about 20 Russian women from a group in Los Angeles, I think called the "milk eaters," all middle aged or older women with babushkas. They sat at sewing machines and worked very busily and didn't get much pay, of course. There was a vacancy for someone who would run the office and sweep the floor, also do some errands and deliver merchandise. There was another candidate for that job, a doctor of law from Germany, but I got the job. Maybe the other fellow didn't look strong enough or his German accent bothered Mr. Cohen.

I stayed there for several weeks or maybe months. Mr. Cohen was himself the cutter of the brassieres. He had a wife and daughter who helped him to distribute the materials. These three were in constant arguments about money. It was not the job I dreamed of, and I wanted to get something better and more promising.

Based on my studies in the making of ladies' purses while in London, I considered myself as having some idea of how to make leather goods or manufacture them. I thought I might find work in such an enterprise. So while working at the brassiere factory, I looked for some companies that made bags. Where would I find such companies? In the Yellow Pages!

I looked in the Yellow Pages for names that somehow were promising, that is, Jewish names. I saw there Friedman Bag Company. I thought it was worth trying. I called and said I would like to apply for a job. They didn't say no and didn't go into any details. I took the streetcar to Friedman Bag Company. I was looking for a firm that made bags. The bags were there, but they were bags for potatoes, onions, and other agricultural products! That was a disappointment. But since I was there, I asked about a job. What could I do? We talked about an office job. The owner was a short Jewish fellow, his English was pretty good. He was a "successful" immigrant from Russia, had started up the company and hired his two brothers.

When you applied for jobs like the previous one or this one, did you say anything about your background? Did they know how well educated you were? Or would that have been a liability for such positions?

I couldn't tell Mr. Friedman that I had a doctor's degree in business economics because he would have been pleased to hear that and wished me much luck! He wouldn't have felt it was a good idea to offer me a job. So I didn't say anything about my education. I just said that I had business experience and was willing to work hard. He hired me. . . .

One day a man came into the bookkeeping department to check the books. I was told that he was a CPA who would help prepare financial statements and tax returns. I thought that was something new and interesting. It reminded me that in Vienna at the Hochschule there were classes to prepare people for this kind of work, to be a *Buchprüfer* [auditor]. That seemed to me to be much more interesting than bookkeeping. I became friendly with that auditor and after a few months he suggested that I should contact some CPA firms in L.A. and ask for a job, which I did.

Before you go on, what were you hired to be at Friedman Bag Company? What was your job?

At first, my job was to be a payroll bookkeeper, to write up the weekly payroll for the employees (maybe 30 people) and then prepare the payroll tax returns. Later, I handled the accounts receivable, where pretty substantial amounts of money went through the books.

As I mentioned before, I began to call on CPA firms. That was in 1942. The war had started and many young men had enlisted and were gone. People were involved in the war effort. The Depression had ended. That made the job situation much easier. I contacted several CPA firms, put on my beautiful, dark blue suit with a necktie to look like a professional, and went for interviews.

How did you decide to whom to apply? The Yellow Pages? Big names?

Yes, the Yellow Pages. Also, I talked to that auditor who came to Friedman Bag Company, and he advised me to seek out large firms that would most likely be hiring people. Most of the time I was asked the usual question about local experience, but there was a scarcity of men who were, so to speak, beginners in the accounting profession. I was offered a job, to my surprise, at Peat Marwick & Mitchell, downtown on 8th Street, in one of the high rises of those days (12 stories). In that office were 15 to 20 people. The firm started originally in London and had established itself as one of the leading accounting firms in the U.S. I was asked to wear a hat and long-sleeved shirts. There was really a formal setup.

I became a professional there, rather than somebody who is willing to do anything and is just a helper. I discovered that the worst thing to say when you look for a job is, "I'm willing to do anything." One has to know something extra, something specific, and to stress that. It may not lead to a job, but it leads to a guided identification of one's abilities.

There was a lot of traveling around in the L.A. area for that job. By then I had acquired an inexpensive automobile from a neighbor, an old Plymouth, gray with a soft top that had some leaks. So I had an umbrella in the car for rain! This was a very good period. I felt I was on an upswing. Things were getting better.

Was it while you were working with this large accounting firm that you got the idea to take classes and become a CPA?

Of course. In that firm it was logical to progress and make more money. The more advanced and better paid people were CPAs. This was the desired position for anyone who had the proper education. I spent a lot of time in classes, reading and preparing. The exams were very difficult, but I passed.

Now let's move on to something else. I'd like to hear about the Gruppe *and its role in your life. I'm curious why the* Gruppe *formed, what it gave you as an immigrant couple.*

The *Gruppe* didn't form according to a plan. We were newcomers in need of finding our place in society. The people that were most like us were other immigrants from Central Europe, people who spoke German, were familiar with soccer and not baseball, people who didn't have much money, were modest in their requirements, and who had the urge to get ahead, in establishing themselves, and who were in a similar age category. As it worked out, we met most of the people through recommendations. One led to another. Then, many of us had children at about the same time. This established a new relationship or connection and exchange of ideas. The basis of the group was for mutual support. We were a group of immigrants who had new children at the same time in a new country and had new jobs. Shared experiences caused a strong connection between us which has lasted throughout the years. In the meantime, of course, the jobs have changed, the children grown up, and people have moved to better homes.

What can you say about your attitude toward being Jewish during your first years in the United States? Did people with whom you interacted know you were a Jew? For example, at your job at Peat, Marwick & Mitchell, did people know you were a Jewish immigrant?

They knew I was an immigrant. They could tell by my language, but the subject of Jewishness never came up. That was a national firm and people were accepting of all. There were some Jewish people there, but not many.

How did persecution in Europe of you as a Jew affect your feelings about being a Jew once you were in the United States? Did it make you feel more Jewish, more eager to assimilate, or what? In short, what effect did it have on you as a Jew?

I was distressed about what happened there and indescribably happy and lucky to have escaped.

How did that affect you in your feelings of being a Jew?

Oh, some people may think they hated themselves because they were Jews. It never came to my mind to raise that question—to accept it or not to accept it. I was Jewish, period. The same as people are white or black.

Did you become more Jewish, or feel that you needed to uphold traditions more because of the persecution? I understand that some people reacted in that direction, while others rejected their Jewishness, ran away from it, ignored it.

No, I didn't run away from it. I admit that in Vienna I was not a Jew who went to temple regularly or was a member of a temple. But I lived in a home where my father was 1,000 percent Jewish, and it came to me quite naturally. I was, too, without really being a practicing Jew. I put on *tefillin* [small boxes containing verses from the Bible, worn during ritual prayer] for several years. Later on, I dropped that ritual. I don't recall when. One omission led to another.

I have the impression that you did not lead a very Jewish life during the first years in America.

We were too busy. To be Jewish was not that important. Important was to make a living, to survive—although there was no fear or anxiety of the future. The wonderful thing was that I had Marianne and you, and that we knew a few other people in similar circumstances. We didn't need any more. When we were able to go away during vacation time for a couple weeks to some other place, that was all that was needed to make me satisfied.

Please tell me your feelings about being Austrian once you were in the United States.

I didn't feel anymore like an Austrian or German. That was a thing of the past. I hated the memory of it, except I knew that I had wonderful experiences there apart from the generally negative way of life.

Was there a point at which you could comfortably say, "I am an American"— that these words fell out of your mouth smoothly? Or do you still feel like a European?

No, I can say I'm American. I'm an American Jew.

At what point did you feel really at home living in Los Angeles or Pasadena?

This may seem strange to you, but I felt at home from the time Marianne and I stayed in the first apartment of our own, the one-room apartment with a wall bed in the living room and a kitchen of our own. I felt we were in America. We found jobs after some time and could support ourselves. What else did we need for feeling American? Well, maybe not necessarily American yet, but certainly not like Austrian Jews anymore.

What were your feelings toward Germany and Austria during your first years here?

This is a funny question. I was glad to get out of there. I didn't hate my past. It was a situation one had to leave—like a fire in the house.

You didn't generalize and feel hatred for all gentile Germans and Austrians?

No. But I had no contact with them, not here, and rarely had any in Vienna.

On another subject, what role did Zionism play in your life before you left Austria and when you first got here?

In Vienna every young Jew was a Zionist.

Every young Jew?

Except those who were socialists, or were nothing. I was both Zionist and socialist, but very moderately. I was a member of Makkabi, a Zionist athletic club, and went to the football games of the Hakoah, Vienna's Jewish sport club. I was a booster of the Hakoah. In college, every young Jew played with the idea of going to Palestine. There were lots of discussions between Labor Zionists and right-wing people, the Jacobinsky wing. I actually went to Palestine with the intent of staying there. That was in 1931, before the Nazis came to power. I went because of the generally anti-Semitic atmosphere and economically dismal prospects for the future in Austria. Why didn't I stay in Palestine? Well, it seemed to be very, very hard and nobody really invited me to stay there. I still had a chance to return to Vienna. So, I was a very mild Zionist! [As told earlier, Otto tried again to live in Palestine two years later, in 1933.]

I was also a mild socialist, and read socialist newspapers. Jews who had progressive (as we call it in America) attitudes in Austria were either socialists, Zionists, or both. Some were liberal, of course, some on the verge of forgetting altogether about being Jewish, and some even got baptized. I really didn't know those people; I didn't mix with them. Most people I knew didn't really care about being Jewish, but they didn't feel like giving it up.

And when you came to the United States? What was your connection to Zionism then?

To begin with I had no connection. Gradually, I read the Jewish newspapers, met people who were Jewish and involved, and I became more involved. The need for Zionism had become so urgent because after the war there was no way to exist for Jews in most European countries. As you see, it didn't affect me here in America. I didn't feel there was any need for me to go to Palestine.

Didn't you belong to a Zionist group in Pasadena?

Yes, I became formally a member of the Labor Zionists and we had weekend meetings. But I wasn't very active. I was more a donor and a helper. I collected money for the Jewish community here and for Israel.

During the early years in Los Angeles, did you encounter any blatantly anti-Semitic incidents directed toward you or other Jews?

No.

Nothing? Ever?

We just knew that in certain areas or towns, Jews were not liked or wanted and that jobs would be difficult to obtain in certain firms, also probably in banks and schools. And we knew about the *numerus clausus* at many universities that admitted only a very limited number of Jews or foreigners. After what we had gone through in Austria, anti-Semitism here seemed to be negligible.

Now I recall that Marianne *did* have one anti-Semitic experience. When trying to rent an apartment for us, she was turned down because she was Jewish.

So, no anti-Semitism in your American experience?

That is correct.

That's pretty incredible.

Well, I didn't stick my neck out in gentile circles.

Here's a very different sort of question. Are there any traditions, either having to do with Judaism or not, that you experienced as a child, brought with you to this country, and wanted to continue with your family here?

Certainly we had Friday nights, Shabbat [Sabbath]. My mother lit the candles. Saturday, my father made Havdalah [ceremony to note the end of the Sabbath]. We celebrated, of course, all Jewish holidays. For Passover, we went occasionally to my grandparents (my mother's parents). That was in the early years. Later on, we had Seder at our house and always had guests. To begin with, we had my mother's two brothers. Later on, we had friends—two, three or four—and there was elaborate food prepared in the best possible manner.

My tradition was to go to the theater or opera at least once each week, usually in standing room because seats were very expensive. In some theaters I went as a *claqueur*. That means I lined up before the event and volunteered to applaud the actors on the stage. That was a custom not only in Vienna but I think in most European theaters. Here, students get reduced tickets. In Europe they had to work for that by applauding.

When you came to the United States, did you try to attend a cultural event once each week also?

Yes, of course. My first impression of Los Angeles was sort of negative, but I was very relieved, almost enthusiastic, when I got to Central Park at the corner of which there was a six-foot tall statue of Beethoven. Beethoven got to Los Angeles! I thought, "Maybe I can be here too!"

That leads nicely to my next question. Was America anything like you expected it to be when you had thought about it during those years waiting to get here? You must have had some ideas about what life might be like, and I wonder whether your first years were anything like you had imagined.

Otto and Marianne Wolman, London, 1939.

That's a very good question. I think I'm almost embarrassed or ashamed to admit that I hadn't any image of what America would be. I just knew, had read and heard that gold was not lying on the streets to be picked up. Quite the opposite. I was scared by stories about the toughness of life here, not necessarily of gangsters, but many stories related to the problems of unemployment and bad years of the Depression. I heard about the Jewish immigrants who went through the misery of Brooklyn or the Jewish side of New York, and that only the pushy and strong ones survived. So I was not looking forward to life in America. I never had heard that art, music, and the higher, better values of life in America were anything like those in Europe. I was a European. Except, unfortunately, I lived in Vienna at the time that Nazis took over.

So the answer to my question about whether America was anything you expected it would be . . .

I think it was better. I didn't feel I was in a jungle. But it was a lonesome place, a lot of strangers around.

Otto and Marianne Wolman, Pasadena, 1992.

Is there someone, some incident, or some object that had special significance in sustaining you through the immigration years?

That's very easy for me to answer because for me there was the goal of being together with Marianne, whom I was separated from. This was a special case in that she left Vienna alone and I was left behind, alone without her. We knew we wanted to be together, even though we were not married. As we separated there was not much hope. But there was also great hope that we *would* meet again. In desperation, hope was the only thing to sustain us.

I don't recall you talking much about the transition years we've been discussing. Did you speak with other people?

There was nothing that encouraged us to remember this period of uncertainty, nervousness, and lack of hope for the future. It was a period in which we didn't see anything good to come to us.

That's a reason not to talk?

Whatever happened was purely for the moment and to be overcome.

You mean in the years afterward, you felt there was nothing about this period to talk about? Some people told their children a lot about their pasts, including immigration years. I don't think you did until I asked specifically.

I wanted to forget those years. The only positive thing that I can remember is that I met Marianne. That made the future after emigration so much more something to look forward to. Of course, that was also a very uncertain thing to hope for. Generally one lived for the moment, very much in a fog and a lot of hopelessness.

What did it feel like for you when you went back to Vienna, and when was that?

The first time we went was, I think, in 1965. I felt in an unreal situation because I went to Vienna and it was not my home. I stayed in a hotel like an American tourist, and my connections with Vienna were only the memory of a place where I had lived with my parents and where I grew up. I went to the high school that I had attended. I went in and looked around. Everything was cold and not alive anymore. I had no more people that I knew, that I went to school with, or friends or relatives. I didn't have anybody. I went to look at houses and remembered people that used to live in them, but who in the meantime had left, either emigrated, died, or simply disappeared—I don't know if dead or alive. I didn't see any store signs with Jewish names. I loved to go again through the old streets and into museums and attend some theater performances. To see the old buildings was a cultural experience and loaded with memories because I had seen them a million times. But I was still a tourist. It was like seeing them in a movie, passing by.

I looked at people in the streets and, according to their age, wondered whether they were Nazis or were too young to have been Nazis. Accordingly, I didn't like the majority of them. I knew they were the infamous type of Viennese—extremely polite and subservient in their service but in reality liars and no-good characters. Even the words they spoke were different from what I was used to. Some used an extreme Viennese slang that was never my language (my language was high German), and I had to make an effort to speak the dialect. There was a strong tendency to use what I used to call Prussian words and intonation, to speak "German," non-Austrian. Others spoke in the Austrian intonation of the Alps. Neither of the two was what I was familiar with.

How does it feel for you to be asked all these questions?

To think back about those years? It wasn't terribly bad really. I was glad you asked those questions. They recalled things to my mind that I had already forgotten, though maybe that's just as well. There's nothing very good to be remembered about it. I think about the past very rarely.

GERTY FRANKEL

Gerty Frankel (signature)

In one way Gerty Frankel was very fortunate. Immediately after the Anschluss, before she even knew the existence of such a document, an affidavit arrived that would permit her to come to the United States. Three months later, her mother died of cancer; her boyfriend, Fritz, was in Dachau; and Gerty was evicted from her mother's apartment. A single child whose father had died earlier, she was 24 years old and suddenly on her own. She lived for a while on family savings, spunk, and resourcefulness until she was offered the position of chambermaid at an English country estate. Some years later, Gerty and Fritz had two children, Miriam and Daniel.

I'll begin with the *Anschluss*, which happened in a very dramatic fashion. Elections had been called in Austria. One of the parties on the ballot was the Nazi Party. During the week before the election, excitement was building up tremendously. Nazis came out of the woodwork. By Nazis I mean people

Gerty Frankel was interviewed in part by her daughter, Miriam Rogson.

51

who belonged to the party or were sympathetic to it. Until that point, the party was actually forbidden and they kept underground. Their only means of identification was that they all wore white kneestockings. It was a kind of peasant-like way of dressing. When elections were called, the party became legal and people started to demonstrate and to wear the Nazi insignia. The elections, I think, were to be on a Sunday. On the Friday before, Hitler marched into Austria and the whole Austrian government folded up. Officially, everybody joined the Nazis, and there was total jubilation. Demonstrations against them stopped. Whoever was against them tried not to make many waves. After the *Anschluss*, by definition, Austrians were not Austrian citizens anymore and were not subject to the protective laws of Austria. They could therefore be treated like aliens—were not subject to the rules and regulations that governed citizens.

For us, it was disaster. I remember the radio program that had the chancellor announce that he had submitted his position to the Nazis. The program itself was devastating. Although Chancellor Schuschnigg was a wavering and indecisive man, he was an intelligent man. His speech was full of literary references and so on and was followed by part of a Haydn quartet. In the background, you heard the *Sieg Heil* and lots of screaming and yelling. For us, it was the end. Some people packed up and left immediately, and were already caught at railroad stations. There were all kinds of rumors around. It was dreadful.

My father was not alive anymore. He had died two years before these events. A year after his death, my mother got very sick. She had cancer and had surgery. But nothing was done because the metastasis was throughout her abdomen. Doctors tried to keep her comfortable, more or less, but she was getting worse and worse and weaker and weaker. Although she was still up and around at that time, she was a very sick woman. I was in terrible conflict because on the one hand, I knew and she knew and most of us knew, that this was the end for us in Vienna. We had to get out of there. On the other hand, how could I get my mother out in her condition?

I was very fortunate because a week after the *Anschluss*, I got a cable from Bella [an American girl who while studying music in Vienna had lived with Gerty's family for two years]: "Affidavit on way to American Consulate." I didn't even know the term *affidavit* yet! We were just coming out of shock and beginning to try to make order out of disorder, and thinking in terms of what does it take (a) to get out and (b) to get in wherever the getting in was possible. I investigated and indeed found out what an affidavit was—a confirmation that there was a sponsor in America who would be responsible for my upkeep and maintenance.

What I still needed was a quota number as an Austrian citizen and for the officials to decide if the financial declaration behind the affidavit was sufficient. I went to the American Consulate and showed them Bella's cable. I asked them about the status of quota numbers. That concept to me was very strange. They explained to me that the quota numbers were for people who hadn't yet registered for a visa. In their projection, if I registered on that day, assuming the affidavit was strong enough, I would get the visa probably very soon. It was then March. A visa had validity for three months after its date of issue. I would have to be on American soil within three months of that date. It was not renewable.

I decided not to register. I didn't see how I could be able to leave that soon. I also found out that visas were issued not only on the strength of the affidavit but also required a certificate of good health from a physician. My mother could never get a certificate that she was in good health, because she was in effect dying. So I didn't register, in order to delay the issuance of the visa until—I didn't know. I just couldn't do it. That was all. I was in the unusual situation of having an affidavit but not registering to leave the country. My mother died three months later. The development of the illness may have gone quicker than anticipated. I don't know. She had ovarian cancer, and I think that cancer usually proceeds very quickly. Nobody told me that then.

During those months, everyday life had become an increased hassle of prohibitions and petty annoyances. You couldn't sit on park benches. I had a job working in a sanitarium for nervous disorders. It was supported by the Rothschild Foundation of Jewish backing. I was working as an X-ray technician. They wanted me to eventually also run the physiotherapy department. I had no training for that. So while working part-time, I was sent to a hospital in Vienna to study physiotherapy in the neurology department.

Over the week-end of the *Anschluss,* the sanitarium was taken over by the Nazis. I came to work on Monday and was invited to come to the office of the hospital director. He was sitting next to his desk. At his desk was a man in a Nazi uniform who handed me a paper and informed me that my job was discontinued as of that day, that I would get a salary for the next two weeks, and good-bye. Dr. Wilder, the director, whom I liked very much, was sitting there and not saying a word. I thanked him and shook hands with him, and I remember he had tears in his eyes. That's all. Never saw him again.

I still went to the general hospital for a few weeks. The head of the physiotherapy department was a Jewish woman. Some leading positions were held by Jewish people. The custom at the time was that you didn't really make it known that you were Jewish. I knew she was Jewish, and she knew I was Jewish. You knew this by osmosis. You didn't talk about it. The woman under her was not Jewish but was devoted to her, really loved her. She had a granddaughter my age who occasionally dropped in on her way from school to home; she and I would talk together. The grandmother encouraged this relationship.

One day, the granddaughter came in all excited. On the way to the hospital, she had witnessed several Nazis who were going into Jewish businesses and had dragged out the Jewish businesspeople, "who were just taking advantage of their clients and finally now were getting what they had coming to them. Now with the Nazis here, we will get our rights, and the Jews are not going to rule it over us anymore." Anna, the Jewish department head, and I looked at her and didn't say anything. The girl's grandmother was in a terrible quandary. She was ashamed of her granddaughter. At the same time, she wasn't going to reprimand her. I could see her struggle and understood that this inner struggle had to result in her resentment of whomever put her into that struggle. If it weren't for Anna, whom she loved, she could have wholeheartedly accepted her granddaughter's enthusiasm. I didn't have to live with that situation for long. By the end of that day, both Anna and I were dismissed. The grandmother immediately became department head. And that was that. I was completely out of work.

The next two months were an intensification of stress, discomfort, and fear. You began to be apprehensive when you heard people walking in the corridors of the house. One day the doorbell rang, and when I opened the door, there were two Nazis, Brownshirts, standing outside. They wanted to see Frau Sonderling, my mother, and to have her come with them. I went, too. They took us to a *Gasthaus,* an inn, in the neighborhood where they had collected an assortment of Jewish business owners. Everybody was sitting there waiting, not knowing what would happen next. The Brownshirts were sitting around tables, drinking beer, leering, making silly jokes and obscene remarks.

Finally, one guy stood up and came to our bedraggled group and said something about showing us Jews what it's like to be on the receiving end, that up to then we had been lording it over them and making money on their backs, that now they would start by having us scrub the floor of that filthy inn. Compared to my fears, I thought scrubbing the floor was not so bad. The other people in the group were all older people, my mother's age and older. I walked up to that guy. He asked me what work I had. I told him I had lost my job. He responded, "You can go home. You really don't belong here." I said, "I want to trade places with my mother. She is very ill and much too weak to scrub floors." He asked what was wrong with her. I was in a quandary because in Europe at that time it was not customary to tell people who had severe illnesses what they had. Doctors told the families but not the ill person. So my mother had never heard the word *cancer.* When she had pain, she was told that it was a result of adhesions that had formed after surgery, that the surgery was successful, that she had a benign tumor. I told him that she had cancer. There was a conference, and then they sent us both home.

We somehow continued to operate in some fashion or another. There were things happening. The time was fraught with fear. Walking through the streets, you saw people huddled together and some Brownshirts picking up this person and that person. I saw Jews who were picked up and then given pails of lye and forced to scrub the pavement. They got down on their hands and knees, and often their stockings tore and their hands started bleeding. Some people climbed up on lantern posts to get a better view and had a good time watching. Others slinked away because they didn't want to see.

But nothing very terrible ever happened to me. I didn't fit into their stereotyped image of a Jewish girl. I was blond and blue eyed. I was not identified as looking Jewish, so I was pretty much left alone in the street. I lived in a typical city apartment house. Such houses had a janitor who lived in an apartment off the entry corridor. These apartments all had doors with glass windows on the top, and the janitor was supposed to watch who was coming and going. One evening I came home and our janitor quickly pulled me into his apartment. He told me that SS men were in the house, going from apartment to apartment. He hid me in the courtyard behind the garbage cans. This was a very decent thing to do. In addition, he was endangering himself. Nothing happened, but it was scary.

I heard about friends that *had* been picked up. And one day, I had a date with Fritz. He didn't come. I called at the Frankels and he wasn't home either. He didn't show up. I think it was three days later that a postcard came from the local police department informing his family that he was "temporarily detained," was all right, and not to worry about him. Fritz had been picked up on the street. The way such roundups worked was that they would close off a number of blocks and everybody within that confined area had to show his identification card. Jews had a card that was yellow and had a large *J* on it. Everybody who was a Jew was collected and taken to the police station. From there they were shipped out to Dachau. At that time, Dachau was beginning to be identified as a place where some people had been sent to and not returned. But we didn't *really* know anything about it.

We went every Sunday to my Uncle Siga, my father's brother, Tante Grete, and their sons. Their home had become a focal point for their friends and the boy's friends. At times of stress, people pull together more. In addition to the stress, I remember really good times and comradeship, fun times with friends who became much closer. Anyway, we were there every Sunday for dinner which was in the middle of the day. One day we were at my uncle's home and my mother got an attack of severe pain. I called the doctor, who couldn't come because Nazis had been in his house making a search. We wanted to call an ambulance, but this was a problem. This was a Jewish household and my mother a Jewess. What hospital would take her? There was phoning back and forth to people who maybe had a little influence. My uncle knew somebody who knew somebody who was an administrator of the Rothschild Hospital, the only place that was at that point still taking Jews. My mother was eventually taken in there.

The next day, my mother's sister was going to move to Prague. Her family had retained their Czechoslovakian citizenship. By going to Prague they thought they might be safe. My uncle and cousin had already left, and Tante Elsa had to leave. I still wanted to see her and say good-bye. In the evening, as I was about to leave my mother's hospital room, a nurse came in and said, "You have to stay. There was a report made to the Gestapo that people here are pretending to be patients. They are looking through the whole hospital for people who are not entitled to be here. I'll lock you in the room, and when they have left I'll let you out." That lasted a few hours. Nobody came to the room. I always somehow got by. Eventually someone unlocked the door. At midnight I left the hospital and got a cab to Tante Elsa. I found her in hysterics. In the morning, I said good-bye to her and returned to the hospital. My mother died. That was one week after Fritz had disappeared.

I went to the American Consulate and registered for a visa. In the three months since I first went there, so many people had registered that the Austrian quota was completely filled for that year and a good part of the following one. Neither the United States nor any other country made any special provisions to absorb the pretty predictable number of refugees. Women could get into England on a domestic visa if somebody requested them from England. Gradually, some men were let in. By and large, it was pathetic how little was done to try to save people.

Two weeks later, I got a notice (an official paper issued by the court) from our apartment landlord that stated that we (now only I) had to vacate the apartment within two weeks because the Aryan tenants of the house found it "unacceptable to live under the same roof as Jews." So I tried to pack up a household that had been established 24 years ago. It was a chore for me, because I never had taken care of anything in our household. Maybe it was my saving grace, because the mood I was in, I just wanted to get rid of everything. But I did pack some things. I had enough sense to realize that eventually I would probably get to America. So I packed some rugs and some dishes and books. There was a lot of stuff left over so I put ads in the paper. At that time, many people were in the same boat and others made it their business to pick up a lot of cheap stuff. I managed to sell a lot for ridiculous amounts. The rest I gave away to our cleaning woman. Some of the things I recall were very nice, but since I'd lived with them all my life, I really didn't treasure them. I'm sorry now. I should have kept more.

In order to ship stuff, you had to get official permission. So you needed to make lists. The lists had to specify every small item. For certain articles you had to have special permission, and the special permission was based on, at first, an appraisal of their value. The appraisal had to be given by an expert. It had to be on official stationary, had to have an official stamp for which they paid taxes, and you, of course, had to pay for all that. Then, on the strength of this appraisal, you had to get special permission to take the object. Finally, you had to find a company that would come to your house and pack your belongings. And during the packing, an inspector had to come too, who stood there with the list of things and the appraisals and the permissions and checked on everything you put in the boxes. The pettiness of the hassle was incredible. So you were involved with all that nonsense, and parallel with that were all the street scenes and the distressing news about people being picked up and for me, Fritz being away. Every day something else happened. On top of it, you had to prepare for your emigration.

MIRIAM: *Were there things you were not allowed to ship?*

Sure. Jewelry. I smuggled it out. I had a little electric travel iron, and we took out the heating element and replaced it with jewelry. It was risky!

MIRIAM: *Did you ship the stuff to America right away?*

Yes. I shipped it immediately to Bella [the American who had supplied Gerty's affidavit], which was a good thing because three months later I couldn't have done it anymore. From that time on, you could take just what you could carry with you.

And I looked for another place to live, which meant renting a room somewhere. In the meantime, I'd found work, volunteer work, at the *Kultusgemeinde*. This was the central body of the Jewish community. It was the umbrella organization for Jewish life in general. It was an important organization. It maintained the synagogues. Charity organizations, everything Jewish, was combined in the *Kultusgemeinde*. The *Kultusgemeinde* began to set up all kinds of things for this emergency. Any Jew who needed assistance knew where to go. You were a Jew by definition if you paid taxes as a Jew. The way it worked was that when you paid income taxes, you designated your religion. A portion of these taxes went to maintain the Jewish community. The rest went to the government.

My loss of a roof over my head was a routine event. That happened all over the city, particularly in areas where very few Jews lived, as I had. People who lived in more or less Jewish-designated neighborhoods were for the most part left alone. People who lost their homes could find a place in these neighborhoods because many people there had lost jobs and were without income but still had their homes. One source of income was to sublet part of your apartment. The Jewish community set up an office and collected addresses of people who had space to sublet and people who were looking for space. The community tried to match these in terms of requirements. I took a volunteer job in this particular department, and I made lists.

From the lists, I picked out something good for myself. I rented a room in the very nice apartment of an elderly widow. I rented her bedroom. She was very pleasant and we got along well. I wasn't home much. I was working during the day, which gave me something to do. Many evenings I spent at Uncle Siga and Tante Grete's. Of course I was very close with my cousins. I was part of their circle of friends. So I spent a lot time with them. Much of the time I spent with them was fun time, nice time. These days were not all misery and worry. But when you heard somebody walk in the corridor, you held your breath and waited. Are they going to ring your doorbell or somebody else's? If it's your doorbell, is it friend or foe? But when the steps passed, you went on with what you were doing. Parallel with that was the concern about Fritz. I wrote letters to him in Dachau, then in Buchenwald. Life itself was so full of stress on the one hand and, on the other hand, release from stress. You somehow coped with it.

Jews in Vienna understood that if they could get out, they were going to different environments, with different languages, different customs, and that they would need to adapt. Being more flexible, being more versatile, having skills that might tide you over until you could do whatever you were originally trained to do, would be important. The *Kultusgemeinde* arranged all kinds of courses. For example, they had courses that taught how to make gloves and belts. We didn't know that in other places people didn't necessarily wear gloves every time they went out into the street! They also had a course in waitressing. I took that course. And I made use of that skill when I came to Los Angeles.

MIRIAM: *How did you live without any income?*

I lived from savings. Our business had been sold the year before. I didn't worry about it. I didn't even think about how long my money would last. It was there and I used it. In many ways, I lived in the sky blue yonder. I thought, "It will last. If it doesn't, something else will happen." I cannot remember that I gave it much thought. But I do remember that for my personal luggage, I tried to get enough clothes that would last me for a while and that would be serviceable. I wanted nice things. I didn't buy cheap stuff. As it was, I pretty much used up what money I had. I couldn't take it along anyway, because when you left, all you were permitted to have were 10 reichsmarks in your pocket. I was too unknowledgeable to try to get money out underground.

In the meantime, I realized that I could not wait out the American visa in Austria. One reason was that the Frankels started working on making it possible for Fritz, if and when he would be released, to leave Austria. The logical place to go was England because his brother Karl was already there. Karl had worked in Vienna with an import/export firm that was actually based in England. Relatively soon after the *Anschluss*, Karl, with his whole branch, moved to England. Karl's position in London gave hope that he could help to make it possible for Fritz to get out. So my plan was to go to England and wait for the American visa there. For girls, there was one way, and one way only, to get to England. That was to get a domestic permit. A domestic permit was issued if a family requested you personally because they couldn't find anybody in England to do the grandiose job of cleaning up their shit!

My cousin Hans had a girlfriend who had such a job already in England, in the home of a country squire. This girl persuaded the lady of the house that she needed a second chambermaid and this chambermaid needed to be me. We actually hardly knew each other. Lo and behold, the request for my presence in England was passed on to the English Consulate and I was invited to present myself to be investigated, to see if I was of sound mind and body, and whether I could, without incurring danger to the English government, be accepted as a maid in the household of Mr. and Mrs. Porrit.

Then began the hassle of working to get out of Austria and into England. That wasn't so simple, because aside from the passport and visa you needed to prove to the Germans [at that point, Austria had become part of the German Reich] that you neither owed taxes or were a person of questionable character who should pay penance for some kind of misdeed. So you needed a confirmation from the local taxing authority and local police authorities. I don't remember anymore all the other papers you needed. But even with this, it wasn't that you just went and asked for the papers. They had to make an investigation about you. You needed to apply, and then they made the investigation, and finally you had to appear at the proper time and place to find out if you were eligible to get the paper. And many of these papers were contingent on getting papers from other authorities. For example, you could only get a tax confirmation if you could prove there was no police activity against you.

During this time, I was of course in close contact with the Frankels. At the end of February, I got a phone call from Fritz's brother Edy, who said, "Fritz is at the Gestapo in Vienna." Fritz was in town! The Gestapo was housed in what had been a hotel, Hotel Metropole. So I went to the Hotel Metropole and waited. He came out, with a shaved head. But there he was! Fritz had to report to the police every day, and he was supposed to emigrate within the month. Departure plans were in process. Fritz's brother Karl was working on an architectural trainee permit to get Fritz to England. At that time, permission was given for leaving the country if you could prove that you intended to go to a non-European country. By that time, Fritz had an affidavit to the U.S., but he still needed a visa.

Once I knew that Fritz would get to England, I went off to be a chambermaid in the English country estate. It was really a very lovely place, way out in the country. There were two chambermaids, a cook, the lady's maid, and a chauffeur. It was a setting you read about in books or see in movies. I had an easy job in a very lovely environment. But the status thing bugged me. I only talked twice to the lady of the house—the day I came and the day I left! Everything was with the other servants. I didn't consider myself one of them, but they considered me one of them, naturally. They had no idea about what was going on outside, no understanding, no information. Nobody did. It was like coming from the cauldron to the moon!

While there, I heard from the consulate that I would get my visa in the beginning of September '39. I gave notice and I went to London. I lived first with Fritz and Karl, then with Fritz alone. I got my visa, which was not convenient for me because I wanted to wait for Fritz to get his so we could leave together. London had an excellently organized aid organization for refugees, the Bloomsbury House. Even in Vienna, one knew you had to go to Bloomsbury House as soon as you arrived in London. People there were helpful with housing, jobs, and other information available through the grapevine. You could meet other refugees there. Most important, when you got your visa, you would inform them and they would make it possible for you to get transportation to the United States. They paid for it, but you obligated yourself to pay it back whenever you could. So I registered, like everybody did, when I got the visa. I thought it would take a long time to get a boat ticket because war had broken out.

Three or four days later, I got a postcard asking me to come to the Bloomsbury House and report to Mr. So-and-So. I did, and the man had a ticket for me on a boat leaving in four days! I was shocked. I didn't want to go and said, "I can't go." He looked at me as if I was crazy. "Why can't you go?" I couldn't tell him that I wanted to wait for my boyfriend. He would laugh in my face. So I gave him a cock-and-bull story about my mother being very ill and that I just couldn't leave her. (I knew that my mother who had died the previous year would understand and forgive me.) I insisted that I couldn't go then. I doubt anybody believed me. He said to me, "This may be your only chance. I can't promise that I can ever have another ticket for you." I replied, "I have to take that risk," and walked out.

I came home and told Fritz about it. He was furious that I had done such a thing. I spent the rest of the week feeling maybe I shouldn't have, but yes I should have. That boat left on Saturday. On the evening of that day, there was enormous excitement and extra newspaper editions distributed. A boat with refugees for America had been torpedoed by the Germans. Yes, it was *that* boat. I was vindicated. Two days later, I got a postcard that I should come to the Bloomsbury House and report to the man of the week before. When I walked in everybody looked at me. Mr. So-and-So said, "Miss Sonderling, anytime you are ready to go to United States, let me know and I'll do my best to get you there." They must have thought I had supernatural powers or something!

Eventually I had to leave without Fritz anyway. A visa was valid for three months and was not renewable. I left in November on the last American boat to carry passengers, *The President Harding*. (It was later converted into a troop-carrying ship and sunk sometime during the war.) Once on the ship, I had to see everything right away. I got dreadfully seasick. After one or two days, I finally *schlepped* [dragged] myself on deck and bumped into a guy I used to go to religious instruction with. (I went to a Protestant school, but I lived in a district where very few Jews lived, so Jewish kids from the schools were collected in the afternoon for religious instruction.) I was pale and feeling terrible. He invited me for a drink. I had never had a drink like that before. It was cognac or whiskey, I don't know. It tasted terrible. But I got it down and I was cured. The rest of the trip was pure pleasure. I had fun. I picked up a boyfriend, danced, and had a good time. I had my first Thanksgiving on that boat.

MIRIAM: *What was it like for you when you first came to this country?*

That is such a general question. I didn't have a choice. If I had come under different conditions, just to look around and see what it is like, to decide if I would want to live here or not, I would have left. I couldn't relate to the way people behaved or interacted or to the values. I came first to Providence. I was very lucky because for the first few months here I was under the protection of people I liked and who liked me, people who tried very much to make me feel at home. Bella knew about me more than anyone else by virtue of having lived with my family in Vienna. In the meantime, she had gotten married, and her baby, Jonis, was four or five months old. So I came to Providence and lived in this very nice, elaborate house, two stories, many rooms.

After that very cozy experience in Providence, where I really didn't want to stay anymore, I moved to New York. One reason was that Fritz finally came to the United States. I had come in the previous November [1939]. He came in February and went to his relatives in Middletown, New York. I wasn't going to go to Middletown, but New York City was much closer than Providence and Fritz could come into the city on week-ends. I tried to find a job. Well, that was in 1940. The United States was still at the tail end of the Depression. To find work was not easy for refugees. People were getting sick and tired of refugees.

I was still under the illusion that I could find a job in the field I had been trained. So I looked up addresses of physicians, I followed up ads, and I went to offices. They all wanted local experience. Of course I didn't have any. How the hell could I? One day I came and introduced myself to a physician. He had a Park Avenue practice. He was German. He had come in the early 30s before the Hitler thing started and had built up a very nice X-ray practice. He asked me questions, and we had a very nice chat. I had the feeling he liked me. He asked me questions like, "How would I do this, how would I do that?" and I apparently answered to his satisfaction. Then he said, "How long have you been in this country?" and I said, "Three months." He responded, "Three months? After three months you expect to get a job in your profession? We had been here three years and my wife was still washing dishes in a cafeteria with a diamond ring on her finger!" I didn't get the job.

I began to work as a maid. I was a lousy maid. That anyone kept me was astonishing to me. I would have fired myself within a week! Mrs. Rothstein was a very stingy woman and paid me very little. She probably couldn't have gotten anybody more efficient for what she was willing to pay, so I retained the job. To work as a maid—with my arrogance of coming from a very good family, of having a desirable background, of being intelligent and fairly well educated, and having a profession, so to speak—was a demeaning thing.

MIRIAM: *Why did you come to California?*

In a way, Uncle Sonderling in Los Angeles was instrumental. I had that job as a maid, and one day I got a phone call that he was in New York and wanted to see me. He was shocked to see me working as a maid. We went out to a cafeteria and he said something about coming to California. He said that it made no sense for me to live under such unbearable circumstances and that he would help me. And I said, "I can go anywhere. I have no preferences for anyplace. But I will go only if my boyfriend goes, too—I am not going anywhere alone." So, "Who is your boyfriend? What can he do?" "He is an architect." Uncle said, "We can make it possible. I have connections."

MIRIAM: *As I recall, he didn't really do much for you.*

True. It was a lot of hot air, but I didn't know that at the time. The following Sunday, I told Fritz that we had the possibility to go to California. He liked the idea because he didn't like it in New York. Another thing was that at that time in New York, there were buildings of strictly traditional architecture. Fritz was trained in the Bauhaus tradition. According to what we had found out, the only place where buildings were a little less traditional was in California. From that point of view, going to California was attractive to him. Then I came with the bombshell. "I have family there. My uncle is a rabbi. If we go to California, we have to get married." Fritz thought it over and said, "OK." So we were going to get married! After eight years! We made a date at the city hall and had all the tests. I gave notice to Mrs. Rothstein that I was getting married. She agreed to give me the afternoon off, but insisted that I return to the house to serve dinner that night.

We got married. Bella came from Providence with her husband, Morry, to be our witnesses. Sam Auerbach, Fritz's cousin-in-law, was another witness. The whole thing was so informal. It was really fun. We appeared before the judge. He probably saw these two little greenhorns standing there who didn't know from nothing and decided to be very lighthearted. After he went through all the formulas, he leaned over that dais where he was sitting and said, "Now who in this household is going to be the boss?" I took it very seriously and began to explain to him that if each one thinks it will be he . . . In back of me everybody began to laugh and the judge also started to laugh, so I realized that that may not be part of the ceremony, but a fun adjunct. Then I went home and served dinner to Mrs. Rothstein.

After finishing my job for the evening, Bella, Morry, Fritz and I, now legitimate, went to the World's Fair. That was the 1940 New York World's Fair. I really enjoyed it. I remember that I ate frog legs. (I always want to try something new!) At midnight, I returned to Mrs. Rothstein and Fritz took the train back to Middletown, New York. I had another week at Mrs. Rothstein's and then I left and visited Bella in Providence. Fritz was still in Middletown. We had arranged to get bus tickets to Los Angeles two or three weeks after the very auspicious wedding day.

Let's talk about your first few years in Los Angeles. What was your life like? Were you able to use your European profession or professional training? What kind of work did you find?

We arrived in Los Angeles in August 1940. One of the first things we did was to get married again! Fritz was anxious to have a Jewish marriage. My uncle performed this religious ceremony. We lived in a small room in the apartment of a Mrs. Vantoch. She was from Austria. She had come with her husband, a journalist, in the early 30s. He had meanwhile died. It was a tiny room with a view of Bullocks Wilshire. It had Austrian-made furniture of Caucasian nut, a highly polished wood with a lot of swirls, and very fashionable at the time. It felt like home! Later, we rented a small apartment, one room with a wall bed. When we wanted a piano, we had to find a bigger apartment.

I was in a position where finding a job was really very difficult. I had the illusion that my uncle's connections would be helpful. As it turned out, his acquaintanceship made it possible for me to get a job as a carhop! At that time, social legislation was in its infancy and basic salaries did not exist. Carhops worked on the remuneration of tips. Some people did quite well. They were quick and efficient and competent. There was an unwritten agreement: carhops stood at the curb of the road and when a car drove into the driveway, whoever called the make of the car first got to wait on it. I didn't know beans about cars. To me a Cadillac or Plymouth were all the same. I only got to wait on a car if nobody else had any time or if somebody took pity on me. Also, the others could balance two, three, or four trays; I could only manage one tray at a time. I got fouled up and couldn't remember what people in the car had ordered. It was so demoralizing. My training at the *Kultusgemeinde* to be a waitress had not prepared me for this scene!

Another of my uncle's connections was with a Jewish community on West Adams. One day, I got a phone call that there was a banquet in a synagogue and they needed another waitress. I went and had a certain number of tables assigned to me. At one point the caterer came up to me and asked for the tickets. I said, "Tickets, what for?" He said, "Tickets, the tickets. Everybody who paid for the meal has a ticket. Don't you know that? What kind of idiot are you?" I had no idea. I had never done anything like this before. I had never attended a banquet. I didn't know the rules for how to behave in this situation.

So I went back and asked people for tickets. I was mortified. Not only that, I was slow. People began with speeches and I was still clattering around collecting plates. It was a total disaster! The man paid me but he said he never wanted to see me again. It was an awful feeling. When I got out into the fresh air from this hot banquet hall, I was still so befuddled and unhappy, I got sick to my stomach and threw up into the gutter. When I came home, Fritz said, "This is it. No more."

I went to an employment agency. The woman running the agency liked me and advised me to get training in lab work that would in some way be related to my European training. She helped me find a trainee position in a hospital lab. I also began to work for an X-ray outfit for no salary to get another local reference.

I had been trained in Europe in medical technology, specifically to be an X-ray technician. I had wanted to study medicine. My father, not trusting conditions in Austria, found that this was an extremely impractical idea under the circumstances. He had a hunch that I would not stay in Austria. He wanted me to learn something that was not language bound and would be applicable anywhere in the world. Besides, he felt that medical school required too many years of study. Since I was interested in medicine, something in the medical technology field seemed to be a decent compromise. And in those days, you did what your father wanted you to do!

Fritz had a job in a cabinet-manufacturing place. I think he got $60 a month. We lived extremely frugally, but that was no problem. Our requirements in terms of daily needs were very modest. We were glad to be here. We had each other. We managed to have fun that didn't necessarily cost any money at all. Soon I got a real job—for pay—through the woman in the employment agency.

You said your father suspected that you would leave Vienna. Why did he have such thoughts?

He didn't trust conditions in Austria. My father had raised me to be aware of my Jewishness. My father was a Zionist. He came from an Orthodox home and had replaced orthodoxy with Zionism. He, I think, never thought he would be able to go to Palestine, but that maybe I would. He had a keen eye for events that would portend evil for Jews. He saw, of course, the rise of Nazi power in Germany and was pretty convinced that our existence in Austria was a limited one in terms of time. He wanted me to be able to go to Palestine or wherever.

Did he have those feelings earlier than did many of the people around you?

I think so. I can remember as a little girl, coming home from school and repeating nonsense about Vienna being the hub of the world, with Schubert and Beethoven and so many famous people, and the Stefenskirche [St. Stephen's Church] being the most gorgeous place in the world. My father told me, "You feel at home where you have people who love you and people who you love. It's beautiful everywhere. When you grow up, you will travel and see other places and they will be just as beautiful to you as Vienna is." And eventually he told me, "You are Jewish and people here don't like you. You are a guest, here by the sufferance of Christian people. Don't feel too comfortable. Don't trust your comfort." I very much integrated those statements and got the feeling in my guts. You could say that this kind of background would be damaging to the psyche of a child, who usually learns to trust its environment. But no. I felt that I knew something others didn't know, that I had privileged knowledge.

I can remember the day I left Vienna and flew to London. That was some adventure! I had never been in a plane before. It was a prop plane that took maybe half a day to fly from Vienna to London. Before leaving that morning, I took the streetcar around the Ringstrasse [the name of street encircling the central part of Vienna]. It was a beautiful, sunny April day, and I stood in front of the streetcar and said to myself, "Take a good look. Remember everything as clearly as you can. You will never see it again." I had only a feeling of adventure and going into something rather than leaving something. I have always been able to say good-bye.

All the way through life?

Yes. It's very helpful to come to a point where you say, "That's it."

Your statement provides a good lead to another question. What about you made it possible to make the adaptations necessary for immigration and beginning a new life?

Well, here you have the answer! It was very early, something that I learned at an early age, due to all the influences around me—not to get too attached and to be able to move on to the next thing. That didn't mean that I adapted easily and readily. It was not so much a matter of letting go as a lack of awareness at that time that there would be so many differences. People interacted so differently here than how I was accustomed. Differences permeated very small things. I remember being very puzzled and really turned off by the way people smiled at each other a lot without knowing each other. I sat in a streetcar and the woman across from me smiled at me. I thought, "That idiot! She's never seen me before, she'll never see me again. Why does she smile at me?" Judgmental as I am, I called that behavior stupid and absurd. Twenty years later I returned to Vienna, sat across from a woman looking glum, and I said to myself, "Lady, for the same amount of money, you can look friendly!" So you see, such things are learned. When you come into an environment that has different ways that are grandiose, you see what they are and can learn to cope. But if the differences are subtle and affect ways of relating and understanding, it is extremely disturbing. You begin to question your own perceptions until you learn that these kinds of puzzling events, social interactions, and styles of behaving are simply different. After a while, if someone smiled at me, it didn't throw me off!

You have talked about some difficulties you encountered. What about you helped you to adapt?

I don't know. I'm a coper I guess. I can sit things out. The more I hear about other people and their reactions to events, I come to the conclusion that I must have had a stable and safe childhood. The insecurities of the time didn't really make a different person out of me. They didn't upset a certain equilibrium I had established. I must have gotten the sense very early that whatever happened, I could manage.

During your first years here, how much of what was going on in Europe did you know about? What and when did you begin to know, particularly about death camps? How did you get information, if you did, and when?

Until December 1941, you could correspond. I still have letters from people who were in Vienna and Silesia at that time and in many ways reported about what was going on there. The letters from Vienna convey a very strong sense of entrapment. To the extent that we were in correspondence, we were involved. You were careful what you wrote. We did not make derogatory remarks about the regime there, but you could get personal information. I got all the information through my uncle, my father's brother. He wrote about the various plans they hatched out, the attempts they made, all the things that didn't turn out to be possible to pursue, including ideas of escaping via Russia by Trans Siberia railroad. He never got out of there. We could correspond until December 1941, when Pearl Harbor made all these communications impossible. After that, if you knew someone in a neutral country, like Brazil, you could use them as a conduit. But otherwise it became very difficult to know anything. If you didn't hear from relatives during the war, you assumed that they just couldn't communicate with you because of the state of war. You assumed that they were living under very stressful conditions. We knew what conditions were like during World War I. We did not interpret from the silence that they had disappeared or been killed. We knew about concentration camps, but I cannot recall that I was aware of the final solution. But it's a long time ago and I'm not that clear about things.

What did you read in the papers? Did you know that President Roosevelt had been approached to allow more Jews into the country?

I cannot recall. There were also a lot of rumors. It was very difficult to sort out what was hearsay from what was really going on. But I do remember certain events. I remember the Germans invaded Norway and were temporarily repulsed. This gave us enormous hope, that this was now the beginning of the end. Whenever news like that came out, one pinned a great deal of hope on it, that it would represent a turning around of the war situation. These momentary things in one's hope took over and you lost judgment about what was real and what was hoped for.

You are talking here about following events of the war rather than what was happening to the Jews.

This was mostly what we heard about. I don't think that news reports were focusing on the fate of Jews. The war was the most important.

At what point did you know what was happening to the Jews? Were Americans privy to that information in the regular media?

I think there was a hierarchy of being privy to it or not. I think the average newspaper reader got a very diluted and distant view of it. Offhand, I have a difficult time to remember as the war progressed how much we knew. Of course, once the war was over, we knew.

How did that news come? What's your memory of becoming aware?

The newspapers reported. Also you began to get—not necessarily directly, but indirectly—in touch with Jewish communities. For instance, occupying forces, American soldiers in Vienna, were inundated by the remaining Jewish people to help them get in touch with their relatives. Through these soldiers, Jews could send and receive letters and receive packages. For everybody, that was enormously helpful. Initially you were allowed to send eight-ounce packages to soldiers, which they in turn could pass on to your relatives.

Within months after Liberation, camp inmates were sent to Vienna, which was occupied by the Russians, French, and the Americans. Fritz's parents had come back to Vienna from Theresienstadt and returned to their apartment, which was in the American zone. Their apartment was occupied by other people. These people were forced to take the Frankels back into their own apartment, but permitted to stay in one room. There was nowhere else to go. Housing had always been a problem in Vienna. Although I don't think there was much destruction, that problem intensified during the war.

I remember Papa telling us the aim was to find somebody who could forward mail to America, to his sons. The logical thing seemed to be to go on Friday to the temple, hoping there would be some American soldiers, which indeed was the case. So, we one day got a letter from Harry Friedenberg, whom we many years later met, that included a letter from Fritz's father. In that letter Friedenberg said that we could send mail through him, to put it in an envelope to him and that he would forward it to Papa. He took care of dozens and dozens of people that way.

Why couldn't you write directly?

It was not allowed. You could only write to people in the armed forces.

How did the Frankels know where you were living?

They had an old address, and their first letter was forwarded. Also, they wrote to all the relatives. There were ways, like a chain reaction. So, you could send eight-ounce packages to soldiers. We were spending days and nights sitting and wrapping things in eight-ounce packages and sending them to Harry Friedenberg. He later on told us that he rented a truck and delivered all over Vienna! He received flour, coffee, sugar, and cigarettes, because these became more valuable than currency in Vienna. It was insane—everything in eight-ounce packages!

To return to my earlier question: How did you first learn what fate had befallen the Jews?

After the liberators came to Auschwitz. Before that you knew about the labor and concentration camps. But you did not know about extermination camps. I don't think we knew of these until the end of the war.

Fritz had been in Dachau for several months. What did he tell of his experience?

He didn't tell much, unfortunately. He only talked about it months later. He wanted to go on with his life. He was not eager to become a spokesman for spreading the news about what was going on there. It is like you put aside something that is so unpleasant, so painful that you don't want to go over it.

I've read that long before the end of the war, attempts were made by Jews to pressure Roosevelt to intervene in the Jews' behalf. In England, I think, there were two people who had seen the camps and told in great detail what was happening. So, it was known.

Yes, there was a Pole. But there were other priorities. There was a war. Also, don't forget that a ship of refugees was turned away from the U.S. There was a big faction that didn't want to be concerned, really. They wanted to make peace with Hitler. It's very difficult to play the blame game now; it's all hindsight.

As you began to hear what had happened, what feelings did you have about being here while this had happened to your family and friends?

The news that came out was so unbelievable, so unimaginable. There was a part of you that thought, "This is impossible." To this day, I think I have difficulty to really understand it. I believe unless one was there, had experienced this with one's own being, it's not possible to know in your guts what it was like. Anyway—back to what we heard: I think we were very uninformed and very concerned with our own lives. When we finally got some notion of what was going on, we felt utter helplessness again about getting people out. There were the rules and regulations of immigration, the consulates, the money . . .

To return to your life here, when, if somebody asked you, "What are you?" could you say unequivocally, "I'm an American," and feel comfortable saying that?

I don't feel like belonging here. If anyone would ask me, "What are you?" I will ask them what they mean by that question. In other words, what kind of category of answer do they expect, like what is my citizenship or what is my nationality? But if they ask me, "Where do you feel you belong?" the question is harder. I don't belong in Austria. I *never* had a feeling of belonging in Austria. But I don't have a total feeling of belonging here either.

You mentioned that your father was a Zionist. What role did that play in your life?

It's like a family background. Jews are important because they're family. In essence, this is the one group of people I can trust in terms of being accepted. They're Jewish; I am too. It's just as primitive as that.

How did you express your hatred of Germany during those immigration years? Did you avoid German products or people if you happened to meet them?

The Germans I knew were all Jewish refugees. To this day, I have a gut-like suspicion of anybody who is German and not Jewish. Then I recognize it and back off and try to get more information. Sometimes I then acknowledge that "they're not all like that," and sometimes I feel quite comfortable to dislike them and stay with my suspicions, nurse them along and feel justified.

What language did you speak at home when you came here? And with your German-speaking friends? With your children?

70

We began very quickly to speak English, even to each other.

By decision?

Well, by decision and reinforced by events. When the war broke out, we were in England. We were in contact with the Jewish organizations there and were immediately warned to not speak German in public places, to not in any way make it obvious that we came from the Continent. That was the beginning. We talked English in the street. Also, of course, we wanted to learn English. When I came to the U.S., I lived with Americans. So I got into the habit of speaking English. I then had a job in New York with Americans.

In the early years here, did people you met know you were Jewish? Did it become evident when you said you were a new immigrant?

To the extent that they asked me. People were not necessarily informed about events in Germany. Also, there was something about these events that was not understandable for anybody who had not been there. I made certain assumptions about people's interest and being informed that I found out again and again were totally erroneous. People asked, "Why did you leave? Why didn't you fight back? How could they throw you out?" They just couldn't believe it. People relate to what they know. The reality was so incomprehensible that after a while it didn't make much sense to explain and describe because I kept bumping into incredulity.

Did you run into any anti-Semitic incidents here?

Personally, I don't think I ever did.

Not in the entire 50 years that you've been here?

Nothing comes to me. I may have heard remarks from people. I remember being startled when people would say, "He 'jewed' me out of something." But that was the extent of it. Part of the language and part of the folklore, of course, has underlying assumptions that you can call anti-Semitic. But I never had personally any discrimination or remarks directed at me.

Pretty astonishing! The other people I've interviewed say the same as you.

So I'm not exceptional. I think that's great.

Let's talk now about the Gruppe. *What were the first meetings like?*

Initially the subject matter of our discussions were our European concerns and approaches to world and social events. We talked about what was not here, like Social Security. We compared many of the social structures with what our European experience had been, like health insurance of employees in Vienna. It was a recapitulation of what was different and how we hadn't really found our way yet. We were still clinging to what we knew. That eventually changed, and so did the discussion topics.

I think Siegfried Eisgrau was very helpful in bringing new ideas. He was in many ways the one who kept the *Gruppe* together. He was always coming up with different projects. He often brought in people to participate with us. At one point, he assigned each of us to read and report about certain things. One day Fritz decided he was going to talk about music. So he gave a talk about humor in music.

Marianne was very active. She is an outreacher; she observes things in the community and wants to do something about them. During the war, she got in touch with an organization through which you adopted children in war zones who were orphaned or deprived. These were children for whom help was warranted not only in terms of sending money but in terms of establishing contact by writing letters, giving these children some sense that there was someone who cared. It may have even been the beginning of the organization CARE. Marianne came with this project and made it her business to see that we all participated. We all contributed pretty regularly. Marianne was a letter writer. Other people wrote letters to our adopted child, too. Eventually our participation petered out, but I think it was only after the war was over. As time went on, projects like this unified us in a subtle and subliminal way and began to tie us together.

For me, there was not so much closeness initially. That took years to jell. As the children were born, it was like an epidemic! That provided an additional connecting link, and friendships with members of the *Gruppe* on a one-to-one basis began to develop. Then came the birthday parties that had nothing to do with *Gruppe* meetings. It was a process of slowly growing together and becoming, in a way, supportive of each other. It became important for me to establish contact with individuals in the *Gruppe* whom I liked. As I became closer to people, in the background, the *Gruppe* became more important and I felt more comfortable in it. The *Gruppe* itself was not my primary attraction. It was a peripheral thing for me. But I enjoyed it. It was a recurring thing that was comfortable. As years went by, it became a more cohesive thing. More people joined.

Were the people in the Gruppe *your primary social contacts during those early years?*

No, not at all. It was only as time went on and I began to get closer to certain individuals in the *Gruppe*. For example, my relationship to your mother was my relationship to her, not as a member of the *Gruppe*. We had established contact with your parents before the whole *Gruppe* experience. Since we lived in close proximity in Los Angeles, and then again in Altadena, we had much more contact. I spent a lot of time with Marianne. This was reinforced by or reinforced the contact between you and Miriam. So this relationship took on a different dimension. It took on a family feeling.

I believe the Gruppe *was more central to other members than to you.*

Probably so.

Still, it seems to me that you and Fritz are the couple holding it together now by having the annual New Year's Eve party.

That became sort of a tradition.

What is the purpose of the Gruppe *for you at this point? What does it give you?*

Family. Kind of a family substitute. There is support I give. There is support I can get. It's just a feeling that there's "commonality," though at the same time, it's astonishing how much I don't know about many people, how much I still find out about them when I ask questions. There is nobody in Los Angeles I know as long as the people of the *Gruppe*. We have a common past. It's like a family where you take a lot of things for granted and don't question. You like some more, you like some less.

Is there anything else about the Gruppe *that we should record?*

My real relationships to people in the *Gruppe* were actually strengthened away from the *Gruppe*. Some of these relationships even developed long after regular *Gruppe* meetings stopped. I became very close to the **Sommers** after we went camping with them in 1960. Up to that point, they were people I liked and with whom we got together. But only when we were camping with them and our children did **Theja** and I begin telling each other who we *really* were. And later, we went on several European vacations with the **Bauers** and deepened our friendships significantly.

73

Was America anything like you expected it to be? Had you heard stories from people who had emigrated earlier, or learned things in school, or perhaps had some notions from films?

I had an uncle who lived in Los Angeles who came every year or so to Vienna to visit his father and brothers. Throughout the years I heard many stories about America where Jews could assert themselves as Jews without the kind of anti-Semitism which I took for granted. My uncle would tell little vignettes showing how Jewish life was visible in the life of the city and was totally accepted as just another way of living.

Bella from Providence lived with us in Vienna for two years, and I was very curious to learn from her what life was like in America. Before Bella's arrival, my aunt came and instructed my mother about what an American girl expects in contrast to life in Vienna, where things were much more frugal. She tried to impress upon my mother that she had to be more generous in certain things like changing towels every day, which we certainly didn't do. As a result of these visits from my uncle and Bella, I was in some way prepared for differences.

Were there any family traditions in your household in Vienna that you brought with you and established in your American household?

I tend to scoff at hanging on to traditions. This I took over from my mother. A making fun in a sly, sarcastic way. I continue to do that, and when I do I feel sort of like I'm winking at her. On the other hand, Fritz has the tendency to say, "These are the things we need to do," because he had learned them at home and "Papa did it."

When did you first return to Vienna and how did it feel?

In 1967. It felt schizophrenic. It was a time of tremendous ups and downs. There were moments of unbelievability—"I'm not really here." I experienced recognition of how people behaved or spoke in certain situations. This was either hilarious or disturbing. There was nothing ordinary about this visit. Everything was either a tremendous high or a comparative low. There were moments that were enormously disturbing, like when I felt that I had never been away, that the years in America were a dream. Those moments when I felt that I had been there forever were really depressing.

At what point did you begin to talk about the immigration years with Miriam and Danny?

Some of it came very naturally. Bits and pieces came out. It's my habit to this day that when I talk about immigration, I don't necessarily talk of the severity or heaviness of it. I talk about funny or ambivalent occasions. I don't make a drama out of my life. Danny was particularly interested, I think, as a teenager. The one who really sat me down and asked me many questions was Gusti [Gerty's daughter-in-law]. She used me as source material for her master's thesis.

How do you feel about these interviews Miriam and I have had with you?

Actually the timing overlapped questions I was being asked by other people. So this was favorable for me because it got me thinking. In fact, I have started to write about my life. The interviews were helpful for me to get into it.

FRITZ FRANKEL

Fritz Frankel was one of few Jews to still have a professional position in 1938. He was an architect for the central Jewish office. He was also a musician. One evening as he was walking to a rehearsal, Fritz was stopped by the Gestapo. Two days later, his family knew only that he had disappeared. Fritz knew that he was in Dachau.

Until 1934, I was studying architecture at the Technischen Hochschule [University of Technology]. After that I worked and lived with my parents. You cannot compare the life of a young man in America today to that of one in Vienna at that time. *Arbeitslosigkeit* [unemployment] was rampant. Very few people coming out of school expected work. It was most unusual to find something. I did work. I worked for the *Kultusgemeinde*. They were building a hospital addition to the *Fersorgenshaus* [home for the aged]. I worked as an architect.

For how long were you, as a Jew, able to keep that position?

Times were in flux, so uncertain. There wasn't a beginning and an end. You somehow floated into life and floated out of it. Hitler was there, for all practical purposes. You could see it.

Do you mean that although he was in Germany, he affected Austrian politics?

From a political point of view, there was the Conservative party. This dominant party of Austria and the one in power was the Christian Socialist. The party was officially anti-Semitic, was very strong, and had a militia. The Social Democrats (which Jews belonged to) also had their own militia, the *Schutzbund*. So did other smaller parties.

Each political party had a militia?

Yes. And each had a special name for it.

What was the purpose of such militias?

For protection, defense and offense against the other parties. There were constant demonstrations in the streets. That was what we called in Wien [Vienna], a *Hetz*. A *Hetz* is fun, lots of fun! The fun consisted of beating up people in the other parties. People had nothing else to do. There was no work around, anyway not enough. So people went around to protest.

At what point in Hitler's "career" did you, in Austria, feel that your existence as a Jew was in more jeopardy than it had been before?

At the university there were students that belonged to the *Burschenschaft* [a reactionary, all Aryan club]. They wore colored hats. They all became Nazis, and they attacked the Social Democratic students, which included the Jewish students. I knew a boy who was blinded when they dropped a bomb right in front of us as we walked down the stairs. I was among hundreds of thousands waiting for developments, but we didn't do anything. We just sat around waiting.

When did you make efforts to get out of Austria?

Already in 1927, when we had our *Matura*, the high school certificate, we knew that the chances were not good to find a job. This was before beginning professional studies. Friends and I were thinking of going to a foreign country. I was a musician, and with a few friends I had formed a band. I was a pianist and I worked together with very good jazz players. Somebody knew that in Dutch India there was a possibility to make a living as a musician because in Sumatra and similar places the white businessmen had very lush clubs. They lived in the clubs, entertained there, and had their own bands. Viennese music had a special note. We tried to put together a program that we could sell in Sumatra. We hoped to find a job there that was well paid. We did not have any plans to stay there, but of course you never know.

Did you begin negotiations with anybody at some clubs, or was this all a pipe dream?

I had a connection through my sister-in-law, Marta. Marta's aunt lived in Holland, and she had connections to Dutch India. Later, while still studying at the Hochschule, my friends all tried to think of ways to get out of town. It was impossible to live in Vienna. We learned English, trying to prepare for foreign life. We made a lot of applications for jobs outside the country. We went to the libraries and looked up telephone books of the U.S., Australia, etc. When we found a name that was similar to ours, we wrote. We wrote hundreds of letters.

These were letters asking people if they knew of work for you?

You wrote such people suggesting they might be a relative and that you have to leave the country. Someone in Gerty's circle wrote a letter and translated a German word literally into English—an *Unternehmer*. In English, the correct translation is "entrepreneur." But this young man wrote that he was an undertaker. He got the job and went to Australia!

We were writing these letters while studying. It was an important effort because it focused our lives and hopes with thoughts of survival. When you studied architecture you knew very well that you could not find a job in Vienna because you were a Jew. The only jobs you could find were with the *Kultusgemeinde*, as I did, or in a private Jewish concern.

So you were unusually fortunate to get the job.

Yes. I was often lucky in my life. That luck continued all through my life. Everything turned out well.

Hitler invaded Austria in March 1938. In June, the Gestapo caught me in the street as I was walking to a music rehearsal and took me to Dachau. That was at a time when people hardly knew what Dachau was, although there were already rumors. We knew it was an established camp where they took different classifications of people.

They just plucked you off the street?

They asked me, "What are you doing here on the street? *Bist du ein Jud?*" I said, "Yes," so they took me to the Gestapo at the Hotel Metropole. That was a dark time I don't remember very well of a day or two. My parents didn't know where I was. I had disappeared from the scene. The interesting thing was that I was taken by the Gestapo and then shipped off by the police. The Gestapo quickly directed the police what to do. The Nazis were in control. That happened in a matter of days.

How is it that you were able to get out of Dachau?

I don't know. They never told me. My father had been an officer in the Austrian army. There were many Nazis in the army of course, and now in the Gestapo. My father knew some of these people in Vienna. He made a lot of applications for getting me out of Dachau. Also, as I learned later, a cousin of mine had obtained a forged visa to Argentina and ship tickets for me. These visas were available in France on the black-market for a while, and until the scheme was known, did get some people out of camps. Perhaps I was one of these lucky people.

So one day someone said, "Fritz Frankel, you may leave"?

Basically, that's what it was. There were seven of us released on this particular day. You had to prove that you had money or had received some, so that you could buy a train ticket. In my case, I needed a ticket from Weimar, because in the meantime they had shipped me from Dachau to a new camp, Buchenwald, which was near Weimar.

How could you have had money?

We were allowed to write letters once a week or two. (I still have the letter form on which you were allowed to write.) I had a postcard that my parents wrote to me telling me that they were sending the money, and I had a receipt for that money sent to Dachau and on to Buchenwald. I had an account in the camps, so to speak. My parents had sent money all along, which went into this account. There was a canteen in the camps where you could buy cigarettes. When you came to Dachau, they took all your clothes away and gave you the prison uniform. They kept a package of your clothes, which traveled with you wherever you went. When I was released, they gave me my old clothes.

For how long were you in the camps?

Nine or 10 months.

And then you returned to Vienna?

First I went from Weimar to Leipzig. There I sat for the first time at a table with a tablecloth and was served on a regular plate. The Jewish community of Leipzig had prepared a meal for us in the railway station hall. Young Jewish girls were serving. I can tell you they were like angels from heaven. We didn't have any girls in concentration camp except for one *Sturmbannführer* [lieutenant rank in Nazi army]. That bloodthirsty girl was in Dachau. Ilse Koch was very famous because she made lampshades out of Jewish skins. She was very pretty. Otherwise we didn't see any women.

Was it the usual route to go from Buchenwald to Leipzig? Were Jews arriving there every day from the camp?

I don't think it happened every day. But sporadically there were Jews permitted out who had connections.

What happened when you returned to Vienna?

Gerty was waiting for me at the station. Before I left Buchenwald, I was given documents that said I had been in concentration camp for such and such time. I had to sign that I'd leave Vienna in 30 days. Then I was supposed to disappear, to get out of town. I had to report to the police every day that I was still there, and if not gone after 30 days, I would be sent back to Dachau. Life was so uncertain from day to day. If you were sent off to concentration camp, everything was destroyed. Your apartment was searched, everything was gone. In any case, you lived with the feeling that you were nobody. You never knew what would be by the end of the day.

What steps did you take to get out quickly?

I hadn't done anything before I was caught by the Nazis. That was a deus ex machina. And now, I had to leave, period. I didn't know where to go. It was a very confused time. Most people didn't know what they were doing. When I came back from concentration camp, I thought I'd like to go to America, that I'd go to the American Consulate and they'd tell me, "Go." But I was wrong! I had to get a number to apply for a visa. Gerty's friend,

Bella, had automatically sent an affidavit for her. I had one from a cousin in New York. He had been in Vienna as a medical student during the mid-30s and we had established a very close relationship. I had painted a portrait of him. Little did I know that I would see it hanging in his New York living room!

In the meantime, my brother Karl had gone to London and was established there. He had worked for an English company in Vienna and was sent to London as a translator. Karl made an application for me through the Jewish organization in London to be an architectural trainee in England, and he found a firm that was willing to take me. (They got a good deal because I was a *licensed* architect in Vienna.) The government accepted this. I remained in Vienna more than the 30 days, but the police were lenient when I showed them that I had a documented plan for leaving. When the police was involved it wasn't so bad. It was only bad when the Gestapo was involved.

So I went to England and worked. Gerty, in the meantime, when she knew that I would get to London, had taken a job there as a lady's maid. She was fantastically loyal and took risks for me. The family where Gerty worked were aristocrats. The eating was done in a very formal way. There were different girls for different functions.

Would you tell me about your stay in London?

I lived with Karl and had a job. I made two pounds a week. Soon, Gerty quit her job and came to live with us. Later, we moved out of Karl's and lived alone. That was a beautiful time of our lives. I remember so many unique moments. You could buy some kind of a device where you had three pots stacked on each other. We used them on a hot plate. We called it tower cooking! Food in each pot got hot that way.

That period lasted six or eight months. The HIAS [Hebrew Immigrant Aid Society], or Jewish Committee for Refugees, was fabulous. They gave people money if they needed it. They bought transportation tickets. Not that they made it easy, but you could get help. They paid for our ship tickets. And when we came from New York to Los Angeles by Greyhound, HIAS paid for it. We paid it back of course.

Did you and Gerty come to the United States together?

No. My visa came a few months later. Gerty and I were not legally together then.

Where did you go in the United States?

I went to Middletown, New York, to the cousin who sent my affidavit. He was very decent to me. I lived with his family and they treated me like a brother. They didn't let me pay them, said I should accumulate some money so I could start on my own. I knew I would go to California. Los Angeles and New York were the only cities with modern architecture. I did not learn the kind of architecture I saw around me, the classical styles. I could have adjusted, but it was against my conviction to design in these styles. Anyway, I had to have a job and I took one in Middletown as an architectural drafts-man. The architecture they did in the company was terrible for me. But I had a job and did all right.

Gerty was in New York and cooked and did other slave work for a lady. On Sundays I went from Middletown by train to visit her. She had a cousin, a bachelor musician in New York, who had an apartment. We met at that apartment and had a good time. We bought food and Gerty cooked there for us. That was still before we got married. We married twice. We had a civil marriage in New York. Why we did that I don't remember. We married again in California because Gerty had her uncle here and we could have a Jewish wedding. He made a big *hasena* [wedding celebration] for us.

When did you come to Los Angeles?

In 1940. First we stayed with Gerty's cousins, the Sonderlings. We stayed for a very short time and then took a room on South Marathon. We lived in the house of Mrs. Vantoch. I can't complain about that time. On the contrary. We were not afraid of anything. We had no money, but who needed it? I still have that philosophy.

How did you earn money during those days? Were you able to find architectural work right away, or did you do other things first?

There were some detours. There was a *Macher* [big shot] at HIAS who was the head of a furniture company, and he gave me the chance to work in his company as a furniture finisher. Then I advanced to a sign printer. In the meantime, I found a job elsewhere as a regular draftsman. Then things started to go. Things went smoothly and I improved my position constantly. With my Viennese diploma I could not do much here. I had to take the California licensing examination for architecture. This was a tough examination. From then on everything went well.

Fritz and Gerty Frankel, Los Angeles, 1940.

The war ended. We tried to find out where our parents were. The Red Cross had no information. Finally, we found our parents, but didn't know what condition they were in. They went to England, first to my brother Karl, then to New York to my brother Eddy. We built the house in Altadena later so they could join us and live nice and comfortably. Then they came.

At the time you built the house in Altadena, were you already working on your own?

I was working for Mr. Miller. I became a big shot in his company and then took it over when he died in 1948. I bought it from his widow. It was a goodwill purchase; there were no assets. We were at 111 West 7th St. Then I had the company under my name and so it has continued.

I'm curious what it was about you that made it possible for you to make so many adaptations to this new country and culture. What in your personality do you think made you able to make this very difficult transition?

Nature works that way. The culture here was so different that it is different still. I'm not yet fully adapted. There are certain features, functions, details that I fully adopted. What I don't adopt, I accept as a necessity, but not as an ideal state of my being. This is very complicated.

If you were traveling in another country and there was a group of people, all from different countries, and someone said to you, "Mr. Frankel, what is your nationality?" what would you say?

I'd say, "I'm an American. I'm a Jew."

Does it feel totally comfortable to say you're American?

I feel very comfortable. But it doesn't mean anything to me basically. What does it matter that I'm an American or I'm an Austrian? That I can yodel like an Austrian? To me it's irrelevant.

When you first got to the United States, how did you feel about the fact that you were an Austrian?

It didn't mean anything. I was born in Austria, period. It was an accident.

When people asked you where you came from . . .

I said, "Vienna." I had nothing to be ashamed of.

Did they realize you were Jewish?

Probably. That was not a problem that ever entered my life.

But during those first years you were considered politically an enemy.

Right. I was an enemy alien and not permitted to be out of the house after seven o'clock.

What was that like?

I could not go out. So what?

What would have happened if a policeman had stopped you in the street after hours?

He could have told me I had violated the law. So, *mazel tov!*

So they didn't make a big deal out of it.

I don't know. I was never stopped.

I guess you didn't tempt fate! In those and subsequent years, how did you express your hatred of Germany? Did you avoid German products, German people, etc.?

Yes, I still avoid their products if I can. Today I tell myself there has to be an end sometime, it doesn't make sense. After all, German philosophy, German music, and German literature gave me a richness that I have not received from anybody else. What Goethe gave me and gives me still is unique.

If the Berlin Symphony comes to Los Angeles, do you attend?

Probably not. But if they are on our series ticket, I'd go. It's not a cause of special emotion.

If you're in a store and need to buy some scissors and you pick one up and it says, "Made in Germany," would you put it back and look for one made in Japan?

Yes, but it doesn't make sense. It's silly in our world today. I did not and still do not buy anything German, but I believe it's silly that I should blame today's German generation. But I react to something emotional in an emotional way. If I think about it, it doesn't make sense that I don't buy anything German. This is a problem. How can I blame a young German who is brought up outside of the Hitler time? Yet they still are products of the German way of education. It is different and I don't like it.

What is it that you don't like? That they are taught that they are the best? That Jews are inferior?

Yes, and they mean it. "*Deutschland, Deutschland über Alles.*" German society is autocratic. Father knows all. What he says is final. In my opinion this belief is an inhuman approach. It's the German way to be anti-Semitic. I do not want to forget that the Germans hate me in principle.

So you continue in your distrust of Germans?

I've never reasoned it out, and I don't trust myself in what I'd come up with. I do not want to forget what the Germans did to the Jews, to *my* country, to *my* nation, to *my* people. I will never forget, and my children should never forget. That does not mean that all Germans are Hitlers. It's the same with Austria. I find the anti-Semitism now much worse in Austria than in Germany. The quality of anti-Semitism there is despicable. It's very emotional. They just don't like Jews and are not willing to change. I think Germans have an intellectual bias—a negative stereotype of the early Jewish street merchants.

Let's return to Los Angeles. What happened in the initial years when you met a German at a business function or at somebody's house?

I would walk away. If I was introduced to a German who was not a Jew, I tried not to have anything to do with him. That has changed much. We have a friend whom we saw yesterday. She's a *Schikse* [gentile], and her husband is a Jew. He was an American soldier in Germany during the war when they met. She's a very fine human being. We have a lot of fun together. Here I speak about qualities that are bound to the individual only. But I would not want her to marry my son! I stay within certain limits in my tie to her. It's confusing of course.

What if you had met her 20 years ago?

I would have rejected her totally. I got milder about my attitudes and actions.

When you lived in Vienna, was your social group all Jewish or did you have some Christian friends as well?

Mostly Jewish. I kept my communications with Christians on the surface. I went to the conservatory, and there were many gentile girls who liked me.

Would you go to have coffee with any of them?

No, no fraternization. I wouldn't have had an affair with a Christian girl. I would not even kiss her. They were outcasts for me. I would not permit myself. In my year of *Matura* there was one girl in my class (this was unusual because there were generally boys and girls separate) and she liked me very much. She did not hesitate telling me. I would not touch her. It was not kosher. Not everything has a deep logic in it. I would just not permit myself to touch a gentile girl. As childish as it sounds, I still ask myself, "Are they different?" This thinking is absurd. Yet that's the way I am.

What role would you say the Gruppe *played in your life back in the 1940s and how did that change over the years? Was it important to you? Why did you all get together? Why bother?*

First of all, it was a group of "like" people. We had the same education. We had the same upbringing. The differences were minor in comparison to the features that were alike. We were of similar ages, had just gone through similar traumatic experiences. It was a welcome opportunity offered to Gerty and me. It was a wonderful opportunity that does not come tailor-made like this in life very often. We knew in advance who the people were, to a degree, without putting a judgment on it. The children were born at the same time, more or less. And of course, it gave an intellectual challenge. This was the original purpose. We all had menial jobs, some more, some less, and we were afraid that whatever intellectual prowess we had, we would lose. We couldn't sharpen our mental knives through work! It's not anybody's fault, but we were not prepared for this American civilization. We did not have the same education. Quite a number of the writers, poets, philosophers were new to us. The *Gruppe* gave us an opportunity to iron that out to a degree.

What can you say about social connections and feelings with Gruppe *members?*

Here, too, how to operate socially was strange for us here. In Europe it was not done like here. There we met friends in a coffeehouse. Here there was a different atmosphere.

In Europe, did you just know that at eight o'clock in the evening a group of people might be in the coffeehouse and that you'd know some of them? Or did you use the telephone to arrange meetings?

Sure we used the telephone. But the social functions were simpler because you met at a coffeehouse. Everything was simpler. You met before a concert or after a concert. It was less formal in Vienna. You didn't have to make all the necessary social preparations as when you have people come to your house. This you did for the High Holidays. For instance, my grandmother lived with us. A High Holiday was an opportunity for the whole family to come to visit the grandmother. I remember Pesach [Passover]; it was a mystical affair. To come to our gigantic Seder was like a family law. One of my uncles conducted the Seder with my father. When everything dissolved in Europe, more or less, because of political and economic conditions and social reasons, Jews were afraid to go out and the family couldn't get together anymore. That uncle died. It felt to us that he had died because the Seder was necessary to his life.

Life in Vienna, in general, was totally different from here, unbelievably so.

Let's talk a little more about the Gruppe *and what it has meant for you over the years. Did it become an obligation to see the people, did you like to, was it a matter of habit? How did you feel when you got together?*

It was very important for us because none of us had any family here. That was our substitute family. Philosophical or political opinions differed, but that didn't matter. It gave us something to discuss. We got together because we liked to. We resonated the way a choir does. It felt comfortable. Relationships developed automatically because people liked each other. No other condition was necessary.

Can you compare the Gruppe's *role years ago with that in the past few years?*

That is hard to say. There is on my part a sort of loyalty—though this is a ghost. There is nothing there. It was part of our youth. We belonged and it gave us a lot of comfort. That doesn't mean it gives us that today. When you analyze it, there were a lot of foolish, even idiotic ideas circulated in the *Gruppe* as time went on. For instance, the role of communism. Now we see we can do very well without it, as a matter of fact, much better than with it. I never saw the virtue of it. Many ideas were prevalent during a time period and surfaced in our group and we talked about them. The Viennese had a song, *"Alte Sitten, alte Zeit"* (Good-bye sweet old time. It's gone. It's gone, we've changed, everything's changed.)

In what ways is the "ghost" important to you?

I cherish it, but it's not important. I never think about it. It's like the prayer book I got for my Bar Mitzvah from my grandmother.

Why do you host the New Year's Eve party each year?

Habit. Well, it's more than that. We enjoy the people. There *is* something in tradition. So much is important in our lives that is only tradition. Going back to the grave of my father. It's just tradition. I create my own traditions. They give me comfort, depth even. Then there is something else. Something that had been a building stone in our lives is not just tossed away when it is no good. It fulfills a function even when it is not "functionable" anymore.

Speaking of traditions, were there family traditions in your youth that you brought with you and established here? These may be Jewish traditions or not.

In our youth in Vienna, the holidays were a great tradition. My grandmother was sitting there like a queen and the family came to wish her a good holiday. There is a certain sweetness about tradition. To relive in a different dimension, a time that is long gone. There is a certain comfort in it.

Again, when you first came to the U.S., what was your attitude about being Jewish? Did you feel more Jewish because of what had happened? Or did you want to step aside and be less Jewish?

Such thoughts never occurred to me. When I came out of the concentration camp, the temple in Vienna was gone. It had been destroyed on *Kristallnacht*. When I came to England and went to *Schul* there on Saturday, it was a delight I cannot describe to you. When we had a Yom Kippur in Buchenwald and tried to celebrate in our modest way by not eating, getting together, and singing a few of the High Holiday songs, do you know what comfort and joy and beauty this was? Totally worthless and senseless, but I experienced this and will remember.

When you came to the United States and could be Jewish openly, did you engage in more of the rituals?

I maintained pretty much the same as we had in Vienna—Kiddush [blessing of wine], the holidays, the duty of maintaining a temple.

Were you ever a Zionist in Vienna or here?

In Vienna, of course. The founder of what is now the Likud party in Israel was in the group I associated with. Theodor Herzel [the founder of the Zionist movement] was buried in Vienna. There was once a year a celebration when the Zionists went to the cemetery to remember when he was born. I always did this.

During your 50 years in the United States, did you ever encounter any anti-Semitic incidents?

I saw some, but nothing ever was personally directed at me.

Is there somebody, some incident, some words, or some object that was of special significance in sustaining you through the immigration years?

There is a saying by Goethe that affected me all my life. "*Mach nicht viel Federlesen. Setzt auf meinen Leichenstein: 'Dies ist ein Mensch gewesen, und das heisst ein Kämpfer sein.'*" [Don't make much fuss with me. Put on my gravestone, "This was a human being and this means to be a fighter."] I had to write a composition about this sentence at the very beginning of high school. I was struggling with it because when I was young I was thinking that life is more than a struggle, that it is not power and strength alone. I tried to defend the position of the weak one. And I wanted there to be more to life. But in the final analysis, I learned that life is a struggle.

What was it like for you the first time you returned to Vienna? When was it and how did you feel being there?

That is a very complicated question. First of all, I don't know if what I say now is what I would have said then. I think I had, like many things in my life, a double experience. I saw how beautiful Vienna is and I would have hated to deny that. Yet I knew that it was not for me. I would not have wanted to live in Vienna anymore. If they would give me a golden car, I would not go. And when I say that, I have doubts about it because I don't know whether it comes from hurt vanity that I say it. It's easy afterward to say I don't want it because I know very well I could not have it anymore. And even if I could, I would not permit myself to have it.

Did you talk to people at all about this emigration/immigration period of your life? Did people ask you questions about it?

Why shouldn't I talk about it? But in general I do not voluntarily give my biography. The period that I did not talk about was of the concentration camp. I didn't want to speak about it. It was my way of blotting out the period. So long a time has passed and I'm not fully aware why I stayed silent. Now I feel it is important to impress it upon people. There are many lessons to be learned. One is about how humans treat humans. Here we saw how the world treats Jews. I consider this one of the greatest injustices there is, because there is no reason for it.

Do you feel that you should talk about it?

Yes, but people aren't interested. I don't want to make a nuisance out of myself. Who wants to hear it? Let's be honest.

How did you feel about these questions I've been asking you?

If you want the answers, I feel all right. I want to be nice to you. I only felt that I have not much to say.

ANN "ANNCHEN" IKENBERG

Ann Ikenberg

Had their lives proceeded as planned, Ann and Fred Ikenberg would have been physician and judge, respectively. Barred from those professions, they facilitated the immigration of German Jews to Palestine, fully intending to go there as well. Before doing so, Ann came to New York for a visit with her mother and sister—and returned to Germany. It was spring of 1938. In less than a year's time, she was back in the United States, this time as an immigrant. Ann and Fred had two children, Danny and Ruth.

My father's family was from Memel, East Prussia. His father was a millionaire. As a partner of David Wolffsohn, later the successor of Theodor Herzl, he had the biggest lumberyard in Germany for construction of railroad cars. My father was a black sheep in his family because he was a Zionist. He was already in 1928 in Palestine. He was one of the first Zionists in Germany and was later a delegate at the Zionist Congress in Basel. Fred and I were both Zionists, independently from each other, already as children.

Did you meet Fred through Zionist activities?

Not originally. Our parents knew each other already for a long time. I must have known Fred as a child, but he was four years older and I didn't remember him. But I did know the whole Dreyfuss family, all old Zionists, who lived in our town. We had a club in Germany called *Jüdische Arbeitsgemeinschaft* [Jewish Workers' Group]. It was founded by **Paul Dreyfuss,** me, and four other teenagers. The *Arbeitsgemeinschaft* met in my hometown, Wuppertal [near Cologne], once a week or twice a month. We studied together Dubnow and Grätz [Jewish historians], and everybody had to give lectures about Jewish topics. Sometimes we also invited outside speakers. After the meetings, we had social gatherings. We went to cafés or our parents' houses. Sometimes we had dances and parties in our homes.

Paul, who was three years older than I, had already left for college in Munich when Fred joined our group. Those two had first met on a train from Munich to Dresden, where they both were going to a convention of their Zionist fraternity, *Karbell Jüdischer Verbindungen.* Paul was very witty, and he sent various printed materials to our group, including a song that goes, *"Denn wo käm' die Schwiegermutter der, hätt'st du keine Arbeitsgemeinschaft mehr?"* (How would you get a mother-in-law if you didn't have this club?) As it happened, very many marriages came about through this club. One of them was Fred and I. We always made fun about it, that it starts with studying Jewish history and ends up in marriage.

When he joined our group, Fred was through with his *Referendar* examination, the first law exam after three years at college. He had three more years until his final exam. I was still in high school, so I hadn't made my *Abitur* yet when we became friends in 1928. We studied together. I took the *Abitur* in '29 and then went to college in Freiburg, Kiel, and Bonn. I studied two-and-a-half years pre-med and passed the *Physicum* in 1931, in Bonn. Fred, meanwhile, had to prepare for the state bar. In Germany, you had to go through six different periods, like internships, for the state bar. These included one in a prison, one as assistant judge (which he did in his hometown of Remscheid), and one working for an attorney. As he went through these various stages and I was studying, we corresponded and telephoned each other.

In '31, Fred had not finished his doctorate. He had written the thesis, but he kept postponing the oral exam. The doctor title is what we called a *Jüdischer Vorname!* You didn't really need it for the state bar. But I encouraged him to take it. He did, just in time, before his professor left. Then Fred went to Berlin to prepare for the state bar. You had to take the exam in the capital of the state. For Prussia, that was Berlin. Because we were friends, I went also to Berlin and studied clinical medicine at the Charité, the leading German university hospital. After Fred passed the bar, I went to Munich to continue my clinical studies and Fred went back to Remscheid to work as a judge.

In 1933, Hitler came to power. He came like a spider. The net got closer and closer. I was not allowed to continue with my medical studies because my father hadn't been a soldier in World War I. (He had been a few months too old.) I was handed my college records and dismissed. Fred, as a judge, was immediately thrown out by the minister of justice (later executed in Nuremberg). Twenty-one years later, in 1954, Fred was reinstated and even promoted, because the dear Germans still had all the old documents in the basement of the ministry. It's not like in America where you are appointed for a judgeship; in Germany, you are a judge for life. Only a certain number of people pass the bar with high enough grades to qualify.

So Fred actually did work as a judge?

Yes, but barely after starting he was kicked out.

When Hitler came, the central Zionist organization, the *Zionistische Vereinigung für Deutschland* (Zionist Federation of Germany) needed people like us very badly because morale was very low and people had no idea what to do. It came as a complete surprise to the German Jews, who were much more assimilated than Jews in Austria. Because Fred and I had always worked for Zionism and there were very few people in Germany with the appropriate experience and education, we were asked to work as employees for the *ZVfD* and give speeches throughout the province. So we gave speeches and helped people to leave the country. We knew all the people who could assist in escapes. Fred spoke sometimes in two cities in one day. He was appointed as the counselor of immigration to Palestine. I still have that letter from the minister of interior, [Hermann] Goering. In addition to his work as Counselor, Fred was the secretary for Rheinland Westfalen within the organization. There were secretaries in every province, one in Rheinland, one in Bavaria, one in Silesia, etc. There were 10 or 11 secretaries.

I, meanwhile, raised a large amount of money from wealthy Jews for the *Keren Kayemet* [an organization that raised funds for the settlement of Palestine]. I was also the volunteer head for the province of Rheinland Westfalen of the women's Zionist group, WIZO (what they call here the *Hadassah*). Then, in 1934, I was employed by the Jewish National Fund.

Fred and you were both working in the same organization?

Yes, and we worked in the same building. When Fred gave lectures, the Gestapo often came. They were always sitting in the first row and recording what he said. Once they came into our office and pointed to a big map of

Palestine. "That's where we want to send you," they said. We were walking on a rainbow. We thought nothing could ever happen to us.

My sister, who had gotten her Ph.D. in economics in Heidelberg, was a journalist, first for the *Frankfurter Zeitung,* a very well-known newspaper in Germany, and later on in Berlin, for the *Vossische Zeitung.* When [Paul Joseph] Goebbels took over as *Minister der deutschen Kultur,* she was immediately discharged. Jews could no longer work on newspapers. April 1, 1934, began the official boycott of Jewish stores and businesses. Fred and I married at the end of that month. The next day, my sister left for England and from there to America.

My mother left in April '36. At that time, you could buy a round-trip ticket to California. She visited my sister in New York, didn't like it there, and went on to Los Angeles. She had even more nerve than I! She got a job right away as a French governess for some movie people. Soon later, she became the matron in the Hamburger Home for girls from broken homes. She was exploited there, taking care of all the girls.

My wealthy grandfather had always helped the poor relatives in Lithuania with money and made it possible for them to escape the pogroms by immigrating in 1901 and 1903 to the United States. They were first in Providence, Rhode Island, where many Jews went because there was an Orthodox community. After World War I ended in 1918, some of these relatives were living in California. They wrote that we should come there. My parents laughed. It was absurd for us to go to California! But later on, when Hitler came, these relatives gave affidavits for us and for everybody we named. Because we had the affidavits and pressure from my mother, Fred and I were among the first to register for immigration at the U.S. Consulate in Stuttgart. We had a very low number, 36 or so, and knew we could get a visa and leave whenever we wanted. But we had no intention to do so. Our plan always was to go to Palestine.

In 1936, the *ZVfD* sent us to Palestine. That was during the riots between Arabs and Jews. We got some practical knowledge about Palestine! This was useful as we continued preparing others for their immigrations.

Before going to Palestine permanently ourselves, I wanted to see my mother and sister once more. I had a very hard time to get a visitor visa because I was on the list for immigration. Very many people had gone on a visitor visa to the U.S. (like my mother) and never came back. I left on a historic day in March 1938. On the *Europa,* a German boat, I opened a newspaper and read that Hitler had marched into Austria. I wondered if I would be able to return to Germany. I visited for about six weeks in the United States. My mother came from Los Angeles to join me and my sister in New York. I compared things to what I had seen in Palestine. The life here was so much easier.

I went back to Germany. A strange thing happened on the boat. The German election was over, but they asked me to vote that I supported the *Anschluss*. I said, "No, I'm not allowed to vote. I'm Jewish." I thought certainly they would keep my passport. Amazingly, they gave it back and nothing happened to me.

When I got home I said to Fred, "Let us go to America. When I was there, I heard more about what is happening in Germany than we know here. I learned about concentration camps." "No," the head of the Zionist organization implored him. "We need people like you here." Fred was hooked and we stayed. I was very mad about such pressure and felt that Fred gave in too easily when told it was his duty to stay.

Then came the pogroms. First, beginning on October 28, 1938, Polish Jews in Germany were arrested. We hid some of them in our bedroom. Others who were working with us at the Zionist organization office were arrested and called us from the police department for help. Fred went with his paper from Goering stating that he was the counselor for immigration to Palestine. But he wasn't allowed to talk to them and couldn't do anything for them. The next time these Jews called us, it was from *Niemandsland* (no man's land), a small corridor between Germany and Poland. Germany had kicked them out and Poland wouldn't let them back in. We couldn't do anything. Fred never put that identification paper from Goering back in the office file. A few days later was the *Kristallnacht*. It really was very good that he didn't put it back because then when he was arrested, we had the paper at home.

November 9, 1938: *Kristallnacht*. The Gestapo began to arrest every Jewish male under 70 years old they could find. That Grynzpan who shot the diplomat, Vom Rath, in Paris, was from Düsseldorf. Unfortunately, we then lived in Düsseldorf, in an apartment next door to the main rabbi, Rabbi Eschelbacher. Arrests began at his house. We were prepared. We had our identification papers in our attaché case. We had all the papers for America, the affidavits, and some money. Most of our furniture was with Fred's parents in Remscheid, not far away.

We walked right past the Nazis on the front steps. They ignored us, not realizing we were Jews. We walked the whole night through the city. I'll never forget the sight of fire burning through the *Magen David* on top of the synagogue. I had a feeling I can't describe to you. I thought, "That's as far as they can go. That cannot work out. There must be a bad ending for people who do something like this." I never had a feeling it could have a bad ending for us. As we walked, people started plundering stores and said to me, "*Fräulein, Warum nehmen Sie sich denn nichts?*" (Young girl, why don't you take anything for yourself?) People took whatever was in the stores.

Nazis were saying those things to you?

They often said such things to me. For example, when I went with Fred in the street, they said I should be ashamed to run around with a Jewish boy.

Is that because you were blond?

I didn't look Jewish. They had their race theory. Little did they know that Hitler looked more Jewish than many Jews!

The *Kristallnacht* was organized all over Germany and Austria. But Jews didn't know about it. Some people got killed that night. As Fred and I walked in the street, we met other Jews. It became clear to us what was going on. After walking all night, I went back to our apartment. Fred wouldn't go back (and never did). The apartment was in shambles. When the Nazis had come to our door and nobody answered, they were so mad that they kicked in the door. They smashed all our silver and crystal. I quickly packed two suitcases of our belongings. We went first to Cologne to talk with our Zionist friends. We learned that men there had been arrested and sent to Dachau. Our fellow Zionist members wanted to take us to Belgium, illegally. We called Fred's parents in Remscheid. Nothing had happened at their house and men of that town hadn't been arrested. It was different in every city. (I later went back to our neighborhood in Düsseldorf and learned that friends' husbands had been sent to Dachau.)

We stayed in Remscheid a week or so, until one day the Gestapo came looking for Fred's brother, who was fortunately in Holland at *hachsharah*. When they asked Fred who he was, he told them. That's how he got arrested. It was terrible. My father-in-law was in the house at the time. He was hysterical with fear and pleaded, "Put me against the wall and shoot me." He didn't want the disgrace of his firstborn son going to jail. The Gestapo took Fred off to prison. I went along. The other young Jewish men of Remscheid were already there.

Fred was well known at the prison because he had been a judge at the court there. I told the Gestapo officers that we had all papers necessary for going to America. They were sociable and said, "Oh, I envy you that you can go to California. I wish we could go." Really, honest to goodness, they said that! They were not all so mean, but they had their jobs to do.

I got Fred out of that prison. I went to the head of the Gestapo there and showed the paper with Goering's signature that stated that Fred was the counselor of immigration. I told him, "The whole immigration to Palestine will stop immediately if my husband is in jail!" He called someone in Berlin to find out if the paper was authentic. Fred got free, but not immediately. He still spent two nights in jail. The remaining Jewish prisoners were deported to Dachau.

From the prison, I called Stuttgart to the American Consulate for Western Germany. Ordinary telephone calls didn't get through anymore. You had to make a *Blitzgespräch* (lightening call) to reach the consulate. Because of connections from work, we were able to get a date for a medical exam, which was necessary for immigration.

Compared to others, we had a very early departure date. Fred was arrested on November 9. In December, we had the medical exam, and in January 1939 we left Germany. That was as fast as it possibly could go. Everybody was trying to emigrate at once, immediately. There were already some men back from Dachau, lucky ones who had the necessary papers. We were on the first boat you could take after *Kristallnacht.*

Why didn't you go to Palestine?

Until 1938, you could go to Palestine if you had 1,000 English pounds. Or you had to have, as we would have gotten as Zionists, a *Watik* certificate. After *Kristallnacht,* we tried to reach headquarters to get the certificates. But at that point, certificates were given only to people already in concentration camps. We had all the right connections and it did us no good! We would have had to wait. I wasn't willing to do that. If you lived through *Kristallnacht* and had a little clear mind left, you got out as quick as possible. It was the biggest affront—to work so hard for Palestine and then to go to America!

We had to notify the Gestapo that we were leaving Remscheid. They came to our house, and we had to pack under the eye of the Gestapo and to present a list of the contents of our suitcases. For everything we took, we had to pay its value to the government. This fine was called *Judensteuer.* I don't know if this was in Austria, too. While the man was in the kitchen, I still threw in some jewelry and gold watches. I had more nerve than anything! Then the suitcases were closed and sealed so they could pass through to the harbor in Hamburg. We weren't permitted to open the suitcases until on the boat.

Earlier, we had shipped a lift of boxes directly to the U.S. Much of their contents were stolen, especially the silver. Also, for several years, we had two suitcases stored in Brussels with **Paul Dreyfuss.** One suitcase was all clothes for Fred and one for me. My *real* jewelry, the valuable pieces, were hidden among the clothes. We knew that maybe one day we would have to leave Europe suddenly. We had an arrangement with Paul that if we had to go, we would send a postcard telling him where to send the suitcases. Paul's attic was full of suitcases from various people in my hometown. I was always afraid he would send the wrong suitcases!

In 1936, I had traveled to Brussels with the two big suitcases. I returned after two days with a small suitcase that had three grapefruits in it! Paul's father, who lived near me, was a diabetic and in Germany you couldn't buy grapefruit. I was bringing them back for him. At the border control, the Gestapo questioned me, "*Fräulein, mit drei Grapefruit sind Sie in Brüssel gewesen?*" [Miss, you were in Brussels with three grapefruit?] "Oh, it was just a pleasure trip!" We really were sort of crazy in those days!

When we got ready to leave, I sent Paul the card telling him from where and when we were leaving. So he sent the suitcases from Brussels to Ikenberg, care of the SS *Manhattan*, Le Havre, France. He sent them collect. We always got such a kick out of it that we don't know who paid for them. We left in January 1939, from Hamburg, with the boat for Le Havre. Then we crossed the Channel to Southampton, England. It was very choppy. Fred was too seasick, but I had to go and look in the basement of the boat to see if the suitcases from Brussels were there. Honest to goodness, they were there! They were our suitcases all right.

We had been able to pay with German money for the trip all the way to Los Angeles. We had the best cabin on the boat, with private bath, but almost no money in hand! We could take out only 10 marks, which at that time was $4. We traveled in high style, wearing our very good clothes that had been packed in those Brussels suitcases. Fred played piano for the passengers.

We arrived in New York and stayed with my sister for the weeks until our boat left for California. She made room for us in her Greenwich Village apartment. Since we knew we would arrive with no money, we had set up a scheme for getting some money out of Germany to the U.S. We had a cousin in Sweden who had married a gentile Swedish man. This husband came a few times to visit us in Germany, once immediately after *Kristallnacht*. He took expensive cameras which we had bought and sold them in Sweden. He sent that money to my sister for Fred and me. Otherwise we would have had nothing. We had a great time in New York. That was the year of a World Exhibition. We could have had a job at the World Exhibit, but we didn't want to stay in New York. Finally, we got to the boat on the Panama Pacific Line which would take us to the West Coast.

And that was a beautiful trip. It was great. We were a rarity on the boat. It was very fashionable to be such interesting people who had just come out of Germany! When we docked in Baltimore, some people took us by taxi to Washington and we were in the town where Roosevelt was president. At that time we were still thinking he was an ideal man. We didn't know what a politician he was! Anyway, we went on and landed in Panama City, where my sister had friends. They took us around and we saw all Panama.

So you had a pleasure cruise!

Ya! We landed in Acapulco. It was a fishing village. Then, in April 1939, we arrived in San Pedro. There, with a car, was my mother, my father's cousin who had given us the affidavits, and her little boy. Ach, we thought it was all so unbelievably beautiful! On Figueroa Street—real palm trees!

It was very fortunate that my mother was here. She had already prepared an apartment for us. There were filled salt and pepper shakers. There was nothing missing. But we had to have money; we had to work. I found something the first day because of my medical studies. Nurses were needed. My good fortune was that during my semester breaks in Germany, I had worked in a hospital as a nurse. I could use that knowledge.

There was an agency where refugees were exploited, like now the Mexican people who are underpaid. Movie people had organized this Opportunity Placement Office in Beverly Hills. There, I immediately got a job with Superior Court Judge Edward R. Brand as a nurse for his mother. I worked for this well-established family because I thought they could get a job for Fred. But they never did anything for us. I got $10 a week and had to pay for my own uniform and carfare. My patient was very temperamental, and I was working too hard. After two months I left, but with a very good reference.

I would have liked to continue my studies in medicine, but we had no money. I would have had to do an internship. But after what we had been through, I couldn't leave Fred alone and stay nights at a hospital.

What kind of nursing did you do?

Private home nursing. I got jobs when patients were discharged from hospitals. I couldn't work in hospitals because I wasn't registered as a California nurse and so couldn't be insured.

In the next job, I got $35 a week. This was a big increase from $10! I had good jobs and I was really treated very nicely. It was mostly home nursing. But I also worked once at the City of Hope. My mother had a car. (She wasn't afraid of anything! She was maybe a worse driver than I, which is very hard to beat!) Fred and my mother took me to Duarte. When they saw the sign that it was for tubercular people, as it was at that time, they got hysterical that I should come home right away. I was the private nurse just for one patient. He had open TB and I had to wear a mask. I stayed with this job for a few days.

When I became pregnant in 1943, I switched from nursing to secretarial work. Nursing is sometimes physically rough, and I was afraid of having a miscarriage. I knew typing and shorthand. So I got a secretarial job in a factory, Superior Handblocked Textile Company. They made and printed on tablecloths, napkins, and towels, and then shipped these to soldiers wherever they were. The soldiers then sent these things home as presents to their

Ann Ikenberg with her husband, Fred, Los Angeles, 1939.

families! Very often those things were so badly printed that we sold mostly to Woolworth's and other dime stores. It was a Russian immigrant who owned the place, Mr. Feldman. He didn't know how to write a letter in English. So I wrote letters for him. When he left the office to see customers, I had "to watch that the Mexican girls didn't steal anything." My typewriter was where all the merchandise was, so I could keep an eye on everything.

After I had quit that job, Gretl Esslau gave me a surprise baby shower. I'll never forget it. The *Keren Kayemet* box was passed in Baby Ikenberg's name. As Gretl said, "It's never too early to start working for Zionism."

How was it for Fred to find work?

For Fred it took time. We came in April. It took till January 1940 to find steady work. Before then he tried various things. He was supposed to sell American flags in movie theaters. He couldn't do that; he was not a salesperson and they wanted him to pay for the samples. Then he cleaned windows in a drugstore for $5 a day.

Finally, we met a man who was able to give Fred a "real" job. We were at a gathering of Zionists, a barbecue at the home of a relative of mine. This relative had worked for years for my wealthy grandfather in Lithuania until he and his family left after a pogrom in 1903 and came to Los Angeles. We met a very decent man, Julius Fligelman, one of the leading Jewish people here. He was one of the founders of the University of Judaism and was very active in the Reconstruction movement. He owned the Los Angeles Period Furniture Company, the biggest bedroom furniture factory west of Chicago, and hired quite a few refugees to work there.

Fred worked there, burning trash and loading furniture. One day, that Mr. Fligelman saw him, and knowing that Fred was a doctor of law, asked, "Couldn't you find work in the office which would be better?" Fred did, and worked his way up until he was purchasing agent for the company. But after 15 years, Fligelman's son didn't want to give Fred a raise anymore. Fred quit. He knew somebody who had also left the company and was opening a new place, the Goldenberg Lumber Company. Fred went to work there as controller.

Something here confuses me. If you had cousins here . . .

Yea, but they didn't give you jobs! They gave big receptions. Their main concern was that we immediately change our name. We cannot possibly be called Ikenberg; we have to change to Ickes. There was an Ickes in the Roosevelt cabinet. We said, "That name was good enough in Germany (and of course we were very snobbish), and who knows what other country we may go to. We can't keep changing our name. We'll keep the name." There were eight or nine of these cousins. They did not want to help us find work because one young man in the family had committed, not a crime, but had not proven very trustworthy. This is also American behavior, I think. They let you in, but then you have to shift for yourself. And we did.

Even if none of these relatives could give you jobs, it seems strange that they didn't even give you names of people who might be able to lead you to jobs.

Right. We had all these people whom my grandfather had supported or given money to, who gave receptions but no work. But they were connected to organizations like Opportunity Placement. It was like with "socially conscious" people today. They have dinner dances, money-raising affairs, like for the City of Hope. They don't help you any further.

Anyway, we made it on our own. My mother also. The European Jews all had good education, and this is what counts in life. You can be kicked out, but they cannot take education away from you. You can lose everything else. That's why it's so important to learn something.

Was Fred ever able to use any of the skills he had learned in Germany?

He couldn't use the German law here. While he worked at the furniture company, he took correspondence courses through Chicago University and studied accounting. That cost less than to go to UCLA.

We never wanted to hear about Germany anymore. That was one of the reasons we went to Los Angeles. We didn't want to hear the word *Germany*. It was such a shock what had happened. Jews who had lived in other places were more conscious of being different and discriminated against because there was more ghetto life elsewhere. But we were completely assimilated. All my girlfriends in Germany were gentiles. In Los Angeles, too, we never read Jewish newspapers. When in the *Aufbau* [a German Jewish newspaper published in New York], they announced you could apply for restitution, we didn't know about it. Then in 1954, at a *Gruppe* gathering, **Rudy Brook** told us that he got a pension of $160 a month from Germany based on his law training. That was a tremendous amount to us at that time. But the offer to apply had expired. Fortunately, it opened again later and Fred applied.

That same year, a letter came from Germany that Fred got reinstated to the bar. I called him at work and said, "*Ist das der Amtsrichter* (the municipal judge) on the phone?" He said, "Yes," hung up, and came immediately home. That was the only time he ever left work early! It meant a tremendous amount of money for us. In addition to the $165, we also got restitution for Fred's father's department store and home, which had not been destroyed. It was what we called blood money. After that, we also got presents from Fred's hometown every year at Christmas. The most idiotic things. And for the month of December, Fred always got twice the salary. The Germans are so religious! Once I called to wish them Happy Easter. Fred was fit to be tied! But it's the German way. Greasy sweetness! And I played into it.

Later on, we read an article in the *Aufbau* which led us to write to the author, Robert Kempner. (He wrote for newspapers in both the U.S. and Germany and was very influential against the Germans at the Nuremberg Trials.) Kempner responded to Fred that he could be promoted in the legal hierarchy because he had passed the *Prädikat* [assessor exam] with a high grade. He would only have to show the right papers. We had these, of course. So Fred became an *Oberlandesgerichtsrat* (here, a superior court judge) and was invited to take a position in Germany. He didn't even ask me. He wrote right away. It would not occur to him to return!

If you had ever decided to return to Germany, for whatever reason, would Fred have. . .

He would have been promoted one step further, to be *Senatspräsident* (president of the senate of the province). Fred had a cousin in Chicago who was also a German-educated judge. He had no children and was very unhappy there. So he went back and became a *Senatspräsident* in Cologne.

As Fred stayed in America, his pension was, I think, 71 percent of the regular salary. I continue to get 55 percent of his salary for my lifetime, because he was a civil servant. When Danny and Ruthy went to college, we got *Kinderzuschlag* (compensation for children's education). I continue to get medical assistance—55 percent of my medical expenses are paid by the German government. Also, they pay for home nursing and for medication, even for dental expenses and eyeglasses.

Is this provided for all civil servants in Germany?

No, only for higher officials. Also, for the time Fred and I worked for the Zionist Organization and I for *Keren Kayemet*, I get social security from Germany. I get 60 percent of Fred's from Germany as well as his from the U.S.

There was something you said a while back that is interesting to me. On the one hand, you wanted to have nothing to do with anything German, and on the other hand, you kept contact with gentile friends of your youth.

I don't blame the whole nation of people for what happened. We even sent CARE packages to some of my gentile friends after the war. There were some very decent people. The husband of one of my very best friends, for example, was the minister of culture in Schleswig-Holstein, in northern Germany, and the dean of the university there. They were socialists, and during Hitler they resisted the Nazis. They were against euthanasia of children. In Westphalia, Germany, there was a famous home for mentally retarded children and he, as a theologian, with his wife, demonstrated against these killings. This girlfriend visited me during the Hitler time. Besides this couple, many of my friends and their parents were anti-Nazi and demonstrated. Some were put in prison. One friend knew a group that planned to kill Hitler. When the group was caught and sentenced for execution, she went to Berlin, where we had a friend from dancing school who turned into a head Gestapo. She went to him and asked for mercy. He didn't want to have anything to do with it. He was an arch Nazi.

As were others: I had a friend in Kiel who wanted to marry me. I saw him again during the night of *Kristallnacht*. Jews were not permitted at the railway station—you were in danger of getting arrested—and, thank God, he didn't recognize me. But I recognized him. He was in full Nazi uniform. We had been together in the *Sozialistenbund* in Kiel on the Baltic Sea. We always used to say, "If you are not a socialist until you are 20, you are a fool, and if after 20 you are still a socialist, you remain a fool." During Hitler, many of my friends got killed for this political affiliation, not because they were Jews.

After *Kristallnacht*, even the principal from my high school called to check if I was all right. (I had graduated nine years earlier!) I know three people in Fred's hometown that hid Jews at risk to their own lives. Some people wanted to hide his parents. The woman who ran the yardage department in their department store had a ranch out of town which she offered to them. But they didn't want to go. Nobody knew what was going to happen. Nobody thought it would come to such an extreme. It came gradually.

During your first years here, what did you know about the fate of Jews who remained in Europe?

We did know about concentration camps, but not about extermination. That information came after the war. People gave up that they would hear about their families. We didn't really want to know what was happening.

Once in Los Angeles, how did you reconnect with your gentile German friends?

I was sought out after the war because my father had made loans on some properties. His name had been entered in the county books as the holder of these mortgages and was still there after the war! When people wanted to sell their houses, this came out. They couldn't sell if a mortgage hadn't been paid off. So the small Jewish community which survived in my hometown tried to find us.

My father had a habit of taking poor Polish Jews into the house to feed them dinner. A Mr. Landau was one such person. He and his family went to Australia. The remaining Jews of Wuppertal wrote to Landau if he knew what happened to us. He did and gave them our address.

Other people from my hometown started writing, asking what happened to us. I got these letters to a nauseating degree. Some people used these letters to write books like *Auschwitz begann in Wuppertal* [an account of the town in the 1930s]. In these books were lists of Jews I knew only from the religious class we had to take throughout school. That had been the time when I, as a Western Jew, mixed with Eastern Jews. In Germany there was this snobbish attitude. *Westjuden* wanted nothing to do with *Ostjuden*. For me, if someone was *Ostjuden* and a Zionist, of course, it was different. Most Zionists were from the East. They had come after the pogroms in the ghettos of Russia. Unless they were Zionists, there was a complete isolation between these groups of Jews and we met *Ostjuden* only in religious class.

It's interesting that you and Fred were such assimilated Germans, yet Zionism played such a significant part in your lives.

For me it was in the blood, maybe from my father. He was ahead of the times in many ways. That's why my father was so happy when I married Fred. And although for Fred's parents he and I could do no wrong, for the rest of his family it was totally unacceptable that we were Zionists. Just as his father had been, Fred was a black sheep in his family. They had big factories and couldn't stand that I would show up there and collect money for Palestine!

Being a Zionist proved to be a good thing. It gave some backbone when Hitler came. That was very important because people felt degraded. Their old style of living was falling apart. Many committed suicide. But we knew Jewish history. Persecution had happened before and I knew that "*Ganz gleich, der Jude wird verbrannt*" (No matter what, the Jew gets burned)— Heine. It's always that way. The Jews get blamed. When something will happen here and in Germany again, too, Jews will be accused. Neo-Nazism exists and some deny the Holocaust even happened!

Did you say that most of your friends were gentile?

Sure, very much. In my *Abitur* class, I was the only Jew.

I ask that because my father had no gentile friends.

It was different in Vienna. Anti-Semitism was worse there. Even though they were free to move about, many Jews lived like in a ghetto. Germany was very assimilated. My family was involved with the whole community, not just the Jews, and was very social minded. For example, my mother and two friends had an advisory office for women who had no money for an attorney and needed protection from the law, like here for abused women. Women could come there for free judicial advice. My father and the husbands of the other two women were attorneys and gave the advice. My father was an old socialist and old Zionist, very progressive, and always gave money to people, besides loaning money so they could buy houses.

You know, during the war, the Germans, too, went through a lot. You cannot blame the whole nation of people for what happened. It could just as well happen here, only worse. There is so much anti-Semitism in America, like I never had experienced as a child in Germany. I *never* experienced any anti-Semitism there, never. Fred experienced a little maybe because he grew up in a small town. He was beaten up for being a Jew.

Let's return to Los Angeles. Would you tell me something about the formation of the Gruppe? *Was it at the furniture factory that Fred met Herman Esslau?*

Yes, and that was the foundation of the *Gruppe!* There were many refugees hired by Mr. Fligelman. Fred always took his lunch from home, and one day, he saw a man sitting on a nail keg eating his lunch out of an attaché case. That was dear Herman eating Gretl's sandwiches! Fred said to him, "You must be a German refugee!" They talked and decided to meet in some other place. That other place was our house on 12th Street near Pico. **Ernest Wolf,** whom we knew marginally through a local Zionist organization and whom Fred had met once through that connection already in Germany, came too. That was the first meeting of the *Gruppe.* I'll never forget that Ernst said to Herman, *"Die Wiener sind alle faul und schmutzig!"* (The Viennese are all lazy and dirty). This slur made them almost as "bad" as *Ostjuden!* Herman, who was Viennese, didn't contradict. He asked that we all meet again next week at his house on Magnolia, where there would be some other Viennese people. So the next *Gruppe* meeting was at Esslaus's, and there came a couple by the name of **Wolman,** and they said they had a neighbor by the name of **Bauer.**

So at the first meeting there were just Ikenberg, Wolf, and Esslau?

Yes. And the founders were **Wolf,** Esslau, **Wolman, Bauer,** and **Ikenberg.** Then Siegfried Eisgrau joined. Eisgrau was always our savior. He was the typical Viennese coffeehouse type. He could sit all day in a café with one cup of coffee and solve all the world's problems. He was willing to give a speech about everything. Willi (a friend of Magda) and Vita and Geo Sommers also came to some early meetings. Our gatherings were an outlet for the physical labor we all had to do during the day. It felt good to get together and have a discussion and *Mehlspeise* [coffee and cake]. It gave us all moral support. It meant a lot to us. In the first years, the *Gruppe* was important because it gave us all a backbone to get adjusted.

During that period we had hardly any money, but managed somehow. And we were very happy. The worst thing I remember was when the Japanese were deported. I thought I was back in Germany. I had Japanese friends and many of them had to sell everything and leave. They were taken advantage of, like we were by the Germans. They were not killed, but they had to go to internment camps. It reminded me too much of the country we had left. We, too, became enemy aliens when war was declared after Pearl Harbor. We were even threatened to be deported—first the Japanese and then the Germans. We were not willing to go to a camp. We had some relatives in Chicago and had already decided to go there. Germans and Japanese became enemy aliens only on the West Coast, I think, because Americans feared there were Japanese submarines off the coast. Whether that was true, I don't know. Anyway, we had to turn in guns, radios, and cameras. We had just gotten a radio that could receive foreign stations and had to give that up along with our camera. Until we became citizens, these things were in custody of the police. It took five years till we could become citizens. When we passed the citizenship exam, we got our radio and camera back and had a celebration.

Did police come to search your house for these items?

Because we were considered enemy aliens, they had the right to come to the house to check that we were home at night. They never came to us, but you never knew. At eight o'clock at night, I had to race home. It was different with the Austrians. Because Hitler had marched into Austria and occupied it, it was unclear whether they were enemy aliens or not. So the Austrians would come and visit us, like Magda Bauer (Frank worked nights) and Eisgrau and the other *Gruppe* members who were not Germans. The Austrians also could keep their radios and cameras.

While you were an enemy alien, did Americans treat you as German or exempt you from that because you were Jewish?

It was so strange. No matter how bad the enemies were, the Germans were always popular. I think it's because so many Americans are of German descent. They were never considered so much the enemy as the Japanese. Maybe it's because we look lily white and don't have yellow color. I never experienced anything bad. We just had to be home at night. We were used from Hitler's Germany to obey.

Was this curfew on week-ends too?

Yes.

What would happen if you went away for the week-end?

We wouldn't have dared. We wouldn't have been one minute after eight out of the house! Especially Fred. Maybe some people took a chance, but he was, through and through, Prussian! If you had to be home at eight, you were home at eight! Not one minute later.

If you were at someone's house, could you stay overnight?

No, you had to be in your own house in case the police came. And that's when the friendships became even closer among the *Gruppe*. The Austrian members visited the enemy aliens. Most of the members came from Vienna. The **Frankels,** also from Vienna, had joined by then.

Toward the end of 1941, Charles and Susan Meyer joined the *Gruppe.* The connection was that my mother was a friend of Charles's mother. The Meyers came from Berlin and they already had a little boy, Michael. He was about four years old then. When we met, Charlie had no work. In time, he found work at a shipyard and later had an electric shop on Alvarado. He was enterprising and did well. Susan, like me, worked as a nurse right away, and she became a very close friend of mine. Little Michael said always, *"Bei uns in Berlin war doch alles viel schöner"* [With us in Berlin, everything was so much more beautiful]. During the day, we would go to Elysian Park and Michael learned Mother Goose rhymes. Sadly, Susie became very sick and died less than 20 years after they arrived here.

Then came the Fischers: Dr. Bert Fischer, eventually professor of physics at City College, and Lilo Fischer. They were ardent Zionists like us. With **Ernst Wolf,** we three couples founded another organization, a labor Zionist group which went kaput. There were not enough people to keep it going.

Paul and Irene Dreyfuss came on Labor Day, 1941. They were able to come with a preference visa because Gaspar Color, the company Paul worked for in Brussels, moved to Los Angeles. Fred picked them up and brought them to our house. When I offered Irene some of my clothes, it became clear that she was pregnant! They had a house first on Fuller, in the back house. That's where the children were born.

The **Sommers** came into the *Gruppe* later. They met the **Dreyfusses** in their citizenship class. Let me count again—**Ikenberg,** Esslau, **Wolf, Wolman, Bauer,** Eisgrau, Willi Frankel, Vita and Geo Sommer, **Fritz and Gerty Frankel,** Meyer, Fischer—that was the *Stammgruppe* [core group]. Later on came **Dreyfuss, Sommer, Brook, Lesser,** Mautner/Stover (Gretl Esslau's sister), **Lampl,** and then **Schwarz.** We all lived, more or less, in the same geographical area.

We were snobbish. Although other people came to our meetings occasionally, not everyone was invited to join. You had to be academic and have information to present. We took turns giving talks about topics we had background in. Sometimes we had guest speakers, like Alexander Granach, a movie person, and Rabbi Franklin Cohn, who was persecuted under McCarthy. Yes, it was a little bit snobbish, that I must say. Also, there was competition. In retrospect, I see that we didn't accept people who didn't have a professional background. It was unconscious I think, but it was that way. There *is* something to it, you know. We had discussions and sometimes they were very ardent and very good. Eisgrau and Fred argued about Zionism and anti-Zionism. Fred talked about Pan-Arabism and some members were very pessimistic about the future of Palestine. Whatever the topic, you had to have a certain level of background to be able to discuss it. Just being

German or Austrian wasn't enough! It was not only snobbism. People had to be able to participate, not necessarily to give speeches (mostly it was the men who did that) but to discuss intelligently. You had to be able to contribute. It wasn't a social club.

In spite of all our troubles from having no money, many of us decided it was time to have children. So in the year 1943, the epidemic broke out, and nearly everybody had a child! In March, you were born; April, Miriam Frankel; then Tommy Lesser. Danny came in October, Bob Bauer in January '44.

For four weeks, I had a baby nurse to take care of Danny. She was also from Germany. She had studied in Bonn to take care of infants. But she scared the hell out of all of us! I was so frightened that I didn't even want her to bring Danny to me. She carried him as if he was the most precious diamond and didn't let anybody see him unless he was under a veil to protect him from germs. I know that by being so scared, I dropped Danny the first time the nurse took off. He fell from the scale onto the wooden floor. But it didn't hurt him, apparently.

Was it common to have a nurse?

Oh yes, and often for more than four weeks. Your mother also had a nurse for you that was recommended by me. Nothing was as precious for people who had lost their families in the Holocaust than that new generation. Having children made it all more bearable.

The *Gruppe* lasted because of our common fate. A close friendship developed among most of the people. Since we all had kids the same age, we had common issues of how to raise a child. Your mother was the expert since you were a few months older than most. We overprotected our firstborns tremendously. We thought they would die from starvation if they wouldn't eat their egg or something! My biggest concern was the children. They were always on a pedestal. This was not so good. I think we didn't raise the children like normal children should grow. Because of Hitler, we were all already much too old to have children. But it was then or never. So we overprotected the children.

In what ways is the Gruppe *still important to you?*

Nostalgic value, I would say. It was an important time in our lives. We had to get adjusted to a new life. And now also, interest in the children's and grandchildren's development.

Now I have a question along a different line. If someone says to you, "What are you?" what do you say?

111

American. Unequivocally. I don't consider myself a German anymore. We never wanted to go back. We never wanted to read a German paper. Nothing again. Completely over. From the moment we got here, we made this home. I told you we had the choice to go back to Germany with full colors. It would have been of great monetary value to us. Fred could have been reinstated as a full judge. And I, as the wife of a high official, would have had a very different life.

Did you speak German at all when you came to America?

No, we did not talk German at home.

Did you make that decision when you left Germany?

No, but when I studied medicine, I learned that you should raise your child in the language of his peers or you make trouble for the child. Some of our friends did not do that. Their children were fluent in German, but had difficulty with their peers. When my mother was still alive, we did talk German sometimes, although she knew English.

When you came to the United States, did you have anything to do with a synagogue?

We were *böse mit dem lieben Gott* [angry with dear God], to tell the truth, because our parents were killed. I will still never go to a temple unless I have to, because I start to cry and make a spectacle of myself. I don't want people to look at me. The only temple I sometimes went to was the Leo Baeck Temple, where Ruthy got married.

In Germany, we were so assimilated that we rarely went to temple there either. Only my father went. He tried to give my sister and me money to go to synagogue on High Holidays! My sister refused to be corrupted. She would not accept his money. But I did! By law in Germany, you had to belong to a temple if you were a Jew. Some of your tax money went to it automatically. On our birth certificates, marriage certificates—everywhere— it mentioned religion, even on the matriculation diploma. You could later on refuse to have it mentioned, but I didn't care to refuse. My father's parents were Orthodox and wouldn't eat in our house. We belonged to a Conservative synagogue. Girls sat upstairs, boys downstairs. All we did was to fool around with the boys until the cantor (who was our religion teacher in school) came up and reprimanded us. Religion class was required. I made a nuisance of myself. For punishment, I always had to copy the "Prophets" three times.

You made a comment earlier that there was more anti-Semitism in the United States than in Germany. Did you ever experience any incidents here?

No, I didn't. In all the years, nothing personal. Fred, yes. At work in his first job he was told, "Go back to the country you came from. You lie. You cannot even write correctly." Although nothing has ever been directed at me, I know anti-Semitism is here. You read it in the paper. You see it. You just know it.

When did you return to Germany for the first time?

In 1963.

How did it feel to be there?

I couldn't even recognize the house where I was born and lived because it had all been bombed. My school was bombed, too. I think only the obstetrician, a classmate of mine, was still living there in his old house. The rest of the town was destroyed by the Canadian and British air force. Most people had moved to southern Germany, mostly to Wuerttemberg, or to Berlin. They couldn't stay in Wuppertal. Everything was destroyed. They, too, had to run for their lives. I visited several friends elsewhere.

Later, we were invited by my hometown to come for a visit. (In Germany they did that; in Austria they didn't.) Some towns paid for the airfare; ours didn't. But when we got there, they paid for the hotel room and board. When we arrived in our room, the table was set with flowers, chocolates, and theater tickets. We could eat in the best restaurants for free. Instead of staying with my friends, as we had done before, we stayed in the hotel and used the food tickets in restaurants. I went to a class reunion. During one visit, we went to a meeting in the city hall and met with a councilman who wanted to know the story of my family, about what my parents did for the city. It got to be too much.

At what point did you begin to talk about the immigration years with Danny, Ruthy, or friends?

I talked about it all along. I have a big mouth! I brought many things with me which I showed to the children. I had nothing to hide.

What do you think about your personality made it possible for you to make so many adaptations?

Aggressiveness. And stubbornness—with my head through the wall! I never took anything lying down. Sometimes I say things that are out of my mouth before I think. I get upset about what I have said, even scared sometimes! But one good thing about aggressiveness—I don't give a hoot what people think about me. That I have learned from the Nazi time. Some people were my friends and some people didn't know me anymore. Some brought us food when it was a risk to do so. Under times of stress you can see who your friends really are.

It's *chutzpah* [nerve, daring] I have! Also, I like people and like to talk with them. Sometimes I say impossible things! I'm not a diplomat! I know better than everybody else!

When they go through a traumatic period in their life, some people have a person, idea, or thing that helps them get through. Did you have anything that helped give you courage?

No, I didn't need it.

How do you feel about this experience of my asking so many questions? Was it a pain in the neck? Or painful to bring up the past?

No, it wasn't painful. I have been interviewed so many times. I think you did a very good job and you did it thoroughly. You deserve credit for doing it. Somebody has to do it. There are many people who pretend that the Holocaust never took place. I know many people don't like to talk about it. But it's important. It's an important chapter. History repeats itself. Now anti-Semitism is going on again.

IRENE AND PAUL DREYFUSS

Inveterate immigrants, both Paul and Irene had already left Germany in the early 1930s seeking work. They were introduced by their brother and sister, respectively, who were in France preparing for immigration to Palestine. Paul's doctorate in chemistry provided income for them, first in Italy, then Belgium. From there, Paul was deported to a camp in France. They fled Europe late, on one of the last ships possible. The only members of the Gruppe to return to the Old World, they immigrated for the final time, to Switzerland in 1957. They had two children, Judy and Michael, the only Gruppe children who do not live in the United States.

Irene left Germany after 1933, at first went to the Alsace as an au pair, or to take care of a household and children. I do not know whether this was a Jewish home or not, but I presume so. Parallel to her leaving home, while

This contribution on Paul and Irene Dreyfuss was written by their daughter, Judy Navon.

her parents still remained in Germany, her sister Gretel, who was Zionist oriented (while Irene was not especially), joined a *hachsharah* in Nazareth, southern France. (This was "preparation"—a farm on which Jewish youth prepared for *aliyah* [immigration to Palestine]. There were several such farms in Europe, preparing youth for the big step.) Gretel influenced Irene to come to this *hachsharah*. Heiner, Paul's already married brother, was also preparing for *aliyah* there. He made the introduction of Irene to Paul, who had also left Germany.

In 1933, Paul had finished his doctor's thesis in chemistry in Germany, with no chance of getting work there. Like many young people at the time, he was aware that he would have to leave the country to find work. Jews generally went either to America or to Palestine. Paul was not inclined to go to America. His outlook was Zionistic and Palestine oriented. But he also knew that he would not be able to work in his field in Palestine and was not ready to compromise. What possibilities/alternatives did he have? A vacancy for assistant chemistry professor was open in Calgliari on the island of Sardinia. I don't know if he knew Italian when he went there, but he learned soon enough. Later, he transferred to Catania on Sicily, where he also taught German to the Italians (who later used that German in their contacts with Nazi Germany, I suspect).

Sometime during or between Sardinia and Sicily my parents met, and apparently the *shiduch* (match) worked. Irene came, I think around 1936, to Catania to join Paul, where they were married in a civil ceremony. No Jews were there, so no rabbi, and no money to be able to afford to go farther north for a rabbinical ceremony. (Today in Israel, civil ceremony alone could be a problem for the offspring, but if the mother is Jewish, all is well for the children's Jewishness.)

They remained in Catania, I assume, for one or two years. I know that Paul did research with olive oil, but know no details. He added to his earnings by teaching German. Irene did not have a usable profession (in Germany she had worked as a secretary to a doctor), but here she utilized other skills. As a child and teenager, she had loved gymnastics and rhythmic dancing, which, gathering from the literature I saw at home, was well developed at the time. So Irene taught gymnastics, I don't know if to children or grown-ups. She continued later in that line when they were living in Brussels, where she also began studying remedial massage and anatomy.

When fascism became too hot in Catania, they moved northward to Pavia, Italy, for a period and later to Brussels in Belgium. There, Paul worked for Bela Gaspar, a Jewish Hungarian emigrant who was a pioneer in color film research and had transferred his work to Brussels. Bela Gaspar, maybe more aware than others of how the political winds were blowing, left Belgium for the United States and began arrangements for transferring his company there, while his employees remained in Belgium.

Paul's parents left Germany and lived with Paul and Irene in Brussels. (Later, his father died there of diabetes. His mother was deported and died in Auschwitz before extermination, Paul said. But who really knows?) Irene's parents (I do not know in what year) left Germany for England, where Irene's other sister, Annie, resided in Nottingham with her husband. Her sister Gretel and Paul's brother Heiner successfully made *aliyah* after *hachsharah*.

Hitler invaded Belgium. Paul, like other Jewish and German men, was arrested. Women apparently were not. I know that Paul was deported to Gurs, a deportation camp in southern France. I know that Irene, in trying to reach him, went though hair-raising experiences, including being in Dunkirk during the invasion with all the bombing and strafing attacks. She must have gone through a terribly frightening period (from which I don't think she ever completely recovered). How did she know where Paul was? I assume the correspondence route went through Wil St. Gallen, Switzerland, where Hans Guggenheim, a good friend of Irene's from her hometown, Freiburg, was living.

Irene made her journey to find Paul in southern France with the wife of another Gaspar chemist who had been taken at the same time as Paul. In her efforts to get to Marseilles, Irene was arrested by German soldiers. From her recounting, the interrogating German, upon learning Irene was from Freiburg (his hometown as well), helped her by falsifying information—by "forcing" Irene to state "she was coming from Marseilles and trying to get to Brussels." She was therefore sent "back" to where she supposedly came from, namely, Marseilles. This period was rarely spoken about, and then with great emotional difficulty.

While Irene was trying to make her way south, Paul was in a camp, or perhaps in several. I know of Gurs, but the name St. Cyprien comes to mind also. As Paul recalled, to keep morale as high as possible, the inmates would organize study groups among themselves. I know that Paul was not always confined, that he had occasion to go out to the village and return. I don't know how the discipline went. They probably did business among themselves (cigarettes, food, jewelry, money), maybe also bribed the guards. From this same camp, Gurs, those who didn't get out in time were later deported to Auschwitz and exterminated.

Irene managed to get to Marseilles. The stories of queuing at the U.S. Consulate in Marseilles for hours and hours, from early to late, being sent away, having to return with more papers, and on and on, provided the subject for Gian Carlo Menotti's opera *The Consul*. Affidavits were supplied for my parents' immigration to the United States by Irene's cousin, Else Lisman, in Richmond, Virginia, as well as by Bela Gaspar through his connection with Franklin Roosevelt; also through that connection, preference visas were arranged. I assume these enabled Paul's release from Gurs.

I don't know how soon after Irene's arrival Paul got out of the camp. But sometime during the Marseilles period, I was conceived by a war-traumatized young woman, underweight and nerved-wracked, using all her human and animal instincts as energy to get papers to save herself, her husband, and her just conceived child.

How to get out of Europe? They went illegally from France to Spain and finally to Portugal to get on one of the last ships out of Europe. Arrival in Los Angeles was on Labor Day 1941. Fred Ikenberg picked them up. (Paul, Fred, and Ann had been good friends in Germany.) Paul came, knowing that he would continue in his profession, also with a moral obligation to Gaspar for helping to save his and Irene's lives.

I don't know much about the beginning in Los Angeles. The first home I know about was a rented house on Fuller Avenue off Sunset, but possibly there were previous rented rooms or apartments. I was born on February 12, 1942, at the Queen of Angels Hospital. Money-wise, things were very tight and Gaspar felt no obligation during the years Paul was working for him to increase his salary much (at least, that was what I felt, though I don't really know), and Paul was incapable of demanding what he thought he was worth. As **Annchen** says, "Gaspar treated Paul very badly."

To make ends meet, Irene, as far as she told me, sewed aprons, maybe other things, too, together with a friend, Elizabeth Frankfurter. (Her husband had been a judge in Germany.) I'm not sure how much success they had at that. Possibly there was some hot-dog stand work in Hollywood?

Then, when we lived in the Valley, Irene helped **Rudy Brook** with his greenhouse, maybe also with the chicken coops. I'm aware that those years were very trying. Irene did not have adequate education, I presume, to enable her to return to school to learn a profession. Or did she? I don't think that would have been encouraged by Paul, for whom the woman's role was raising the children. As a child and later, I got the repeated message: a career woman was something negative, not to be striven for; or rather, the price was too high when seeing what happened to children when the mother's personal career gained importance.

I remember having heard that Germans in L.A. were considered enemy aliens during the war and were limited in their traveling around. But I didn't feel anger on Paul and Irene's part for being considered enemy aliens; rather, cynical irony.

First friends were definitely all Jews and all immigrants. It was always this way. In Cincinnati where we lived from 1954–57 (after which we returned to Basel), the friends were again all Jewish immigrants. Through **Ann** and Fred in L.A., the circle of friends, immigrants, widened. **Ernie** and **Theja** apparently met Paul and Irene soon after their arrival, in evening high school where they all studied for American citizenship. And then came friendships through the *Gruppe*.

When the Gaspar Company went bankrupt in 1950 or 1951, it was a difficult and most unsettling time. Irene got very nervous, smoking incessantly. Paul "escaped from bondage," but was out of money. He looked for employment in color photography research, as he had been doing. He had great difficulty in finding anything in the United States. I do not know how many alternatives there were and why he preferred Ciba in Basel, Switzerland, although I have my ideas. In the Dreyfuss home, problems were not yet discussed in the presence of the children. I am aware that while Irene felt very happy in the United States, Paul felt happy among his friends, but America was foreign to him. He could not see himself "playing baseball with his son," as he sometimes said, and maybe that was symbolic of his difficulty in adjusting. Maybe the years of feeling himself to be an underdog at the Gaspar Company made him need to get as far away from Gaspar as possible. I think he was afraid of Gaspar's wrath and wouldn't have been able to regain his independent footing had he stayed in the United States. (But wouldn't Kodak or Eastman Color have been happy to absorb Gaspar's scientists, who brought with them an enormous wealth of scientific knowledge, if not even unpublished secrets?!)

What language was spoken at home?

I presume a mixture of German and English. Or German when we children were not supposed to understand! I don't know for sure. I'm aware that in 1952 when we first moved to Switzerland, although I didn't speak German, I must have understood enough so as not to be completely lost. Irene's and Paul's broken or accent-rich English led to flaws in my English—so that I remember teachers correcting me, "You don't say 'Mammy,' you say 'Mother,'" and correcting my *th* and *s/sh*. I remember being embarrassed about my parents speaking English with an accent. I was called Judy and not Judith, a more Jewish name, because my parents had difficulty saying the American *th*, and didn't want me called Judit.

How did Paul and Irene feel about being German?

While in America, I don't know if it was an issue. They adopted America as their home. The question might be phrased differently—how did they cope with European culture and values versus American?

Hatred of Germany?

When living in Switzerland, Paul and Irene very rarely went to Germany. Once, on a trip, they showed Mike and me where they grew up, where their grandparents had lived, where childhood memories were. It was early postwar

Germany, still before the *Wirtschaftwunder* (the economic miracle of postwar Germany). We drove through Germany in an American car and village children would surround us and stare. I think Paul got some satisfaction from seeing "important," not being belittled as a German-Jewish child. His memories were of anti-Semitic insults, being beaten up by children. While living in Switzerland, most of our travels, hikes, and vacations were in Switzerland and not in Germany.

On the Swiss-German border there is a town, Lorrach. Food items on the German side were cheaper, and I think Irene occasionally enjoyed getting something cheaper there, especially products she wouldn't have bought otherwise. They owned few German electronic products, although I remember a Grundig radio.

Non-Jewish friends?

No, no connections with non-Jewish friends were maintained, not by Paul or Irene. Also, I'm not sure whether there were non-Jewish friends in their youths. They had associated mainly in Jewish circles. Perhaps in later years, this reflected an incapability of reconnecting to the painful past.

Attitude about being Jewish?

They were very aware and conscious of being Jewish. Also sensitive, with painful memories of childhood beatings because of being Jewish and being weak, especially Paul. Paul had been a Zionist and remained so—so that when I decided to make *aliyah*, I had full support, with his awareness or not, that I was fulfilling the step that he hadn't taken. Israel also was the country to which Paul's brother and Irene's sister had immigrated, as well as cousins. The main concentration of surviving family went to Israel.

Joining a synagogue in Los Angeles?

When living in the Valley, definitely yes. It was not a traditional synagogue with acceptance of cart-blanche customs but, I believe, a Reconstructionist congregation, looking for a modern, "this world" orientation. Rabbi Franklin Cohn, the very progressive rabbi there, spoke once at a *Gruppe* meeting. I don't know whether Paul was active in this temple community, in addition to the *Gruppe,* but I don't think so.

When in Basel, we joined the synagogue, but this was and has remained an Orthodox community to which Paul could not make a satisfying connection. Also, there were few immigrants who had settled down to Swiss-style lives, and those who had were very different from us, particularly with the

Los Angeles addition to our immigrant baggage. Most were East European Jews who were foreign in mentality and background to Paul's and Irene's German backgrounds.

Anti-Semitic incidents?

I don't know about Irene and Paul. I was aware on Blewett Avenue, Van Nuys, of living among people, not of our kind, and there was some anti-Semitism from neighbor children who threw mud on our house and yelled, "You dirty Jews." The children must have learned that somewhere!

What role did the Gruppe *play?*

It is natural for people to look for other people who speak their language, share their culture, have similar past experiences, and among whom each member is respected for what he is and what he was, with whom the trauma of the war and the difficulty of adjusting could be talked over. I see today how I, although born in the United States, have become, through my many years in Israel, an Israeli. When abroad I look for fellow Israelis of similar status.

The *Gruppe* remained very important also during our years in Switzerland. Vincent [**Rudy and Eva Brook**'s son] remarked how our leaving, "deserting," was experienced by the others. For us, the Dreyfuss family, leaving Los Angeles was a great loss, the loss of our extended family, our friends. The *Gruppe* and Los Angeles meant an open door to us—laughter, holidays, birthdays, vacations together, friends, extended family, normalcy, belonging, loving relationships.

Upon moving to Switzerland, I felt a darkness enclosing us. There was no one to open the door, no extended family, no old friends, no new friends with whom spontaneous meetings were possible. Loneliness. Sadness. I don't know how much of this Paul felt because I think he was very satisfied professionally, or at least at the beginning. (The work project was small to begin with; later it exploded in size and he was pushed aside by younger people and again had to fend his way as a Jew among non-Jews.) Also, he was financially much better off, a compensation for his Gaspar years of "slavery." For Irene, leaving Los Angeles was very much more difficult—leaving friends, good friends.

I became aware of what the Los Angeles *Gruppe* meant to me when visiting L.A. in 1981—and aware of why I immigrated to Israel in 1962. In 1954, we had visited Israel the first time. We came to Israel on a holiday after two years in Switzerland, which I call the "loneliness period." That visit meant to me the meeting of aunts, uncles, and cousins for the first time, all of whom

Irene and Paul Dreyfuss, Catania, Italy, 1936.

lived in settlements of various kinds. The excitement—theirs and ours—over our coming, also the excitement of their friends and neighbors—all of whom were involved in making us welcome—was overwhelmingly warming. It gave me the feeling of being wanted, loved, accepted—and of belonging—so it was quite natural to return to that place. (That in reality life is not quite so is another matter, but the feeling of belonging has remained.)

The heartwarming reception of friends in Los Angeles in 1981 (and again now in 1989) made me aware of this loving, big family we had lost by leaving, and I appreciated the *Gruppe* all the more.

EVA AND RUDY BROOK

Eva Brook

Rudy Brook

Childhood sweethearts, Rudy and Eva went off to Berlin together to study at the university. Upon completion of a law degree, Rudy was forbidden to practice law and turned his efforts to helping Jews immigrate to Palestine and to working secretly for the Jewish underground. Above ground, both subsequently worked in Sweden, this time preparing Jewish youth for aliyah. Fully intending to immigrate to Palestine themselves, when visas were not available they came instead to the United States. Rudy's new agricultural skills bore him in good stead as he gathered a star-studded clientele for his landscaping business. Rudy and Eva had two sons, Tom and Vincent.

Rudy's grandfathers on both sides were bankers in Aachen. His father, Oscar, moved to Magdeburg to start a wholesale yardage business. Rudy and Eva both grew up in Magdeburg, where Eva's father, Hans, owned a drug store.

This contribution on Eva and Rudy Brook was written by their son, Vincent Brook.

Eva's mother, Alma, died of cancer when Eva was 10; Hans died in a concentration camp, as did Rudy's mother, Elise, and his sister, Margot, though Oscar was spared the ignominy, dying of natural causes in Aachen in 1938.

As legend would have it, Rudy and Eva became childhood sweethearts at ages 11 and 9, respectively, when Rudy wrote on the school blackboard: "Eva's sweet, even though I haven't tasted her yet!" After *Abitur,* both Rudy and Eva went to Berlin, Rudy to study law, Eva to study art and physical education. They were married there in 1931 at ages 27 and 25. Eva was the breadwinner for the first few years, teaching art and P.E. at various schools in and around Berlin. Rudy eventually earned his law degree but was never able to practice owing to the anti-Jewish laws imposed by the Nazis. Instead, being an ardent Zionist, he went to work for *Hechalutz* (Federation of Zionist Pioneering Organizations). Rudy became what he called a "high-ranking member" and was instrumental in enabling thousands of Jews to get visas to Palestine, arranging "phony" marriages and otherwise circumventing the restrictive quotas imposed by the British. Once, however, he "overstepped his bounds" with near drastic results.

That happened in 1937, when Rudy, "in a moment of weakness and strain," sent an angry letter to a German immigration office about its delay in processing a visa. He went so far as to threaten going to a higher office if no action was taken. Luckily, he was only branded *unverschämt* (impertinent) and sent to jail for a few days. It could have been much worse! For Rudy was also working secretly for *Haganah* (the underground Jewish defense organization based in Palestine) and had been entrusted with the equivalent of $60,000, which he was to pass on to another operative. Had the police found the money in Rudy's possession, it obviously would have been curses for him, but instead they informed him that they would be picking him up the next day, thereby giving him time to dispose of the money. Thank God for German correctness!

And as it turns out, the jail experience, far from being an ordeal, was something Rudy actually enjoyed! "It was a great experience," he recalled. "I was put into a large cell with 24 others—drunks, Seventh Day Adventists, socialists, homosexuals. There was a good-looking gay (the son of a wealthy industrialist) who wore a flashy tie with stripes. The cops would let him out every afternoon to act as bait, putting him on a street corner to attract other gays. Then there was a funny transvestite who dressed in black panties. He was very popular, but if anyone asked him to take off his 'breasts,' he got all huffy and said that was going too far! The whole thing was a big circus."

Rudy could say this in retrospect, of course, because he was let out fairly soon. He knew he'd be a marked man from then on, however, and with a keen sense of the political climate, realized it was high time to get out of Germany. My mother, however, happily engaged as a teacher in Kaput, a small town outside Berlin, still "didn't believe it could happen." Rudy went alone to Sweden in late 1937, where he stayed for about a year. He found a position as a gardener and maintenance man in a boarding school for Jewish refugee children. In mid-1938, Eva joined him and worked there as a teacher. The school was also a *hachsharah,* a preparation center for youths intending to immigrate to Palestine, meanwhile working on farms and learning agriculture. At that school, Rudy met **Ernest Wolf,** the school director.

Rudy and Eva were not able to go to Palestine because by this time the few visas that were available were being reserved for the worst (that is, concentration camp) cases. This was fine with my mother; she didn't want to go to Palestine anyway. Instead, they arrived in New York on November 9, 1938—the infamous *Kristallnacht.*

Rudy remained in New York, while Eva went alone to Hollywood. A German friend of hers, Gerda Weinman, had been making quite a go of it as a "masseuse to the stars" and told Eva, also trained in massage, that she couldn't miss. Fortunately—at least for me—she did. She had trouble making friends and making ends meet. After about six months she sent out a distress signal to Rudy, who eagerly responded. Someone else who responded to Eva during this period was a famous actor and *Gruppe* speaker with whom Eva had a brief affair.

Eva's massage practice was discontinued for the most part, I believe, when Tom was born in 1940. She pretty much remained a mother, housewife, and chicken farmer until 1951, when she started her beloved and successful 20-year kindergarten teacher career. She was also quite creative and continued to do portraiture and art in general throughout her life.

Rudy started off in Los Angeles as a self-employed gardener, remaining so throughout most of the 1940s, then branching into landscape architecture and real estate in the 1950s and 1960s. My parents moved in 1945 from their first L.A. apartment on Glencoe Way in the Hollywood Hills to Sherman Way in Van Nuys, where they bought their first house (and farm!). It was a monumental move, both geographically (the Valley was truly the sticks then) and financially. The purchase price for two acres, complete with fruit orchards, chicken farm, and a large old Spanish-style house—was $6,000! Yet incredibly, Rudy was advised by almost all his friends—I don't know about the *Gruppe*—not to do such a crazy thing, and he had to hock his shirt and borrow up the wazoo to pull it off.

One of the people who did encourage him, both verbally and with a loan (to be paid off through deferred salary), was Peggy Gershwin (Ira's wife), one of Rudy's first gardening customers in Beverly Hills. This brings us to the "gardener of the stars" stories.

The relationship with the Gershwins wasn't all roses. One time, in fact, Rudy almost poisoned them! One of his duties, besides keeping the large grounds immaculate, was supplying flowers for the weekly piano display. "There wasn't a magnolia tree in Beverly Hills I didn't rob for the Gershwins,"

Eva and Rudy Brook,
Los Angeles, 1942.

he recounted. "One day I was driving through Benedict Canyon and saw that it was aflame with fall color. So my Belgian helper and I got out and picked some branches and the secretary arranged them. The next day when we arrived, Mrs. Gershwin greeted us with powdered arms, and I said, 'Oh, Peggy, you got poison oak!' 'Oh, that's what it is? My Beverly Hills dermatologist didn't know!' "

Rudy was forgiven, and even when his helper, Jack, fell into the swimming pool with the power mower, the Gershwins looked the other way. The vines Rudy planted along the tennis court were the last straw, however. "Like wealthy people are," Rudy explained, "they didn't like to be seen when they played tennis, so I had to plant vines all along the front side. I chose beautiful bougainvillaea, but not yet being knowledgeable enough, my choice back-fired. One day I arrived and the vines had grown so strong that the fence had fallen over. Peggy came out to greet me, but she stumbled over the steps. Then she said, 'Rudy, we have to part.' For me it was a big blow. It was one of my bigger jobs. But I recovered."

One job that kept him going was "taking care of an empty place that was going to be rented. One day I came to the place and there was a very handsome young man who introduced himself as the new tenant. I asked him what his profession was and he said, 'Oh, I'm an actor.' Then he asked if I could lower my rate from $17.50 to $12.50 a month. I reluctantly agreed, but he eventually became one of my nicest customers. After some time I asked him why he still called me Mr. Brook, all my other customers called me Rudy. He said, 'Yes, I'll do that, but under one condition. If you call me Cornel' "—short for Cornel Wilde. Rudy counted among his other famous customers: actors Robert Ryan, Peter Lorre, Hildegarde Kneff; German-exile directors Fritz Lang and Douglas Sirk. Another was Judy Garland.

On more mundane matters: I always pretty much accepted my parents' casual explanation for why they changed their name from *Bruch* to *Brook*. "Nobody could pronounce Bruch," they insisted, justifiably. "The average American would've pronounced it to rhyme with 'crutch!'" Now, alas (too late to probe further), I'm not so sure this wasn't an unconscious "crutch" on their part, or even dissimulation.

Rudy remained a staunch (if chastened and always irreligious) Zionist, though he retained a certain Germanic pride and Prussian authoritarian streak, in addition to his famous Old World charm. Eva was decidedly the "religious" one, though not in an especially Jewish (and certainly not Orthodox) sense. Both my brother and I went to Hebrew school at the Valley Jewish Community Center (now Adat Ariel in North Hollywood), I was bar mitzvahed, Tom confirmed, and we observed the major holidays: Sabbath, High Holidays, Passover, Hanukkah, and such.

At the same time, however, my mother in particular maintained a good deal of attachment to things German (and Christian). Christmas Eve, for instance (when German children opened their presents—as did we), was unabashedly her favorite holiday. Easter ran a strong second and we ended up celebrating both (minus the religious trappings, of course) with gusto. It was only later that my "best-of-both-worlds" became tainted. Our Christmas trees got smaller and smaller and were dubbed "Hanukkah bushes," and we started rationalizing our bireligious festivities as a partial concession to my two immigrant German cousins who, while half-Jewish themselves, had officially opted for Protestantism.

A stronger-than-average ambivalence toward both "Germanness" and "Jewishness" prevailed. German was spoken extensively in the home, to the point that both Tom and I picked up the language quite naturally (not out of any conscious bilingual program). On the other hand, Yiddish didn't exist—this was something truly "foreign." While I was growing up, we had no contact with any Yiddish-speaking American Jews. Only later would I discover how deep my otherwise extremely tolerant parents' selective anti-Semitism went for these "loud, uncouth, reactionary boors." I, and my parents, too, came to like many of this "special breed" very much, and a whole new appreciation of what it meant to be a Jew unfolded.

This first-hand experience of the rifts within the Jewish community also led to my own tendency of approach/avoidance to being a Jew. This is relevant to the *Gruppe*, I think, because the dichotomy within me was at least an indirect reflection of a similar schism within them—the "assimilationist" syndrome, one generation and continent removed. In our predominantly Protestant neighborhood and public schools, for example, I made the most of my non-Jewish name and nonstereotypical Jewish appearance to play

WASP to the hilt, with only occasional twinges of self-betrayal, such as when a peer would drop a penny and blurt, "Whoever picks it up is a Jew!" In Hebrew school, on the other hand, I could secretly indulge in being one of the "chosen people," feel special and superior, yet, paradoxically, also act out, be a "bad boy," since in the mundane scheme of things the Valley Jewish Community Center didn't really count!

My parents spoke sparingly with me of the Nazi period until later years, only a little more of the early immigration period. There was a definite opening up toward the end of their lives, prompted by reaching out and nostalgia on their part, a belated search for roots on mine.

THEJA SOMMER

Theja Sommer [signature]

Theja was independent and adventurous. At 24, she left Germany for Holland to pursue her career as a musician and teacher. She met and married Ernie, then returned with him to Germany in 1934. When the Nazi vise tightened, Theja decided to come to the United States as a "tourist" and from here find a way to bring Ernie and their young daughter, Sybil. The plan that evolved took her to Havana, where she lived among a small group of Jewish refugees, while Ernie tried to obtain a visa for Cuba. Never hesitant to push her luck, Theja's efforts expedited that visa as well as the additional ones required for entry into the United States.

I'll start with my birth. I was born in Dresden, East Germany, in 1904, from Polish parents, and spent most of my youth in Dresden until I moved to Holland. I spent seven years in Holland.

Most of this interview was led by Debbie Kirshbaum, Theja's granddaughter, and Sybil Goldenblank, her daughter.

129

DEBBIE: *Why did you move to Holland?*

It started out that my parents had friends who invited me to spend a summer at the beach there in 1928. I was 24 years old. I liked Holland. I felt that there were some pressures at home and I wanted to be independent. This was quite unusual at that time, when women stayed at home until they got married. I was a musician and was already performing piano in Germany. I started to play in Holland and especially to teach. I was perhaps one of the first to play for radio, which was pretty new at that time. I remember vividly how I gave a lecture/demonstration on the "Carnival" by Schumann for the Dutch East India station. In 1933, I picked up my mother and brought her to Holland.

DEBBIE: *Why did you do that?*

Hitler was gaining popularity in Germany. And both my brother and I were living in Holland. My brother lived near me, in an apartment. My mother moved in with him and I kept my room. I felt sorry for my mother because she didn't speak any Dutch and couldn't speak with anybody, so I took her to a German Jewish club. It was very, very boring for me. Then I signed up to play chess. I was put at a table with a man and he won one game after another from me. I looked at him. He had an intelligent face and the hands of a worker. I said to myself, "Who is this?" We didn't talk, just played. At around eight o'clock a bell rang and I asked, "What does that bell mean?" "It's the end of the evening." I said, "That early?" He said, "I have to get up early too." I asked, "How early do you get up?" That's how our first conversation began! He said, "At 5:30." " What do you do at 5:30?" "I'm a vegetable man. I go to the market to buy vegetables and then resell them to my customers." Realizing that he was a new refugee, I felt maybe I could do something for him. I said, "Why don't you bring us vegetables?" So he started to bring vegetables to the house where I lived. We had a maid, and she asked how did the vegetable man know that I like spinach. So it came out that we knew each other. Ernie and I played more chess!

DEBBIE: *Were you worried about what was happening in Germany at this time?*

Not too much. All during those years I went back and forth between Holland and Germany. I saw the whole development from both sides, from Holland and in Germany proper. I visited my parents while they were still in Germany and saw what was going on. While there, I played for the Berlin radio. In Holland I felt safe and secure. Nobody knew what would happen there later. This was unpredictable.

One day at the end of 1933 or beginning of 1934, I received a letter from the German Consulate to appear there. A man said to me, "You cannot be a German citizen anymore. You are originally Polish [in Germany at that time, children took the citizenship of their parents] and became a naturalized German citizen. Unless you can prove that you did something for the fatherland, we have to take away your German citizenship." I said, "What *could* I have done for the fatherland? I wasn't in a war. I never fought for Germany." He said, "This is confidential, but I know you have played on the radio here. If we can put down that you brought German culture to Holland, we can leave the passport with you." So I said (and of that I'm proud today), "I'm sorry, I did not just bring German culture. I played whatever I wanted." Then he said, "I'm sorry, I have to take your passport away." And he did. I became *staatenlos*, a person without a country.

DEBBIE: *Why didn't you just go along with his idea for your protection?*

At that time one didn't feel the need of protecting oneself. If it was a matter of life and death, or even if I had felt in any danger, I wouldn't have done what I did. But at that time there was no danger for me. There was just pride that made me feel, "Damn you, I'm not just going to bring *German* culture to Holland!" Until I married, I was without a country. I became German again through Ernie.

DEBBIE: *When did you and Ernie get married?*

We married on December 23, 1934.

DEBBIE: *What did you plan to do?*

My brother, who had a cigar factory in Döbeln, near Dresden, had a job in Germany for Ernie. So we went there. I had no objection to going there. Nobody knew what was coming. Up to the time when I left Germany in '38, I always thought when I heard rumors of people being taken to prison that they had done something wrong. I really never thought that any of it would come to me or my family. We lived in a small town, very much to ourselves, and I got pregnant. Then the cigar factory was confiscated by the Nazis. Ernie lost his job, and we went to Dresden. Through the Jewish community, he found some kind of a half-time job in a smelting plant. We felt this wasn't a safe time for me, and income was so small that I went back to be with my mother in Holland. She had arranged a place for me to stay with friends, a wonderful young couple who just took me in. We knew their parents in Germany. They were all good people; all later perished.

Until I was very pregnant, I earned a little money by playing piano for performing dancers. Then I had the baby in the Jewish hospital in a charity ward because Ernie could only send me 10 marks every month. One was not allowed to send more than that out of the country. It was 1935.

I had made an arrangement with Ernie that the moment a baby came, I would send a telegram and he would come. To get permission, he had to show the Germans that I had a baby. So I went to a photo store to get a picture of myself to show me being pregnant. It was a little store on the main street, and when I went in, the man asked, "You want just a head or a half picture?" I said, "No, I want the whole figure!" I still have that picture with the big belly! My mother sent the telegram, a short one to save money. It said, "Come."

Ernie came. When he saw Sybil he started to laugh and said, "She looks like my grandmother." Sadly, he couldn't stay, because as a foreigner he couldn't have gotten a job in Holland.

I stayed in the hospital for two weeks. Because I had nowhere else to go, I went to a home for unwed mothers. I had to pretend to be unmarried. At that home, I could see the baby only to feed her. Otherwise she was kept somewhere else. I had to do jobs around the home, like beating the carpets outside. I was very busy. I could only stay there a few weeks. Our very good friends, the Pollatzes (he had been my teacher and school principal in Germany and now was living in Holland), had arranged for me another home where I could stay with a doctor's family. Neither the Pollatzes nor this family was Jewish.

I stayed there until Sybil was about three months old and the woman got sick. I went back to Dresden in the beginning of '36 to join Ernie. In the meantime, he had made out of the half-time job a whole day job. We rented a bedroom in a family's house. Later on, we had a bedroom and a dining room. I cooked on the stove in the kitchen with the house owners. They all liked our baby very much. Sybil had rickets because she was born in the dark month of November and had no sun. She had really bowed legs. We took her regularly to be checked by a pediatrician. He didn't know we were Jewish. It was hilarious when he explained to his nurse, "This little girl has a typical Aryan, long head."

SYBIL: *Were you aware by then that there were problems with the Nazis? Were there restrictions on your movement within Germany?*

Everybody spoke of leaving Germany. I remember the Pollatzes asking how I could go back to Germany. "Don't you have more pride than to go

Theja and Ernie Sommer, Dresden, Germany, 1935.

back to Germany?" they had asked. But Ernie had a job there. Nobody ever had a thought what would come. We lived very much to ourselves. We didn't go out much. Our neighbors didn't know that we were Jews.

We were restricted in many ways and had all kinds of incidents in Germany. Once we went to a summer resort where they felt a Jew shouldn't go swimming, shouldn't sit on a bench, shouldn't go to a movie. We didn't participate much. The people with whom we stayed there were gentile and treated us very well. But at home, we had some neighbors with whom I had a very unpleasant incident. That was at a time when people said even if a baby cries, she has to wait four hours between bottle feedings. Because the doctor had prescribed natural sun for Sybil to treat her rickets, we sometimes left her outside. So she cried outside. Some neighbors wrote us a letter saying that it's absolutely cruel to leave a baby outside, that only Jews would leave a baby outside, crying in the sun.

There was a girl across the street, maybe 10 years old, who often went with Sybil to a nearby playground. She was so sweet playing with Sybil. One day her mother came to us and said, "This is the worst day in my life. Susie cannot come to you anymore. In school, the children had to write that they are never going to have anything to do with Jews."

DEBBIE: *At that time did you celebrate Jewish holidays?*

Yes, but the setup in Dresden was like this. Dresden was a city of 500,000 people. Five thousand were Jews. Most Jews didn't go on Shabbat to temple; as a woman, especially not. You went on the High Holidays. You lit candles and you had Pesach. But that was it.

DEBBIE: *Did you light candles on Friday night?*

Yes, that we always did.

DEBBIE: *Did you ever sense that you needed to hide that?*

No, not as long as I was in Germany.

DEBBIE: *What weren't you allowed to do as Jews in Dresden? Could you go into a movie theater?*

At that time, yes. I left in summer 1938, and until that time you still could. Also, Jews had their own entertainment. They had the *Kulturbund* [the Cultural Society of German Jews, which created jobs for Jewish artists and musicians]. I'll give you an example. I probably was one of the last Jewish pianists who still played for the *Deutschlandsender,* that is, the radio for all Germany. Many years later, I got restitution money for that. Jewish doctors could only treat Jewish patients. You could not have household help under the age of 45 if she was gentile, while Jewish help could be any age. [The purpose of this policy was to "protect" gentile women of childbearing age from being seduced by the Jewish men who employed them.]

SYBIL: *How did they check that Jews obeyed these restrictions?*

They just knew. Children talked about their parents. They would even betray their parents. Everything for the fatherland. Also, I could not teach piano to non-Jews. I only had a few Jewish students at the time.

DEBBIE: *What happened next?*

By early 1938, people were talking all the time about leaving Germany and where to go. We hadn't even thought of that! Then one of Ernie's bosses went to America and wrote a letter about it, how wonderful it was, all the things that he enjoyed there. More and more, something started to work inside of me. I felt that I wanted to get out. I must honestly say, it was not so much that I had to escape something but more the sense of adventure. I wanted to go to America. And when I got a letter from Oscar, a distant cousin with whom I had been close in Germany, I started to think seriously about it. He wrote, "Come here, come to Chicago. You can stay with us as long as you want. Don't worry about anything. We will find everything for you."

Restrictions intensified and it got worrisome. The Germans invaded Austria and there was a conflict with Czechoslovakia. At that time, I felt, "Out!" Ernie and I made a plan. I would leave first. He and Sybil would follow later. Ernie is a little slower in deciding such things. Somebody had to take the initiative! We didn't have much money and borrowed some from the Jewish community. We left our silver and other things and I bought a round-trip ticket to America. I should mention something here. All German Jews already had Sarah or Moses put in their names on their passports. But because our passports were issued in Holland, we didn't have the J in the passports. That helped a lot later with the immigration. When I left Germany, they didn't know I was Jewish. I could just say it was for a pleasure trip.

DEBBIE: *Couldn't the three of you have gone to America as tourists?*

It would have looked suspicious. As it was, when I came to New York, many people were taken from the ship to Ellis Island for questioning. You had to act "touristy." You couldn't show any worry. If I had taken a child with me, it would have been a dead giveaway that I wasn't going back to Germany. Once in America, I would find a way to get visas for Ernie and Sybil. I must tell you frankly that I don't know if I would have been able to do what I did during the next months, if instead of 1938, it was later. All the horrible things happened right after that summer when I left. But we were still thinking that the situation was temporary, that soon there would be a different government.

As I made my plan to leave Germany, this was my thinking: Now there is conflict with Czechoslovakia. Who knows what will happen. I cannot leave Ernie alone with a small child. He has to have the chance to run away and will be handicapped with a child. Where can I bring our child to a safe place? So, I asked my good friends in Holland, the Pollatzes, for help. Quakers, they had left Germany and bought a little house in Haarlem (about 20 minutes from Amsterdam), and were taking Jewish and half-Jewish children into their home. These were schoolchildren. When I asked Manfred Pollatz to take Sybil (two-and-a-half years old), he agreed to take her. She would be in good hands, but without parents—like an orphan.

I paid ahead of time for a good hotel in New York, both room and board, for two weeks or so. We were only allowed to take 10 marks out of Germany. I decided I needed some more money. Since I would be going through Holland and had played quite frequently there over the radio, I wrote to a radio station and got an engagement to play for half an hour. That little extra money I was able to keep and use when I got to America.

I took Sybil to the Pollatzes and then took the boat from there via Belgium to America. I was as a tourist. But on that boat there were already Austrians who had run away from Vienna. On the ship, I spent my German money on toothpaste and things I might need later, things that would have been cheaper in America. I spent a fortune just to use up all the money that I was allowed! Once you got to America, any money over the 10-mark limit had to go back to Germany.

I got to New York in August 1938 and was met at the boat by a good school friend, Trudy Glauber. I went to the hotel that I had paid for in advance. I talked to the manager of the hotel and asked if I could transfer the food cost into a longer stay. My English was a school English. I could ask directions from a policeman, but when he answered, I didn't understand where I should go! When people talked to me on the phone I got scared to death! Trudy was really a friend to me. She told me all her experiences. She advised me not to phone places but to write penny postcards and ask others to call me. That would save me money. I had so little. We went to a cafeteria, for instance, and would not eat. But lemon, sugar, and water were free, so we made lemonades. Or we would go for a nickel from New York to the Statue of Liberty. We would stay on the boat and never get off! When my stay at the hotel ran out, I found another place in the east part of New York.

So, how do you get to stay in America for good? I went to the Council of Jewish Women and asked what to do. They told me to go back to Germany, that I had no chance whatsoever. "A man can bring his wife on a preference quota, but a woman cannot bring her husband. You better go back and come with your husband." Well, I was *not* going back. I *had* to find a way. The situation was that I had come to the U.S.A. as a tourist. In order to immigrate legally, I would have to leave the country and register elsewhere at an American Consulate. There I'd receive a quota number. In addition, I would have to find somebody in the U.S. to sign an affidavit to guarantee that I would not become a public burden. How was I to find a person to do that for me?

The wife of my cousin Oscar in Chicago was a good friend of mine. She had a sister in New York who invited me one evening at seven o'clock. I thought that was for dinner, but nobody gave me anything. I was so hungry and so tired from struggling to speak English. Finally, I asked her for something to eat. She was surprised that I thought seven o'clock was for dinner! I told her my situation, that my husband was in Germany and child in Holland. She said, "I want you to meet somebody." That somebody was a Mr. Gelbhaus. He became an angel for me later. He had a hardware store

136

and came right over with his sleeves all rolled up. I thought, "He cannot do anything for me." But she wanted me to tell him my story.

DEBBIE: *Because he had his sleeves rolled up, you thought he was just a worker? And that he couldn't have any money?*

That's exactly what I thought. But the next morning, my cousin's sister-in-law told me that Mr. Gelbhaus had decided to give affidavits for me, my husband, and child. As I told you before, I had talked already to the women at the council and I had pestered them so long that they finally said they would pay my way to Havana. Once there, I could apply for a visa to return to the U.S. as a legal immigrant. Entry was under the quota system. Ernie and I both would have to come as Germans. By that time, German Jews had already gone to the different consulates in Europe to apply for visas. These went eventually into the thousands as the situation got worse and worse. In Cuba, however, there were very few applying and that's why I went to Cuba. Also, I knew that a business associate of Ernie's had come from Germany to Cuba and then to the U.S. He had then been able to bring across his wife and children on a preference quota.

The Council paid for my ticket to Cuba, and Mr. Gelbhaus loaned me $100 extra. As he said, "A woman doesn't go without money." I took a bus to Miami first, which took ages. In that bus was a boy who had lived across the street from us in Germany! We talked. Then we took a boat overnight from Miami to Havana. That was September 28, my birthday. Some of the people on the boat knew it was my birthday and gave me cigarettes. This was a big thing at that time. Jews on the boat with the same plan as mine talked about arrival in Havana, that they would go to the hotel and make themselves nice, fresh and good looking, before going to the U.S. Consulate. I said to the fellow who was with me, "Do you know what? We are not going to the hotel. We are getting a taxi and going right to the consulate. First things first. This is why we came to Havana." That made later a difference of three months! I got my number and so did the fellow with me. The other people had to wait three months. At the consulate, the girl said right away, "Oh, it's your birthday today," and I got a number.

Then I lived in Havana. I was the only woman on her own among the 100 or so refugees. The others were in couples and the rest were men. I went to the Council of Jewish Women there and they gave me $10 a week. This branch had been set up specifically to take care of the refugees who would arrive in Havana. Later, when Ernie and Sybil came, they gave us $15. I made a little extra money. I played music and taught a little. I made friends in the Jewish community. There were two kinds of Jews in Havana. There were Eastern Europeans who were on the way to America and had to wait for the Polish or Russian quota, which was very small. While waiting, they started businesses in Havana, got settled, and never made it to America. Then there were American Jews, who were quite well-to-do. They had a beautiful synagogue. I played a concert in the synagogue. Don't forget, I came from a cold country, and there I was in a tropical country and it was really beautiful. I went swimming at a very cheap place. I had a friend there. His name was Brie. He had a girlfriend in Germany, but we became good friends. He gave me big advice, "When the council asks how you spend the $10, don't say you went swimming. They want to know that you eat and sleep!" I lived with the $10 very comfortably. One didn't need much. That was until November.

Ernie, in the meantime, had booked a ship. *Kristallnacht* came on November 9. When I heard about this, I bombarded him with telegrams that he should definitely take that ship. But he had been taken and put into prison. I didn't know what had happened to him, but knew terrible things were happening in Germany. I was frantic. I had earned a little money, enough to get a lawyer, and I asked him to bring me to the government. I had learned a little bit of Spanish. He brought me to the right office and I talked to a high-up person and said, "You have to help me!" Have you ever been in such a situation? You feel close to tears and you can suppress it or you can let go. At that time, I thought it would be advantageous to let go. And I did! He said, "Come with me to the Western Union and I will send a telegram to the Cuban Consul in Germany to give Ernie permission to come to Havana." That's how Ernie got a visa to Cuba.

The visa was secured, but then came another problem. By that time, things had become stricter in Havana. In addition to the visa, we had to have $500 as a deposit to show we would not be a public burden. Where would I get $500? I was in touch with the people in New York. Once again, Mr. Gelbhaus was our angel. So I had the money and was waiting for Ernie and Sybil.

They came in December. There was a sad part to the reunion. Although Ernie had told Sybil during their journey, "We're going to see Mommy," when the time came, she turned away from me. I interpreted it as a mixture of embarrassment and anger. We had been apart for six months.

We lived in a very fashionable area. It was right across from the president of Cuba. We had an empty room and full board. This meant beans and rice for lunch and beans and rice for dinner. Havana was beautiful, and I loved the Cuban people. During my two-and-a-half months alone, I often had a good time because when I played piano somewhere, I was invited for dinner and was with interesting people. I went easily to the beach, and I went to the old Jewish school and practiced the piano there. When Ernie and Sybil came, things changed. A friend who had a child asked me to take care of her child sometimes. That was fine, since I was taking care of Sybil and would get a little money. One day I met through her a man who was a producer.

When he heard that I had such an early quota number and he had one that would keep him waiting for about a year, he asked if I would sell him my number for $100. I considered it because Ernie and Sybil had much later quota numbers and I would not have left them behind. So we made an arrangement to meet in front of the consulate at nine o'clock to see what could be done.

This event was like a miracle. If one thinks of some sort of a higher power, this is a good example. I was standing there and the man didn't come. Finally I thought, "Maybe he is indoors." There were elevators, open so you could see inside them. As I went up, I saw him going down. Suddenly, I had the feeling he had double-crossed me. I went directly to the consul general's office. When he saw me, he said, "Since when does one sell an American visa?" So I told him, "Look, I have a family and it is not in the interest of the American government to separate families. What would I do in America without my family? And $100 is a lot of money for a refugee." He said to me, "I don't know what I can do, but if there is anything within the law, I will do it." That was the end of December 1938.

SYBIL: *What had the man done to double-cross you?*

Instead of going *with* me to the consul, he went and told him there was a woman who wanted to sell her number. He didn't say that it was his idea and that we had agreed to approach the consul with this question together.

On New Year's evening the phone rang. We were called to the phone and it was the consul general. "I wish you a Happy New Year and am happy to tell you that your whole family will be allowed to move to America this month." I don't know what he did. People thought I must have slept with him! We figured out that Sybil was on the Dutch quota and there weren't yet many applicants in Holland. Also, I had the right to take her on the German preference quota, as the mother. Originally, I had thought I would be able to take Ernie on a preference quota. But while men could do this for their wives (as the businessman friend of Ernie's had done), it didn't work the other way. Anyway, we figured out that the consul didn't take a number away from anybody because Sybil was entitled to two!

The condition for our immigration was that we could not travel together. So I went first to Miami. Ernie put Sybil on a later plane and I picked her up. Finally, he came on yet another plane.

The next event was that Sybil got a terrible case of tonsillitis. I thought it might have been because she had to sit in a cheap plane seat, which was very cold. She had a high fever. Again, the Council of Jewish Women had a branch in Miami and took care of us. They saw to it that Sybil got to a hospital and had a doctor and that I could move in with her in the hospital room because Sybil couldn't talk any English. Some things stand out in my memory. Sybil was given jello to eat. This was for us the funniest thing. It wasn't a food; it trembled! Then once there was a knock on the door and in came two women to see the poor refugees. They brought a blunt scissors and a book Sybil could cut up and a purse. In that purse was a dollar. Probably somebody had told a women's group that there was a sick refugee child in the hospital.

The Council of Jewish Women again provided us with room and board. It was at the home of a refugee family, where we were taken care of quite nicely. We had to think of our future, where we could earn some money, where I would be able to function as a pianist. Ernie didn't want to go to New York. In addition to that, Sybil was very sensitive and the doctors said she should be in a warm climate. We stayed in Miami from January until the beginning of March. Then we decided to go to Los Angeles, which also had a warm climate. Also, Ernie's Aunt Marianne was there.

DEBBIE: *Did you know her before?*

No, but we knew it was very difficult to deal with her. We had written to her that we were coming to Los Angeles, but she didn't invite us to come and stay with her. We didn't know what would happen to us once we got to Los Angeles. We went by train. We took things to eat with us. We didn't stop anywhere. I think it took two days and one night.

DEBBIE: *Weren't you uneasy about coming here?*

Ernie thought that something would happen when we got here. As you know, he's very family conscious! And what do you know? When we arrived, there were his cousins, Jodi and Max, at the station. They brought us to their house and showed us where our room was! They had prepared a fabulous breakfast. A fire was burning in the fireplace. They were very, very nice to us. We stayed there about two weeks. Then we moved to Westmoreland.

DEBBIE: *Let's talk now about how and when you met other refugees, especially the* Gruppe *members.*

First we met the **Dreyfusses.** Ernie and I went to evening school, to Hollywood High, for a citizenship course. Ernie was a very good student and liked the course so well that he took it a second time. I took, in the meantime, a music course, so I'd learn the English expressions for things I knew in German. Ernie told me one day that there was a fellow in his class that looked like someone he might have always known. It was Paul Dreyfuss.

Irene was also in that class. She was pregnant with Judy and didn't fit in the desk bench anymore! They lived in a furnished duplex. We told them, "You have to come to us. We rented an unfurnished duplex and you should see it. We furnished it by buying things for $5 and others for $2.50." (We still have some of that furniture in the den today!) The Dreyfusses were our first good new friends. We spent just about all the holidays and birthdays together. They were actually our only friends at that time.

One day, Paul said, "I want you to meet some nice people." We went to a *Gruppe* meeting. In the beginning we didn't go each and every time to meetings. Some of the people knew each other already in Vienna or Germany. We always made lots of fun with each other because German is different from the Viennese German. Even the words are different. We felt the Viennese had a sloppy and incorrect German and they made fun of us that we were stiff in our language.

Let me tell you what my feelings about the *Gruppe* were. What struck me was that they were really highly intelligent people, very knowledgeable. Each time, somebody spoke about a field where they were really experts. What I found interesting was that when we first came, everyone spoke just German. The topics were mostly on how to relate to America and the differences from our former lifestyle. Later, more and more people started to speak English. We weren't newcomers anymore, needing to adjust. We had adjusted, spoke English, and were experts in various fields.

DEBBIE: *Did you ever not want people to know you were from Germany?*

No. I always liked them to know. I also wanted them to know very soon that I'm Jewish.

SYBIL: *Was this so even when you first came to Los Angeles? Did you want people to know you were German or Jewish then?*

I don't think that bothered me. But I remember once on Westmoreland, somebody came to Ernie and said, "We really have a variety of nationalities here. You are German and there are also some Jews." That irked me. Many people thought a Jew is the one that speaks Yiddish; somebody who speaks German is German. I tried to clear that up. At first when we came, we had the feeling we had to whisper things, that things would be overheard. When you come from a totalitarian place, as we had, you don't feel free to speak.

DEBBIE: *Are you saying it took you a while to get used to being free?*

Definitely.

SYBIL: *How did you feel about the Germans? How did you feel being German?*

At that time, the Germans were my enemies, absolutely. But I can't say that I hated them. Maybe people who got out of Germany later or were in camps had different reactions. Part of me is German and part of me still has the tendency to see what's good in Germans. Ernie has that, too; sometimes, I think, too much. He doesn't see that there's some neo-Nazism going on in Germany. He still will try to defend them with, "But the youth is different." I don't agree with him. I'm very much worried about the German unification.

DEBBIE: *Did you have any different feelings about Judaism because of what you had just been through?*

I was naturally Jewish, like I was in Germany. I was once asked to be on jury duty. When the judge said it would be a long trial and asked if anybody would not be able to stay, I felt so proud and happy when I said I couldn't do that because the Jewish High Holidays would be soon. In Germany, you could never say that. Then I felt really good to be in America.

DEBBIE: *How long did it take you to feel "American"?*

This is a very big question. Do I really feel American today? I feel German. I feel Jewish. I feel Polish. I feel Dutch. I feel Cuban. I feel very much American also. I have spent most of my life in America. But basically, the first years of one's life are much more important. That's where you got your upbringing, your education. So basically I'm still European.

SYBIL: *If you are asked, "What are you?" do you unequivocally now answer, "An American"?*

I would probably put Jew first.

SYBIL: *Are you 100 percent at home now in Los Angeles?*

Of course. I'm living here. But I don't have the nostalgic feeling that some people have. What bothers me is that you have Thrifty here and Thrifty there and Bank of America everywhere. The uniqueness that you find in some of the European towns, cities, and villages gives you the home feeling of, "This is mine." Even when I'm thinking of some of the places where I lived in

Germany, I get more of a home feeling. I don't have the feeling when I come to Ventura Boulevard in Van Nuys that this is home.

DEBBIE: *Don't you think that's because of the times more than the shops themselves? There are probably chains of stores in Dresden now.*

You might be right.

SYBIL: *How long did it take you to feel Los Angeles as your home?*

I think right away because there was no choice. Where else? I did not think it was a nice home, obviously. But this was where I was. There was my family, my furniture, and my piano. That's home.

DEBBIE: *Were you involved in any political groups in the early years?*

No. We were really very busy. Ernie always worked long hours and I was teaching and I made a home and cared for a child.

DEBBIE: *When Sybil came to Havana at age three, I guess you spoke to her in German. I know that at some point she only wanted to speak English. When was that?*

Especially in the beginning, we spoke German. But when other kids were around, she wanted us to speak English. If we talked German when her friends were around, she became 150 percent American. She felt talking German was equivalent to talking with Hitler! I was the same with my parents. When other kids were around, I didn't want my parents to speak Polish to me.

SYBIL: *What about you made you able to make all the adaptations necessary for living a new life?*

I like changes. I like adventure. And another thing. This was it. There was no choice. And this was the best there could be. It couldn't have been better! I couldn't have made a better choice.

DEBBIE: *Was America what you expected it would be?*

I thought many things very funny and I still do. And I still find many things should be different and many things I do not like. My friend, Trudy

Glauber, told me Americans never grow up. They're teenagers all their lives. There is something to this. Much here is superficial, very businesslike. I don't know whether people go really into the depths of life and of what life can be. In many ways, Europeans have much more substance.

RUTH: *As Sybil was growing up, did you talk about the immigration years with her?*

No, we did not talk about that period. It had been a difficult time for us and for her. We didn't want to talk about it.

RUTH: *When did you begin to talk about the years of immigration with her or other people?*

With her we talked very little because she avoided it. I talked much more with Debbie. She was genuinely interested and wanted to know much about it.

RUTH: *Do you talk about it with Sybil now?*

She's still avoiding it.

RUTH: *What about talking with other people? For example, at your synagogue, if people asked you questions, did you talk with them? Did that change over time?*

I told it more or less as a success story. How we came out and all the adventure that was connected with it. How I managed to avoid Ellis Island, how I managed to come out of Cuba, how I got Ernie out. I was proud of all that and liked to talk about it.

RUTH: *How did it feel for you to have these interviews with Debbie, Sybil and me?*

Mixed feelings. I admire what you're doing. But I did find it a nuisance to go through the whole thing once more.

RUTH: *Did you remember things that you hadn't before or that you might rather not think about? Did it lead to some conversations between Ernie and you?*

144

We like to think back and speak about the past. We speak among ourselves. We try to tell people about it. We always find that we have to make a lot of shortcuts because it's a long story. But you want to know it in detail. That part I enjoy.

ERNIE SOMMER

After breaking the skull of a Nazi student group leader, Ernie Sommer knew he wasn't safe in Germany. He went to Holland and sold vegetables—and found Theja, who would become his wife. A job offer brought them back to Germany, where they lived in a small town. After Theja's departure, first to the United States and then Cuba, he tried to get a visa. The very morning that he received permission to enter Cuba, he was arrested. It was the morning after Kristallnacht.

The German inflation, of which you really can have no conception, was terrible. My parents wrote to a relative in Hamburg who was able to get me a job as an apprentice at a big bank. At the same time, I studied at the university there, but I had no time to take many classes. After two or three years, I quit the job and then I was a full-time student and made my matriculation. Then I worked for my doctorate, which I never finished. All that time, I was connected with my friends from the youth movement.

I was once arrested in a group that was probably Communist. I was saved by a newspaper article which I had in my pocket about me getting a medal for heroism (I had saved a drowning woman). The police told me, "You don't belong with these guys. Get out of here."

So I was in Hamburg, working on my doctorate, no longer taking courses. I made just enough money to get by, by writing for newspapers. Once when I was a reporter at a student demonstration, Communist or anyway leftist, the meeting was broken up by the Nazi storm troopers. I got involved in a fight in what we called *Saalschlacht* [a hall battle]. I broke a chair in the way we had learned—to smash a chair down so that you have only one leg left in your hand that you can hit somebody with. Well, I was fighting and I broke the skull of one of the leaders of the Nazi *Studentenbund* [a student group]. When it ended, I was stuck with a knife. I ended up in the hospital with a badly injured finger, which I still can't move.

After that, I wasn't safe anymore in Hamburg. I immigrated the first time then, in 1933, and I went to Holland. In Holland, I eventually made a living by selling fruit and vegetables on the streets. I had a route of many firm customers. And then I met Theja. We met playing chess! Then we made the mistake to go back to Germany. That was supposed to be for only a short time, but we got stuck. The Nazis took over the plant where I worked. I was without work and then started over as a half-day bookkeeper. Finally, I was the manager of an aluminum smelting plant for four Jewish firms that were in the scrap metal business.

We stayed actually much too long in Germany. Everything was worse by the month. My job was not secure anymore. By 1938, things were darker and darker for Jews. It was so that Theja decided, already before I had made up my mind, to leave Germany and to explore the possibility to go to the United States.

DEBBIE: *Why America? Why not South America or Israel or somewhere else?*

America was the place closest to us in cultural and economic affairs. Besides that, we had relatives in America, actually very many relatives. In the 1850s, two brothers of my grandmother went to America and settled. One of them came to visit in Germany and he told my grandmother, "Let me have your two boys and bring them to America. There is the future." So, two brothers of my mother immigrated to America in the 1890s. One of them settled in San Francisco. That was Uncle Louis. The other one settled in Flagstaff— my Uncle Julius. So, naturally, we had closer connections to America than anywhere else. Besides, everybody at that time wanted to go to America from Germany if they had a chance.

DEBBIE: *Continue with the time you decided to leave.*

Theja left in June 1938. She wrote me, "I'm not coming back. I'm trying to do everything I can that you have the possibility to come here, too." At that time, the easiest way to come to America for us was the way over Havana, Cuba. I was doing my regular job. Sybil was in Haarlem, Holland with good friends of ours.

DEBBIE: *How often did you go to see her?*

You did not go so easily from one country to another one. I don't think I saw her until I picked her up to leave for good. In the meantime, we had in Germany what we called *Kristallnacht*. Many of the Jewish men were sent to a concentration camp. Jewish houses were entered by Nazis, and furniture, crystal, and dishes were thrown out of the windows. It was the ninth of November 1938. I was on my way back from Hamburg, where I had tried to get a visa for Cuba without success.

DEBBIE: *Was Theja already in Cuba at that time?*

Yes. She had gone from the United States to Havana. That was no problem for her. But for me to come to Havana, there were new restrictions. You had to make a deposit of $3,000. Of course, we didn't have anything like that. So I had left Hamburg without hope that I could take the boat that was bound for Havana and for which I had reserved space. I cabled Theja that there was no hope that I could make that boat, that I could not get a visa. I took the train back to Dresden. While I was in the train, people got in at Leipzig and said, "The Jewish synagogue is in flames. They are plundering the warehouse of Schoken." I did not know then that it was an organized action throughout the country.

But when I got to Dresden and took the streetcar home, I came by the place where the synagogue was. But there was no synagogue anymore. There were just burnt-out walls. On top of the rubble I saw, like a sign, a *Magen David*. (That was later on saved by firemen and is now part of the new synagogue.) I got out and mixed with hundreds of celebrating people. They didn't know and didn't recognize that I was Jewish. Standing in front of the shell of that burnt-out synagogue, I saw one of the most terrifying views I ever have encountered. The elders of the temple, dressed in *talleisim* and high silk hats, each carrying a half-burnt Torah, were forced to parade back and forth. The howling masses were making fun of them and shouting insults toward Jews. I was standing there and my insides were screaming. It was too dangerous to open my mouth.

Earlier that night, while I was still away, they had taken most of the Jewish men of Dresden as prisoners and later sent them to a concentration camp in Buchenwald. I didn't know that then. I actually thought I was safe because I had applied for an exit visa and was ready to leave. But early the next morning, two policemen came to my apartment and said, "We have to arrest you. You have to come with us." They were normal police and were quite decent. They gave me time to call my secretary and tell her what happened and to tell her to send a cable to Theja in Havana.

DEBBIE: *When you were arrested, did you think you were going to be sent off to a concentration camp? What did you know about concentration camps?*

By that time we knew what a concentration camp was, but we didn't know details and we thought normally people wouldn't be brought to a camp. We thought that happened only to people who tried to smuggle money out or something illegal.

The police told me, "Why don't you take a sandwich along? We don't know when you will get to eat again." I was brought to a police station and had to wait. In the afternoon, I was taken in a prisoner wagon, all by myself, to a big prison. The men who drove said, "We are not going to do anything to you, but where you go now, it will not be so good for you." That meant the Gestapo, the black-shirted SS men would be there. I was put into prison.

That same morning, I had gotten a telegram from Hamburg that said I had been granted a visa for Havana. That was the work of Theja. It was one of the first visas ever given out not by the Cuban Consulate in Germany but directly from the government in Havana. How she did it I don't know. I gave that cable to the prison warden and asked why if I could leave Germany I had to go to prison. It didn't help. The worst thing in the prison was the uncertainty what would happen to you and how long you would have to stay. The boat to Havana on which I had reserved a ticket was going to leave some time at the end of that month.

We were not treated cruelly. I was together with another young Jewish fellow. I could tell you stories about how we spent our time in prison. Anyway, after several weeks, I was called out. We were standing in line, 15 or 20 of us, and told that we were dismissed and could go home. We got back all our belongings and papers in good German order and left the prison.

Then started about 48 hours in which I don't think I slept for more than one or two hours. Once my passport was returned, I took the train to Hamburg, back to the Cuban Consulate. All the necessary steps fell into place. There was no trouble. I had to go to a doctor for a medical checkup. Then I paid a small amount of money and got my visa. I saw one very good young friend still in Hamburg, whom I had known very well while we studied. (I found out later on, he was one of the first to be sent to one of those extermination camps in the East.) The boat I had a ticket for had left Germany by then. But I still had a chance to get to it because it was not going directly to Havana. It was going first to Le Havre in France and then to Antwerp in Belgium to get some freight. That would take 8 or 10 days from the time it left Hamburg. I had to get a transit visa from the Belgian Consulate.

DEBBIE: *Was this boat primarily for immigrants?*

No. It was one of the regular shipping line, the Hamburg-America Line. Unfortunately, my ticket was no longer usable. At the travel agency in Dresden, they told me that my ticket was in the meantime sold because the Nazi officials had told them it would take at least three months before I would get out of prison.

DEBBIE: *Did you get your money back?*

No. I went to Hamburg-America Line and got another ticket. The only thing left was in the lowest class. We used to call it *zwischen x deck*. That meant that there were often 120 people in one room at the bottom of the boat. But I was glad that I could still get these tickets for me and my daughter.

With visas for the U.S. and Belgium in hand, I took a train back to Dresden. I had phoned my parents from Hamburg. They thought I was already on my way out of the country. In Dresden, I packed up two suitcases, as much as was allowed, and went once more to my hometown and saw my parents. My mother was very, very ill. But she got out of bed as if nothing was wrong with her. I don't know where she got the strength. I spent one night with them, and then I had to say good-bye—which was forever. My mother and I knew it. She died two months later.

From there I went to see my sister-in-law. I had already heard from my parents that my brother, a doctor, had been taken to Dachau. So, I visited his wife and their little girl. My sister-in-law said to me, "Please take my girl with you to Holland. When you pick up Sybil, maybe those people would take care of Monica." I said, "Yes, no doubt, they are the kind of decent people, Quakers, who would do that." I had a picture of Sybil in my passport. She was two years younger than Monica, my niece, so we were taking a risk. I smuggled her out of Germany on my passport, with the picture of Sybil. Nobody checked too close. And there was no trouble getting into Holland. There, I went to our friends in Haarlem to pick up my little girl. Sybil was calling the Pollatzes *Opa* and *Oma* [grandpa and grandma], and they treated her like their own child. Sybil, of course, hardly knew me anymore, after half a year of being away from me. But I had to take her away. I said to my friends, "I brought you another little girl, Monica, my niece. Would you take her?" And of course, they did.

DEBBIE: *Where did they get the money to take care of all those kids for free?*

They had sold their house in Germany and bought the one in Holland. They wanted to do something helpful for Jewish children while the Nazis were deporting their parents.

In Germany I still had a little money, enough for the boat and train tickets. And I also had some money, what we called *Bordgeld,* money to buy things on the boat. I took Sybil on a train to Antwerp, Belgium, where that boat, *Orinoco,* was at that time. We just made it. It left the next day. So we took the boat to Havana.

It was not so easy to get into Cuba. The people in first class had no trouble to get in. But in lower classes, and I was in the lowest of the low, people were transported at first to a kind of Ellis Island in Havana. An American Jewish help organization put up money for them. (At that time in Havana you could still do a lot with American money.) But I already had left the boat. I smuggled myself and Sybil through the controls without being caught. Downstairs on the pier was Theja and we all three met again. But I wasn't there legally. Theja had brought a lawyer who told me to go back on the boat and to go through the regular controls. With the help of that lawyer and Theja, I got in. Then, we got into a taxi and drove to the official place where you could get the stamps on your passport that you were admitted.

Theja had taken an unfurnished room for us and had rented furniture. I'll never forget it. There were about 20 grapefruit on the table! Some boyfriend of Theja had given them to her as a welcome for me.

We were supported in Havana with a weekly allowance by a Jewish help organization under the auspices of HIAS. They provided services and money for immigrants. Theja had gotten $10 a week and when we came, we were three people and got $15 a week. It wasn't much, but Havana was cheap. Housing was cheap and we could live there.

DEBBIE: *And in the meantime you waited for your visas to the United States. Talk a little about the time when you actually landed in America, some of your first impressions and feelings about finally being there. What did you do then?*

First I must tell you that it was not easy for me to get into America. By that time, there were three to four thousand refugees in Havana who wanted to go to America and there was a quota. When Theja got there, the quota was 100 a month, but by the time I got there, it was only 10 a month. My waiting time would have been three to four years. At the time I arrived,

Theja could already get a visa. And she was entitled to take her child with her on the preference quota. But I would have to wait.

That's when I saw for the first time the difference between American and German officials. The consul general, who was for us bigger than the president of the United States, did something that he never told us, but we know more or less from what happened. The quota was based on your place of birth. Sybil was born in Holland, and the Dutch quota was completely open. So she could enter the U.S. She also had the right to go with her mother on the preference quota. The consul probably decided that since Sybil had two quota numbers, by giving me one of them, he wasn't taking one away from anybody. He gave me one of them.

We left Havana after the first of January. I remember the consul general called us and said, "I have good news for you for the New Year. You all will be permitted to enter America!" But we could not travel together. If Sybil traveled with her mother, she would be on the German preference quota. I needed to enter on that quota. So, Sybil would have to go by herself on the Dutch quota. We entered the U.S. one by one. First, Theja took a plane to Miami. Then, I put three-year-old Sybil on another plane. She was one of the youngest ever to enter the U.S. by herself. After she had left, I had to go back to the consulate to prove that I was still there and to get my visa. The next day, I could fly to Miami, where we all three were together again.

In Miami, we were helped by a committee of the Council of Jewish Women. They took care of all of our needs. They put us in a home with another Jewish family who had come earlier and had established themselves. The Committee paid everything for us. I tried to find a job, but there was nothing open except a job as a dishwasher which paid very little money.

DEBBIE: *You said earlier that you had noticed a difference between German and American officials. Do you mean that Americans bent over backward to help you instead of following precise rules?*

That's right. The consul general stretched the law. He didn't go against the law, but he certainly didn't have to do what he did. He had sympathy when Theja had said, "I can't be separated from my husband for three more years. It doesn't make sense."

DEBBIE: *Had you planned to stay in Miami?*

It was not possible to stay there. I could not find a job. I had written to my relatives in Los Angeles and got a letter that I should come, but no details about what would happen to us when we arrived. We were in Miami all during the month of February. In the meantime, I had a letter that my mother had died. I went to say *Kaddish* [the prayer for those who have died] in a synagogue there and didn't have a *yarmulka* [skull cap]. I had to buy one. But those were kind of carefree days.

We had trouble persuading the committee to buy tickets for us to Los Angeles, where we wanted to go. They wanted to send us to New York because the fellow who had given us the affidavits—who actually was a stranger but posed as a relative—lived in New York. We knew that we did not want to go to that big city, also that we could not be a burden to this man who I never met. Theja met him only one or two times. We figured that if we had to start life all over again, we might as well go to a place where conditions were favorable.

In Havana, one of the girls on the committee had told us in glowing colors about life in Los Angeles, that you could drive on one street all the way from the middle of town, without stopping, right to the ocean. That was probably Sunset Boulevard. Finally, the committee made it possible for us to go to Los Angeles. We took the train for, I think, three days and three nights. We took all provisions with us—sausage and bread.

Then we got to Los Angeles. There at the station were three of my cousins, Jodi, Maxine, and Rita. My Uncle Julius had passed away already in 1913, a very young man, only about 38. His wife, Marianne, was a very smart and efficient woman, and took over their business and properties. All during the big recession in the 30s, she held onto everything. She and the children left Flagstaff and went to Los Angeles finally, and bought a big house, which they still have now. My cousins brought us to that house. The funny thing was, my aunt had written us in German, but her German was not very good. She came from Lithuania. She never wrote us that we could stay with them. So we still did not know when we came there where we would sleep that night. We had, of course, no money. But when we came to their house, they took us upstairs. There was a big room, two beds in it and a little bed. My cousin said to us, "This is your room."

We were comfortable at my relatives' house. We were guests, but we knew that was only temporary, that we had to find a way to be on our own. Theja had her profession as a pianist and could make money wherever she went. She could always play music for dancers and give piano lessons. I tried to find a job in my line of metal smelting. I had a list of foundries and smelters. I went from one to another. There were no jobs to be had. America was in difficult circumstances. Somebody finally sent me to the plant of the American Smelting Company. They had just opened a new plant in Los Angeles. I went to the end of the bus line. There was nothing anymore—no houses, no paved roads. That place was on East 26th Street near Vernon, and I started walking over rough roads. I finally came to a building and found the office. I, of course, was dressed in my best suit, with a briefcase under my arm. I spoke to the manager of that plant who was very nice to me. He said,

"I really don't have a job for you, but you said you would do anything. If you want to work at our furnace, you can have a job." So I got that job.

DEBBIE: *How did you feel when you got the furnace job?*

I was happy that I got any kind of a job. I was relatively young, but not that young anymore. I was 35 or 36 years old, and I had never done any manual labor in my life before. I knew the theory of building a furnace and working at one, but I'd always had other people working for me. I had never worked with my own hands. So I started on that new job and it was not easy. I remember one day when the heat in the place was especially high. I was the ladle man. That means I was pushing a big crucible with 4,000 pounds of metal along on a rail and had to pour that metal into molds. Everyone of our crew got sick. The heat was about 140 degrees! My heart pounded to the breaking point from the terrible heat, my stomach turned over. But I would show them that a Jew could do it! Between the time I emptied my crucible and filled the other furnace, I had to run to the water dispenser for water and salt tablets. After a while, there were only two men still working. I was one. The other was our foreman. Finally, they shut down the furnace because they didn't have people to work anymore.

DEBBIE: *How long did you work there before you got a different position, one that was not so awful?*

I worked in the furnace for about two years. There were some job openings, for instance, in the laboratory. We had a very bad manager who was anti-Semitic. He told me always, "Oh, you are too dumb for that. You cannot have a job like that."

DEBBIE: *I understand that you were grateful for having a job, but to have gone to college, to have other goals, what was it like to be in such a position?*

I had some guilt feelings maybe during the years in which I did not do what I should have done. I think I have to make up for those feelings now. I also had some feelings that I wanted to prove that a Jew could work well at such hard labor. Throughout my life, I always had the ability to pick the hardest job possible! This was one of the hardest. We did not have a union. I was one of the charter members when they finally opened a local union. I was very afraid about joining. I had a funny kind of relationship to my boss, who was also Jewish and who took me in his car to work sometimes. I even asked him if I should join the Union. He said, "By all means do that, and tell me about everything!"

RUTH: *What about you, your personality, your style, do you think made it possible for you to make all the adaptations necessary to adjust to a new life in a strange country?*

The same as Theja. I, too, was kind of adventurous, trying new things and adjusting pretty easily to different circumstances. For example, when we came to Los Angeles, we stayed with relatives we had never met before. And then I became a common laborer at 50 cents an hour in a metal smelting plant. That was a completely new experience for me.

RUTH: *When you came as a German, you were considered an enemy alien. How did that feel?*

Actually, it was only after the war started that we were considered enemy aliens. We were kind of citizens, second-class, although it didn't really affect us much. We just lived our lives. As during the last years in Germany, we were not much involved with other people. We were quite closed up. I worked hard. I had to be home at seven o'clock. I remember when my boss tried with the commanding general here to get me permission to work longer. "He can work longer if he wants, but if we catch him, we'll put him in jail."

RUTH: *How did you feel about being German at that time?*

I had no minority complex. I was very much surprised that the American attitude toward Germans was to hardly consider them enemies. Several times we found out that Americans had a pretty high opinion of Germans. We lived in a little duplex and the owner wanted to sell it to us. I said, "How can we buy it? We have no money." The owner said, "I know you are Germans. Germans are honest. You will pay me somehow."

THEJA: I have to say something to that question, too. Already before the war, when we lived in Holland, we boycotted German merchandise. I remember an incident shortly after Ernie and I had moved into a neighborhood there. I was very much insulted when Ernie came home and told me that one of the neighbors had talked to him and said, "How our neighborhood has changed. We have Russians here. And now we have you here as a German." I did not feel I wanted to be under that term *German*.

My feelings have changed and my feeling about Germany is different from Ernie's. I have quite a love for Germany for many things. It's a beautiful country. I owe Germany a lot. I had my whole education there and my whole culture is actually German. But I feel that we Jews are really what Hitler used to call *Internationales Judengesindel* (international Jewish trash). We

Jews have something very wonderful. Through all the centuries, we have been in different places where we gave something and took something away with us. It's like a bee that gets some pollen and returns it in another form. We give and we take. I have that feeling very strongly. I was born in Germany from Polish parents. We know how anti-Semitic Polish people can be. But I have also quite a love for certain aspects of the Polish people. I admire them in many ways. I lived for seven years in Holland. Now I'm certainly not Dutch, but I've gotten a lot from Holland. I have lived for a few months in Cuba. From all these places, I gave and I took. That is a difference between Ernie and me. He was born in Germany from many generations of Jewish Germans, in a small town, a beautiful little town in western Germany, and has a different outlook.

RUTH: *Does that mean that you, Ernie, identify more as a German than Theja does?*

ERNIE: Yes, I think that might be true. Of course, Germany was Hitler. And Hitler was Germany. We hated Hitler. So we hated Germany at that time. But we said, "This is not the *real* Germany. This period will pass and there will be another Germany"—as it later on really happened. So, I don't think in my inner feelings I was really anti-German at that time, even though we went through quite a bit of bad, bad things.

RUTH: *In the first years that you lived here, if you were confronted with something or somebody connected with Germany, how did you feel and/or behave?*

ERNIE: We probably boycotted German goods, but there were not many here. We did not have German neighbors, German friends, few contacts actually with anybody who was of German gentile origin.

Germans we met were very nice to us. I remember the first time we went camping. It was very improvised. We made a trip with the car to San Francisco. We didn't have the money to sleep in hotels or motels. Theja and Sybil slept in the car and I slept on the ground. We had no equipment. At a campground on a lake near Fresno, at the foot of the Sierras, there was a German family camped close to us and they felt sorry for us. They gave us blankets and a cot. They wanted us to be more comfortable. He was a baker. They were simple people. And they were German.

RUTH: *When was that?*

ERNIE: Maybe 1941.

RUTH: *So can we say that you didn't avoid Germans if they happened to cross your path?*

ERNIE: In fact, we felt much more familiar with them than we did with strange Americans!

THEJA: We absolutely did not have hatred of Germans. During the time that we still were in Germany, we had some very good experiences with some Germans who were very nice. I even worried that they might say things that would put them into danger with the Nazis! The problem was Hitler and the group that supported his ideas, not among the regular people. Among the people that we knew in Germany, I don't know of anybody toward whom we would have any personal resentment.

RUTH: *During the war, what did you know about the fate of the Jews in Europe?*

ERNIE: We only had general news, like every other American. We never knew exactly what was happening. There were many rumors, but no facts really until after the war.

RUTH: *And then when you did know, how did you feel that you had gotten out before this great tragedy?*

THEJA: *Very* mixed feelings, and I have them, I would say, almost up to this day. I sometimes have a nightmare seeing myself on a bridge where my mother would go to one side and I would have to go to the other and I have guilt. This is a motif that repeats itself.

RUTH: *After the war, did you resume any relationships with gentile friends in Germany?*

ERNIE: No. But we went back to Germany for a visit in 1954. That was our first contact with old German *Bekannten,* people we used to know.

RUTH: *What was it like to be with these people?*

ERNIE: In my hometown, we spent some time with a friend my own age. He took us out to drink with him. We had lived in a more or less Catholic

158

neighborhood. Catholics with whom we talked tried to tell us they could not really have been Nazis because Hitler was the same way against Catholics as he was against Jews, that they too felt persecuted. This, of course, is ridiculous. Lots of Catholics were Nazis.

RUTH: *How did it feel to go back to your hometown?*

ERNIE: It was like digging in graves. It was very, very depressing. There were a few people left whom we had known before. One neighbor showed us a book with something written in it. She said, "Your father gave this to me." We went across the street to another neighbor. There was a crystal bowl on the table and she said to look at that bowl. "That was yours. Your father gave it to me when he was driven out of his house. The Jews were all put together in a 'ghetto house,' and then sent to extermination camp." And so, I heard a report about the end of the Jewish people in my town. They had been on the last transport.

RUTH: *Do you believe those neighbors who said that your father gave them the book and bowl?*

ERNIE: Oh yes. I'm very certain. We knew these people well from childhood on. But there were other people in town. I did not trust some of them, and some were very reluctant to talk about Hitler time. I heard about another neighbor. He was a head man of the Nazis. He hated Jews.

We talked to a neighbor very close to our house. She told us how it was when the alarm sounded and they had to run into the bunker. When they came out, the houses and the whole street were on fire. They kept telling us, "We went through terrible times during the war. You cannot imagine what we had to go through." That was foremost on their minds, not what happened to the poor Jews there.

THEJA: Still, Ernie has a very close feeling for that town.

RUTH: *After that visit, did you keep contact with any of these people?*

ERNIE: Not by letter. But we went back to that little town two times more. Things had changed. I had made up my mind, more or less, not to forget but to forgive the German people. I never really believed that people could change all that much. So, although some were still died-in-the-wool Nazis and they spoke to me the same way as they would have already before Hitler, generally the young generation somehow wanted to wipe out what had happened. They didn't feel part of it and didn't want to think or talk about it. It was as if that period had never existed.

Before our last visit, I had written a letter to the mayor of the town and told him that we would visit at a certain date. I even had put an ad in the local paper asking that if there were any classmates of mine around to contact me. Not one was alive anymore as far as I could find out. No answer except one man who was somewhat younger. The mayor referred us to the city archivist. We were received with open arms, I must say. He had published a little book called, *The Persecution of Our Jewish Co-Citizens in Soest*. In it was document after document about what was done to the Jews generally and specifically in that small town. The book was out of print, so he made a copy for us. He didn't know many details about the fate of the local Jewish people. I could fill out quite a bit of what he didn't know, especially with the report which I have still from one survivor who was transported together with my father to Theresienstadt and then Auschwitz.

RUTH: *Were there any Jews remaining in your town?*

ERNIE: When I had lived in Soest, of the 20,000 inhabitants, 300 were Jews. Two people of the whole congregation returned. They were not alive anymore when we returned in 1954.

RUTH: *So the entire Jewish population of that town was annihilated.*

ERNIE: Except the young people like us who had emigrated before. Of those who stayed, almost none survived. There was no Jew there when we came back. The town was *judenrein*.

RUTH: *I'm curious about your use of the German language once you settled in Los Angeles. Did you speak German to each other, with Sybil, with friends?*

ERNIE: In the beginning, my English was still pretty poor. We spoke mostly German with each other and also with Sybil. Later on, Sybil did not like it anymore. She would answer in English. We developed what we called *Immigranto*, a mixture of languages even in one sentence. Sybil would only speak in English.

THEJA: Gradually, I had to speak much more English because I was teaching in English.

ERNIE: I learned English in the smelting plant where I worked, and that was not the best educated English! Every second word was some cuss word.

160

My fellow workers made fun of me. Our foreman once told me a sentence to say to our superintendent. It was very dirty and demeaning. I didn't know what it meant and said it to him. Fortunately, he realized that I had been put up to it!

THEJA: Our neighbor complained because Sybil started to use the cuss words when she was outside. That was between the years when she was three to six. Then when we wanted to buy a house, somebody loaned Ernie money without interest. Ernie sent a thank you letter and wanted to say that some day he hoped that he could reciprocate. Instead of *reciprocate,* he wrote *retaliate!*

ERNIE: The reason I didn't speak English better was that I worked very, very hard, and when I came home I fell into bed. There was no time, no strength even, to pick up and to do anything. I worked very irregular times, depending on the way the furnace was operating. One day, from 10 at night till six in the morning. Then I might have to come back, not at 10, but at six in the evening and work till after midnight, and so on. It was a very rough time. I came home dead tired sometimes after a night shift. Theja was teaching rhythm band in the living room and the children made noise with their instruments. I tried to sleep!

RUTH: *When you came to the United States, how did the experience of immigration affect your Jewishness? Was there any change in your identity and wish to practice as a Jew?*

ERNIE: We actually continue more or less the way we did it in Germany. I came from a rather Orthodox family, one of the two or three families in town who kept kosher. After Theja and I married, we kind of let down our Jewish connections. I don't even remember if we went to temple on Saturdays. I don't think we did.

When we came here, my mother had died and I was saying *Kaddish* for her. This is a holy obligation, and I had to do that. We went to a temple in our neighborhood.

RUTH: *At home, what were your Jewish feelings and/or activities?*

ERNIE: We always kept Jewish customs. Every Friday evening we made Kiddush. On Pesach we had a Seder. We did this also during the Hitler time in Germany. I remember our first Seder in Germany. We had Sybil there in a basket. She was a baby still. We were lonely, but we made our own Seder together.

161

RUTH: *Were you ever Zionists?*

THEJA: I belonged to *Blau-Weiss*. Not that I was especially Zionist, but it had a better ball team!

ERNIE: No, my friends were actually die-hard anti-Zionists. We were fighting the Zionists with every means possible. We felt they were not quite as bad as one member of my class who later on became minister of justice! They were just not our kind. We were German Jews. We wanted to be German and Jewish at the same time. The Jewish Youth Movement, which I joined, *Kameraden Deutschjüdischer Wanderbund,* called Zionists traitors of the fatherland. I remember our first *Bundestag,* a meeting in the woods of all groups from the whole German Reich. We were maybe five or six hundred there. There were very intellectual discussions. I remember that the whole afternoon discussion was about the word *deutschjüdisch*—if it should be written as one word or with a hyphen. We felt that the difference was significant in its implication. This youth movement is something very hard to describe. Our whole life revolved around that movement. I mean, I might work during the days, but I would spend my evenings always with the same group of people. On week-ends we were hiking together. So it actually took over our whole life.

I really became, if I may call it, a Zionist only after we visited Israel in 1967 and I saw what the spirit was there. I got *angesteckt* [infected] with that spirit and I had to watch that I did not become nationalistic Jewish. As I said before, I was anti-Zionist to a certain degree. In my Jewish German group, we gave money for Palestine but not for the Zionist movement.

RUTH: *I think you said before that your first friends here were mostly Jews, although you met non-Jews through work.*

ERNIE: Hoping to meet people, we went to the Jewish Club of 1933. That exists still today. Then there was a Quaker family, the Harveys. He was a professor at Whittier College. They had heard from our Dutch Quaker friends about us, and they looked us up when we first arrived. They opened their home to us and remained friends until their deaths.

THEJA: Talk about the **Dreyfusses.** They were the best and only friends we had in those early years.

ERNIE: I went to Hollywood High for citizenship classes. During intermission, in the corridor I saw someone walking (I can still see him!) like a German professor, slowly, one step at a time. This seemed very familiar to me. I talked to him. That was Paul Dreyfuss. He was in the same class as I. Also, Irene was in the same class, as long as her belly wasn't too big to fit behind the desk! I took them home one day. They lived in a furnished place and were not too happy with it. We had just rented a house and furnished it very, very cheaply. I brought them home to show that you can buy a piece of furniture for $5 and fix up your place for less than they were paying.

That was our first contact with anybody from the *Gruppe*. They were our first real friends. Anything we did was with them. We had the holidays together and the birthdays. We visited, we ate together. They then later said to us, "We want you to meet some nice people." They told us that they were members of a group, a very intelligent group, who came together, listened to each other giving speeches and then had discussions. If we would be interested . . . Well, we were interested. We more or less joined the *Gruppe*. But even there, we were not at home in the beginning, at least I was not. I was aware that I was the only manual worker. I was the only man, I think, who didn't have a doctorate degree, although I worked five years on mine. I still remember once when everybody got a chapter to read in preparation to present it at the next meeting. Nobody offered one to me, and I felt very hurt.

RUTH: *I'm curious how the* Gruppe *continued to fit into your lives during the following 50 years. How did its meaning change over the years, and what does it mean to you now?*

ERNIE: It became more or less an important part of our lives. At first, the *Gruppe* was relatively large. Gradually, we lost more and more people. The first ones who really left after the war were the **Dreyfusses**. Then people kept on dying. We were less and less. But we still speak of the *Gruppe*. The *Gruppe* still means something to us, and even if we don't see each other often, we feel real close to each other.

THEJA: I see it a little bit different from you. To begin with, I did not feel that the *Gruppe* as a whole meant much to me. The **Dreyfusses** introduced us to it, and then the **Brooks** joined and we were close with both families. Gradually, other people became friends—the Esslaus, the **Wolmans**. I never saw it as a complete thing. I think even later it was parts that broke into pieces. I don't see it as a whole. But it became sort of a telegraphic agency that connected Pasadena to Santa Monica and so on. The *Gruppe* as such wasn't the important thing to me.

ERNIE: There was something else. There was also I would not say animosity but some difference between the people from Vienna and the *Yekes* [German

Jews]. We were teasing each other about that. There was a certain difference in culture and education. At least, I felt it that way. That only slowly disintegrated.

THEJA: I didn't feel the difference between the Viennese and the rest. I feel that was mostly kidding. In feeling, there was not much difference.

RUTH: *The Viennese are a bit snobbish aren't they?*

THEJA: Actually, they felt that *we* were snobbish with our old German language. There was constantly an issue about language and kidding about it.

RUTH: *So now the* Gruppe *is individuals, whom even though you don't see very often, you have warm feelings about.*

THEJA: So little is left. This is the tragedy. But for many years that warm feeling was there, and if something happened to anyone in the *Gruppe,* you knew it immediately. You got a phone call. News would travel very fast, disregarding the distances. This was nice.

RUTH: *By any chance, did you have any kind of political involvement in this country during your early years here?*

ERNIE: Not officially, but we came together with people who were very much oriented to the Left. I joined the National Guard and was in a unit that had only Jews and Koreans, all immigrants who wanted to show our solidarity with Americans. But when war was declared, the unit was disbanded. We became enemy aliens.

RUTH: *If somebody said to you, "What are you? What's your nationality?" when, if ever, could you say, "I am an American," and feel comfortable saying that?*

ERNIE: Now, yes, I would say, "I'm an American." But pretty close to it, I would say, "I'm a Jewish American."

RUTH: *When did you begin to feel American?*

ERNIE: When the war ended and there was a general feeling of euphoria, we half-Americans were part of it. During the war against Hitler, we were on the side against him. Naturally I said, "I'm American."

RUTH: *When, if ever, did you feel 100 percent at home living in Los Angeles?*

ERNIE: Maybe because we had pretty close relatives here, we felt at home faster than other people with no close connections. I think I felt at home in Los Angeles very fast, as much at home as you can feel once you are transplanted from your real home into foreign soil. It can never be 100 percent the same as being in the country and surroundings where you have grown up, where your roots are.

RUTH: *In those first years here, did you encounter any anti-Semitic incidents, either directed toward you or somebody else?*

ERNIE: Sometimes I felt I didn't get the same treatment as others. At work, I was also a member of the working class. There was some underground feeling that Jews were different. I felt this especially when we got a new superintendent who said he would see to it that all the Jewish foremen would be thrown out. I remember especially one incident when we had a foremen's meeting with management. There was a big Oakie, L.J. Anderson, and he was probably drunk. Suddenly he blurted out about a superintendent named Art Cohen, "I won't take orders from a kike like that." That caused a big uproar. He was fired the next day. The other superintendent was very friendly to my face, but we all knew he was anti-Semitic. I felt it in the beginning because I did not get promotions. When there was an opening for a better job, I didn't get it. This was the case, even though the company was originally owned by Jews and still had a Jewish manager.

RUTH: *Was anything anti-Semitic ever said there directly to you?*:

ERNIE: No, not that I remember. Not directly, but I felt it was there.

RUTH: *Before you came to the United States, you must have had some notion about what it might be like here. In what ways did it turn out to be similar and in what ways was it different from these expectations?*

ERNIE: I found the people here were actually lazier than in Germany and that while you were pushed in your work, those in charge were not in such a hurry. In general, I was surprised that life was more or less the same as we had it in Germany. But one thing that was very different was dependence on automobiles. I lived far away from my working place, and so after a while one of my coworkers told me, "I know where you can get a pretty good car." In Germany, we figured members of the union are brothers. You held together for common goals. You wouldn't take advantage, one of another. So

Theja and Ernie Sommer, Los Angeles, 1987

I trusted him. I found out it was different here. The fellow who wanted to sell me a car was behind in payments on his own car and wanted to bring a customer to his dealer. So I got stuck with an old wreck that was a headache for me. How did I spend my free time? More underneath that car than in the car! But from that experience, I learned quite a lot and became quite a mechanic!

RUTH: *Was there any person, thing, or incident during the process of immigration that was especially significant in keeping your morale or wits together?*

ERNIE: If there is any person who made it easier, it was Theja. She always was the adventurer and had ideas and acted on those ideas. I was much more the conservative type. I could stand up to all kinds of unhappy times, but I was not the one who actively would change where I was sitting. I would stay in a job, which I did for 20 years with my first company, or where we lived or whatever. So I would say it was Theja who made not only our immigration possible but also our integration into American society.

RUTH: *How did it feel for you to spend time going over these pieces of your past?*

ERNIE: It was not painful. In fact, I enjoyed remembering things, some which I had long forgotten.

FRANK BAUER

As children, Frank Bauer and his brothers had been baptized. Their parents felt that life as Lutherans would be simpler. Years later, Frank was in line at the U.S. Consulate, waiting to register for a visa and was seized by the police. His next weeks were spent in Dachau. Release from there was contingent upon a plan for immigration to Finland, which was secured through efforts by his wife, Magda. Frank and Magda had one son, Bob.

I was born in Vienna, as was my father. In 1933, I was 26 years old. Already for some years, the economic conditions were deplorable. There was a creeping depression all the time. At the time that I got started with my working life, it was very difficult to get a job unless you had somebody who pulled strings for you.

Was that as true for gentiles?

Yes. At that time there was no official discrimination against Jews. When I started my first job, I was 19 and had just finished the technical school. I didn't have a *Reifezeugnis* [high school diploma]. I had interrupted my high school education in order to go to technical school. The reason for that was that my father was very old and was worried he wouldn't be able to finish paying for the children's education. So my older brother went to the Hochschule für Bodenkultur instead of what he wanted to do. (He wanted to be a doctor.) I went to the Technologische Gewerbe-Museum (a school, believe it or not) which interested me only as far as math, mechanics, and physics were concerned. In mechanical engineering, I was neither talented nor did I like it. When I got out of that school, I got a technical job, not very responsible and very lowly paid.

After a while I was really unhappy. I decided to finish my high school education. To earn the diploma, I had to pass several tests, one in Latin, one in English. I don't recall what other exams. I prepared on my own and took the required exams. With the results of these tests, I got a college-preparatory high school diploma [the *Matura*] and started law school at the university.

I took all the required courses for law school, but couldn't take the final exams because by then Jews were no longer permitted at the university. This was 1938. The job I had meanwhile with a big chemical outfit in Vienna was terminated two days after Hitler marched in. It was known that the main owner, Mautner-Markhoff, was of Jewish heritage, but his grandparents got baptized at the right time and he was accepted at all the clubs. He was considered an Aryan, although not by blood. He was nice and paid me two weeks salary. But I was out on the street.

From then on the question became one of emigrating—where to and when to go. I was sure I wouldn't be able to make a living in a foreign country. Language difficulty was really minor, but with my broken-up education, I didn't know how I would make it. At one time I had a visa to Yugoslavia. What would have happened there, nobody knows. Maybe it's lucky that I didn't get there. I might have been picked up. I stayed put until I was arrested at the time of the *Kristallnacht,* right in front of the American Consulate.

Were you waiting there in line?

Yes, I was in line to register for a visa. Many of us were rounded up and taken to the police station. The next three days and two nights were quite terrible. We were standing up most of the time, like sardines. We couldn't sleep and didn't get anything to eat, so far as I remember. Then the Gestapo came and we were asked a few questions about our emigration intentions. I actually had been promised a visa to Australia at that time. But that didn't satisfy the Gestapo. They assigned us right and left. Right—you go back home, and left—you go to a concentration camp. At that point, I knew I was going to Dachau. And that happened.

I was in Dachau for 10 weeks. Then I was released under condition that I report to the police every day or every other day to confirm that I was still in Vienna and that I would soon emigrate.

The release was contingent upon your promise to get out of the country?

Yes. While I was in the camp, Magda was in touch with people in Finland whom we knew. They were able to arrange for a visa, and I went there in March 1939. I was lucky enough to get Magda out within a very short time after that. I talked to the police president who was in charge of immigration, and he was very sympathetic. So Magda was able to get me out of Dachau, and I got her out of Austria.

How was it that you knew people in Finland?

There was a close relationship between my mother and the aunt of the girl who later married my older brother. This aunt had a close friend who got to Finland by a proxy marriage. She immediately became a Finnish citizen and got her friend, the aunt of my sister-in-law, to Finland. When I was in Dachau, Magda wrote to these two ladies that I was in danger and asked whether they could help. These ladies contacted a Finnish member of Parliament who had the connections to get me the visa.

So when you got out of Dachau, it was because you had a visa to Finland?

I think so. When the visa was actually issued, I'm not sure. I'm not certain that I had it when I was released.

Were Jews ever released without some documentation of pending emigrations?

Things were very irregular. They were not yet very organized. On one hand, people wanted to get rid of all the Jews. On the other hand, the camps became overcrowded. When I was in Dachau, Magda's sister's husband and Magda's brother were there, too, and were released a day earlier than I.

Are you saying that some things were really arbitrary?

Yes, but most of it was organized in a spectacular way. For instance, when the Hitler army walked into Austria, within an hour or two, every big office had a Nazi head. That was prearranged. Every branch of the government and police had a predetermined new boss.

Would that have been an Austrian or a German?

Both. There was an illegal Nazi Party in Austria long before Hitler came. It was a fifth column and very well organized.

How were you informed of your release from Dachau?

You went every day to the big *Apellplatz* [central square] where you stood in rows like military formations between the administration building and barracks. All kinds of things happened there. Every morning there was a count as we stood at attention. If one person was missing, we all stood until there was an explanation. One time a prisoner escaped and the whole camp had to stand at attention in the cold weather in pajamas. While we stood at that square, over the loudspeaker they read out the names of anybody to be released that day.

Did that happen very often?

At that time, yes. Families were working at home to get some results. There were releases every day. I heard the releases of my brothers-in-law. I got scared then. "Why not me?"

While you were in Dachau, could you communicate with your family?

Once a week we could get a letter and were permitted to get about 10 marks to use at the canteen to buy some extra food, like candy or extra bread or butter. I could write a postcard, which of course was censored.

How fortunate that Magda's efforts coupled with those of the people in Finland made it possible for you not only to get out of Dachau but of Austria as well. Why was it that Magda didn't obtain a visa then, too?

The people in Finland had gotten a working permit only for me.

Does that mean that a visa was contingent upon having a work permit?

Yes, that's right. The reality was that men *had* to get out. They were in greater danger at that time. I don't know whether women were left alone, but the concentration camps were mainly for men.

What was your relationship with Magda at that time?

We had been married since 1935.

What happened when you got to Finland?

I didn't get the job. The people who signed for the job said, "We helped to get you out, but that's it." So, I set out to learn some Swedish, which was much easier for a German speaker than Finnish. In Helsinki, lots of Swedish was spoken. I could also speak English well enough to talk with officials. Soon Madga joined me, and we lived quietly and modestly.

How were you able to support yourselves?

We got some money from America, I think $40 each month.

Who in America was providing this money?

The people who gave us our affidavits. This is the story. Before I went to Dachau, I wrote a lot of letters to America, to people with my name. I wrote and wrote and there was no positive answer. I also wrote to some organizations. The Council of Jewish Women in Los Angeles got our names and found some people to provide affidavits for us. These people were four sisters who were spinster schoolteachers. With the affidavits came the promise of $40 each month so we could survive the waiting time.

We got the immigration visas for the U.S. under very difficult conditions. Russia was attacking Finland. There were airplanes flying and bombs falling. The war there ended with the Russians getting a naval base, as they wanted. They apparently didn't try to conquer Finland. The Finnish soldiers fought a ridiculous war against Russia. It was just unbelievable. But before peace came there, we were trying to get out. We were in Helsinki, but all consulates and embassies were evacuated out of the city and in temporary quarters. The temperature was 40 below, the snow was high, and transportation was hard to get. How could we get to our visas? We had to find some buses to go to the different embassies, and they were all in different places. We needed the Swedish and Norwegian as well as the American consulates. We couldn't get to America without first going through Sweden and Norway, because the only way of leaving the continent was from Oslo, Norway. It was a hassle. First, the Swedish said they couldn't give us transit visas without seeing the Norwegian ones, because without these we might get stuck in Sweden. But people were generally nice. It was hard work, but we managed to collect all the visas.

Then we got boat tickets on the Norwegian America line that departed from Oslo. Under normal circumstances, we could have gotten to Oslo by boat via an island between Finland and Norway. But since Finland was at war, the only way to get there was by train. The train from Helsinki went all the way up and around the Gulf of Ostsee Bothnia, between Finland and Sweden, and then down the other side to Stockholm. We were warned to take some bed sheets with us, so if the Russians attacked the train, we could get out in the snow and cover ourselves. Wartime! We had a small amount of American dollars with us. It was illegal to carry them out of the country. But we did and sweated it out. At the border between Finland and Sweden there was a big border check. We were lucky.

We got to Stockholm. We had a letter from people in Finland who had friends there, so we stayed overnight with them. We went on to Oslo, where I had some cousins. And then we got on the boat. It was exactly four weeks before the Germans moved into Norway. Our boat was the next to the last that could still leave for America. That part of our trip was very pleasant. In a sense, it was a vacation trip. Along the coast to Stavanger and Bergen, it was uneventful. There was a big Norwegian flag painted on the boat so that the Germans wouldn't attack. The trip across the ocean, too, was uneventful; nothing happened.

We landed in New York on March 7, 1940. The procedure in New York was fascinating, in a way. We didn't have time to worry about where we were going to sleep or eat. We looked at the immigration officers sitting in their chairs with their feet on the desks. We never saw anything like that in Europe. They had big cigars and sunshields [sunglasses]. It was an amazing, but somehow expected, sight. Some cousins of Magda's met us at the boat and asked if we needed a few dollars. We still had a few dollars on us. I don't think they were really ready to help us to any extent.

Did you stay with them?

No. They lived somewhere in upstate New York. What happened to us in New York is probably what happened to many. We got referred to the HIAS. That corresponded to what in London was called the Bloomsbury House. In both cities, that was where Jewish refugees were received and helped. There was a lot of red tape and it was done very inefficiently, but we were provided with rent and food money. They gave us chits to use for such payments.

Did you know before you arrived in New York that such help would be available?

174

Frank Bauer and his wife, Magda, Los Angeles, 1940.

I'm not sure. I think there was somebody at the boat who told us. We stayed for a few weeks with some relatives of my sister-in-law. Magda got a job in a milliner shop for $15 a week. From her salary, we paid these people for room and board. I couldn't find any work. We decided to go to Los Angeles, where the four schoolteachers lived.

We went on a gruesome Greyhound trip across the country. I think we stayed in Kansas City one night because we couldn't stand it anymore without a stop. We arrived here on the first of May, 1940, with a lot of luggage.

I didn't realize you could take much out of Austria. Had you accumulated it in Finland?

The restrictions were mostly on money and jewelry. You could take clothes out. The suitcases were closely checked when you left the country. We had that luggage all the time in Finland and brought it to Los Angeles. The four teachers didn't understand. They thought we would come naked! They were thinking of the people who had been pushed out of Poland years before with nothing. They just couldn't understand that we arrived with clothes. Magda even had a fur jacket. That was just terrible! They had helped rich people! I shouldn't be ungrateful for what they did because they helped us to come over. We stayed with these old ladies in their duplex apartment for a while. Only once while we stayed there were we permitted into the living room. Otherwise, we were in the kitchen or "our" room that was servants' quarters. There was friction all over the place. When Magda went shopping and bought a loaf of rye bread instead of that cotton that they ate, there was a big stink. "How could you do that? You're not satisfied with what we give you to eat?" It became intolerable for us.

We moved out. Magda started working soon, sewing some little things, and I finally got a job also. I rolled up woolen pieces somewhere downtown for $60 or $80 a month. But we were on our own. We had a little apartment very close to where the **Wolmans** lived near Pico and Alvarado. The Esslaus lived there, too. After I left that job, I started driving a cab. That gave us a decent living, and we could save some money.

As an Austrian, you were an enemy alien . . .

This was a strange thing. People at the immigration office weren't quite sure of official policy. I understand that some people who said they came from Austria were registered as Austrians and then were later not considered enemy aliens. Some officers said, "Austria doesn't exist anymore; you're a German." And these were registered as Germans and hence became enemy aliens. We Austrians never really knew for certain what we were considered! I had an interesting experience with this. I was driving a cab at night. As an enemy alien (perhaps!), I was under curfew and wasn't supposed to be out at night. One day there was a knock at the door and two or three people from the FBI were standing there. That was scary! But they were very nice. They asked me why I had immigrated and whether I was Jewish. Under what flag they put me or whether they made an exception for me, I don't know. They obviously found that I was not a danger driving a cab at night.

After immigration, did you speak German or English at home?

I really don't remember. It's very likely that we mixed the languages. As soon as we worked, we had to speak English. I know that some people got home from work and immediately started to talk German. I don't think that was the case with us. Bob was born in 1944. At that time I drove a cab. Magda did some leather or milliner work. When Bob started to speak with us, he didn't want German. He didn't even want to hear it. When we spoke German, he said, "Speak English!" That's why he never learned German. We didn't insist on it. It was too difficult to get him to learn German. That he asked us to speak English must mean that we spoke German sometimes.

176

How did you express your hatred of Germany during those years? Did you avoid German products, German people?

I didn't do anything like that. I said many times, if I would be able to catch an individual German who was my concentration camp boss, I probably could step completely out of character and kill him in cold blood. However, I refused to let the past bother me in the sense, let's say, not to buy a German car. I know people who couldn't understand when I bought a Volkswagen in 1966. I said, "Look, this VW is probably the best deal in a car that I ever made in my life. Why should Germany, that did so many bad things to me, also prevent me from getting that bargain?" I was rationalizing probably.

When you lived in Austria, did you have any close friends who were not Jewish, and if so, after immigration did you reconnect with any of them?

I was fairly close with one of my fellow students at the Technical Institute. In my opinion, he already showed very anti-Semitic tendencies at that time. Why we stayed the way we did, discussing philosophy as teenagers do, I don't know. There were no real friends. When I went back years later, I looked up class lists and got together with a few people with very limited success. You heard that from other people, probably. When you go back as an emigrant, many Austrians complain that they were not able to emigrate, that they had it so difficult. They point out that we got free and had it so good. They want to tell you what they went through during the war. They don't want to hear what you went through. If you had some relationships before, such discussions threaten to destroy them.

Do you have any idea what proportion of your Jewish friends in Austria survived the war?

I know of two who committed suicide shortly before or after the *Anschluss*. But I think that quite a few did emigrate.

In those years just after immigration, what was your attitude about being Jewish? How had your recent experiences affected it?

There is a story that might be peculiar to me. I grew up as a Lutheran. A few days after the last of my grandparents died (my mother's mother), my father picked up his three children (I was the middle one at age two) and had us baptized. He did this because he wanted our lives to be easier. I didn't go through any Jewish education. In school, during religion classes, I went with the Lutherans.

Did you know about your Jewish heritage?

Of course. I knew exactly. There were our relatives who were Jewish. So how could I not know? One of my uncles also got baptized. He was an officer in the Austrian army and in order to advance he could not be Jewish. That family baptized their son. He was sent to Buchenwald anyway. That uncle's wife never felt Jewish, but she was. She got deported, too. Anyway, my brothers and I knew where we came from. It just didn't get discussed. . . . My contacts in school were to a large extent Jewish.

Did you ever tell your classmates about your background?

I don't think so. I think I was ashamed. That's a wrong word. I was told in my family that it's easier not to be Jewish, not to be indoctrinated.

Here, kids always say to each other, "So what are you?" Didn't you get questioned?

Latent anti-Semitism existed in Austria long before there was any official talk about it. I think some friend of mine once said, "I think you're Jewish. You have dark hair." That guy became president of the Austrian National Bank.

Was there anything Jewish about your family life?

No. There were no *mezuzahs* [parchments with Old Testament verses in a small box, secured to the doorpost of Jewish homes]. There was nothing Lutheran either, except the Christmas tree. There was no religion whatsoever.

After Hitler invaded Austria, I went to temple and converted. That was not an act of heroism. I knew that even if I stayed Lutheran, that wouldn't save me. Had I thought that would allow me to live happily ever after in Nazi Germany, I don't know what I would have done. I'm very doubtful of my idealistic convictions. Maybe it was a protest. I said, in effect, "I know where I belong and don't care to belong anywhere else." That's the way I reconstruct it.

Why were you so certain that your heritage would be exposed?

Our house was already branded by the time I converted. Information about people was recorded very methodically. On *Kristallnacht*, they came to our house. Nobody told them we were Jewish. I don't know how they knew.

They were very efficient at these things. Whenever you applied for a job, you had to show your *Geburtszeugnis* [birth certificate], which stated religion. The Nazis could simply go to the birth records. The fact is, there was no way to escape. If I had applied for a job, I would have had to show my birth certificate. It was illegal to hire anybody who was not Aryan.

So when you and Magda married, you were Lutheran?

Yes, we married in 1935 in a civil marriage.

Did you feel good about your conversion back to Judaism?

Yes. I think it was the right thing to do. Without any other purpose, it was the honest thing to do.

When you came to Los Angeles, what did you do with your Jewishness?

I was really busy with just getting along. Religion never (before or afterward) was an important thing in my life. The conversion had really nothing to do with religion. My Jewishness is basically tradition, but not religious ritual tradition. It's my awareness of what Jews have contributed in the past and what part of society they are still in, what they do in medicine and physics and stuff like that. That's my Jewishness. That doesn't mean that I know all that much about Judaism. I read some now. But not like **Otto** [Wolman] or **Fritz** [Frankel]. They are mavens!

In Los Angeles, did you ever encounter any anti-Semitic incidents?

Most people I met were Jews. Initially, I worked in a Jewish business. But when I started to work at the cab company, I did find some anti-Semitism. The people who drove cabs at that time were a very mixed bunch. Some of them were Jews, some were immigrant actors between films or engagements. The I.Q. range was from way up, all the way down. There were some obnoxious Jews among them. I remember one who was really very hard to take, dishonest and everything else. On the other hand, there were some pretty high-class non-Jews. I think there was a Russian immigrant who used to be a count—very nice and intelligent. I found all shades of anti-Semitism there. Some was just slightly ironic, "Oh yea, you're a Jew." Or, hateful. Every shade was expressed.

Let's talk about the Gruppe. *What's your theory about how the* Gruppe *evolved? What did it provide for you? How did you get into it?*

The first people I met here were the **Wolmans,** Esslaus, and **Ikenbergs.** I don't know how or why they formed the *Gruppe.* I think I was present at the first meetings.

What was the purpose of the Gruppe, *in your opinion, and what did it provide for you at that time?*

People who are congenial like to get together and have an exchange of opinions. Some groups read books and discuss them. Others have topics to read up on and then discuss. Ours, like these, had social and special interest implications. I was happy to get together every month with people I liked and exchange opinions with them.

What did the Gruppe *do for you?*

It kept me in touch with friends. It was the only group anybody invited me to join!

Were most of your friends then from the Gruppe?

I think my social life was within this group mostly. I met some other people and dropped them. There were some others around, but this was the center of interest. By hindsight, I feel very much that it was like an extended family.

How did the Gruppe *continue to fit into your life during the subsequent 50 years, and in what way is it still important for you?*

It was a connection that I held on to. I had no reason to discontinue. More than that, I felt that's where I belonged. It was a common interest situation. We understood each other because of similar experiences. We could discuss our new experiences in this country. It was a natural. I can't give any logical reason.

A different kind of question: If somebody now asks, "What are you in terms of nationality?" I assume you respond, "American." At what point could you say that unequivocally?

I still can't say that. I have emotional ties to Austria. Even Bob does. On the other hand, he has no tie to Judaism. He was confirmed at the Wilshire Boulevard Temple because he wanted to go to Camp Kramer with a girl-friend!

Do you feel 100 percent at home in Los Angeles?

That is a problem. I'm completely used to living here, which has something to do with the fact that so many friends of mine are living here. But I'm very much in doubt about being at home here. I have complaints about the American lifestyle, the American psychology. But I adjust as well as I can.

Would you feel at home anywhere? What does it take for anyone to feel at home?

A sense of home is gone for us. You adapt to conditions and you live the best you can with your family and friends. You forget about defining what is really home.

Before you came to America, you must have had some idea what it would be like here. In what ways was it like and in what ways different from what you expected?

If I think back, I have the feeling that I didn't have time to even contemplate what it would be like. To begin with, I was scared to emigrate because I felt ill prepared. I expected it would be very difficult to make a living anywhere. So, wherever I was going to go, I didn't even try to think out in detail what the conditions would be like. I just thought it would be strange and difficult.

Is it so that you really didn't have any preconceptions of life here?

The only thing I knew was that blue-collar workers drove cars. This was not so in Europe. I also knew that street numbers went up to 20,000, which never happened anywhere in Europe!

When did you go back to Vienna? How did it feel when you did?

I went back the first time in 1965. I started out in Germany, where I bought a Volkswagen and traveled a bit. When I came to Vienna on the West Autobahn and saw the sign, "Wien," I had a very strange feeling. I can't say whether it was pleasant or unpleasant. It was just a very strange feeling. In Vienna itself, I looked up my old landmarks. I didn't have bad feelings about what happened to me. I closed them out of my mind. They were gone and didn't influence my life anymore. I found Vienna as beautiful as it ever was. I had no particular negative feelings. I still now enjoy going there every once in a while.

Did you wonder whether people you met or passed on the street were thinking, "Is he a Jew?"

Yes, and still do. And not only in Vienna. In both Austria and Germany, I go in the street and wonder about them, "What did he do during the Holocaust?" I judge the age and think how old he was then and I have certain feelings. The first time I came to Germany in a train from Amsterdam, I saw a station manager on the border. His behavior, stature, and uniform could have been that of a Nazi officer. I felt something strange. Just a first impression, just the minute I got into Germany. Later on I forgot about these feelings. Times have changed. People have changed.

Did you talk about the immigration years with Bob or other people? About Dachau?

We spoke of our previous life, as friends do. Particularly when you meet new people, you exchange your experiences. I was very free about talking about what happened in Dachau. In fact, I talked openly about it as long as I was still in Austria. People were amazed. I was probably very loose with my concern for safety. I had to talk about it, couldn't keep it in. When I got to Finland, I published an article about my experiences in the camp. I wrote it in English. It was translated and published in Finnish. Then I sent it to my brother who had gone to India, and it was published there in an English newspaper.

When did you tell Bob about your experiences?

That's difficult to remember. He was born four years after we came. Obviously for the first years, there was nothing we could tell him. Probably I was pretty negligent, because once when we talked about the concentration camps with other people, Bob was surprised when I said I had been in one. Then we started to talk about it. In his late teens, early 20s, he was very, very interested. A few years back he wanted to go with me to Dachau and we did go. In fact Bob and I were there together twice.

Magda and Frank Bauer, Los Angeles, 1987.

Is there someone, some incident, some words or some object that was of special significance in sustaining you through the immigration years?

If anything sustained me, it's that Magda was here with me throughout. She always stood by me, was unbelievably loyal, forgiving, and faithful.

MARTHA
SCHWARZ

Martha Schwarz left Vienna with her parents for Versailles, where a wealthy uncle had rented most of a hotel to house his relatives. But Martha was restless, and besides, she was engaged to a man who had already immigrated to Shanghai. Martha followed him, but by the time she arrived in port, she had concluded that he was not the right man for her. The right man, Kurt, did not come along for a few years. Meanwhile, Martha and a friend had established an international nursery school, which continued operation throughout the Japanese occupation. Martha and Kurt arrived in the United States with their son, Tom, in 1947, and subsequently had a daughter, Patricia.

My religious upbringing was really not Jewish. I grew up with a mixed group of friends. I can remember from junior high school there were girls that were anti-Semitic. I was aware of it, but it didn't affect me really. Most of my friends were Jewish, but I had other friends, too. I was not politically very interested at that time, so I wasn't part of a socialist movement or conservative movement or whatever. What interested me was music and theater and art.

I was involved with those things and having a good time. As I look back to the early years, I had a *very* good time. My education in art and music comes from being exposed to a tremendous amount of the very best. I still think back with fondness to this time. My mother was very bright and well educated. She tried to give me an awful lot of cultural education. She dragged me to concerts when I didn't want to go because I thought they were boring. And finally I enjoyed them. She knew what she was doing.

Did you study music privately or go to a conservatory?

I took some singing lessons. And I sang in a choir in big concerts, like under Bruno Walter and Wilhelm Mengelberg (who was a Nazi), and many other famous conductors. I enjoyed this very much. It was during the time just out of high school. I studied piano, but I was lazy and never practiced enough and never achieved anything. Every boy and girl from a middle-class Jewish family had to play an instrument, but it didn't always work out! What I really enjoyed was singing in the choir. That gave me a great deal. I did that until Hitler came and there was no more of it.

Was this a city choir?

In Vienna there were several choirs. It was not something that you got paid for. People sang for enjoyment. Some had done it for many, many years. In Vienna, the old ladies who had done it for 20 years were in the front row and the greenhorns were way back. There were several choirs you could join if you could read notes. I got into my choir through a friend who already sang in it.

What did you do during the day at that time?

I went to a commercial high school. I was sent to that school because my mother was a friend of the director of the school. I didn't particularly want to go there. I really wanted to be a social worker. I always liked to deal with people. So I graduated from the high school and went to work in my father's office. That was it. It was not all to my liking. At that time, you did what your parents told you to do.

What was your father's business?

He was in the wine wholesale business. There was an office with a head bookkeeper. I worked for him and am still in touch with him. But it was not something that I really wanted to do.

In 1938, what was happening in your life?

The morning after *Kristallnacht,* my sister and I stepped out of the streetcar at the terminal near where we lived outside the city. There were some SS men, and they said to me, "You come with me." My sister said, "I'll come along too." They said, "Not you." She looked less Jewish than I did, for some reason. She said, "Yes, I'm coming. I'm her sister." We were taken to a house and had to wash bathrooms. It was in a villa of some people that I knew who had left already and was not far from where we lived. After many hours, we could call my father. When he came, he was as white as my shirt and fuming.

When did you begin thinking about leaving the country?

Hitler came in March. Very shortly before that, we started thinking about it. Kurt, by the way, got out a week before Hitler came, with the idea of returning and getting his mother. That never happened.

Did you know Kurt at that time?

No, I met him later in Shanghai.

So when Hitler marched in, people realized that they better get out fast. What steps did you take?

We were lucky because my mother had a brother who was at that time in Paris, a director of Lever Bros. He brought out a great number of relatives. Not only us, but 50 other people. My uncle bribed the mayor of Versailles. We all went to a hotel in Versailles. Most of the hotel was taken up by our family!

My father's business had a branch in Fiume, Italy. My brother was on his own there. He had to flee from there and ended up, after a very difficult time, in Alexandria.

When did you leave Vienna?

We left on December 2, 1938. Many people left earlier than that, but it took us that long. At the German-French frontier, we had to get out of the train and we were frisked. We had to take off our clothes. Every toothpaste tube was squeezed to check that there were no diamonds inside. We missed the train to Paris. When we finally crossed the Rhine, my father spat into the river. I'll never forget it, because he was not that type of person. He was *so furious*. It's one of those little things that you still remember.

What were you allowed to take out with you?

Clothes. I don't know about jewelry. Maybe my mother wore some.

Any household goods?

No. My parents had two lift vans, and I had one which was supposed to go to Shanghai. I was engaged to somebody who had left earlier for Shanghai. So my mother gave me a lot of very beautiful things like Oriental rugs and silver, furniture—things for a *very* nice household. It was *all* stolen by the Nazis. We never got one thing of these lifts. Not my parents and not I. The people of this very big moving company were caught in Trieste.

I keep hearing the word "lift." How large is a lift?

It's very large, enormously large. You could put all the furniture of this room into it. It's like a big van.
So, the three lifts were all paid for, my parents' to France and mine to Shanghai. My parents' idea was to go to France with some of their possessions and then see what to do next. We had our clothes and very little money. Some people had money outside Austria, like a Swiss account. We didn't.

Before you left Vienna, did you have a visa for France and also one for China?

I had one for France. You didn't need one for China. What I had was a ticket for the boat, first class to China. (Why not use up some money?!)

Could anybody go to China at that time?

Yes, it was an open port. Twenty thousand went there—Germans, Austrians, Hungarians, Czechs, all those refugees. You just arrived and you could do whatever you wanted to. If I wanted to be a ballet dancer, I could! I decided to be a nursery school teacher, though I had no qualifications whatsoever. You didn't need any. You didn't have to have any certification. Nothing. You just opened the school! I opened a school with a friend who had some training.

Let's go back to Versailles for a moment, and then go with you to China.

We arrived there in the beginning of December. In February, my father took me to Genoa, to get a boat to China. My trip took 27 days. I arrived on March 29 or so. I had a stop in Port Said and saw my brother. He was at that time in Alexandria already. He had no money at all. I had a little bit, and gave it to him. It was the most dreadful encounter that I can remember. It was so sad. We were very close. He was two years older and we were very good friends as grown-ups. He was on board my ship for a couple hours. I never saw him again because he died at the age of 42. That meeting was very bitter. But the trip was interesting. The boat was full of refugees. We had great luxury going first class. I had a beautiful stateroom. That's when I saw my first big cockroach! Under different circumstances, the trip would have been wonderful.

I followed somebody to Shanghai. But I arrived in Shanghai to say no to this man. I was not going to marry him.

You felt that when you arrived?

I felt that it was absolutely wrong and I wasn't going to do it.

You knew that the minute you arrived or before?

I had my doubts already. Somehow I was young enough to be adventurous and to want to see what the world was like. And thinking back, I wanted to break away from my family and to be on my own. I was always a rebel, in a way. I was very close to my mother, and it was very hard to say good-bye to her because she wasn't well. She had a very bad heart condition. I knew I wouldn't see her again, and I didn't. She died at the age of 58, the day that Kurt and I decided to get married. She didn't know about us. We didn't know about her.

So I arrived in Shanghai and was picked up by this fiancé of mine. I told him that I had changed my mind. I didn't know a soul except this young man and his group of friends. After my announcement, they were all against me. I found an ad in the paper that some English people wanted their four-year-old to learn German. I answered, got the job, and we became very good friends.

Did that happen immediately?

Pretty soon, because I needed to make some money. I needed to do something. The woman was half English and half Danish and her husband was

English. His father was British consul general in Peking. They were very involved with Chinese culture.

Did you live with this family?

No, but we became very good friends. This was high society. It was colonial life still when I came. It was already Japanese occupied, but there was still the British club. The family went to northern China every summer, and I went, too. I didn't stay with them, but had a room with an Australian brother and sister. So, I gave German lessons to Anthony Frazier and French lessons to an Italian-American girl, also the child of people from Shanghai who summered at this beautiful seaside resort. Wealthy people stayed in their own houses there, not hotels. They had servants and such. I had it very nice and had a lot of fun. I had practically no money but it didn't matter. I was young enough to have fun. This was the summer of '39. While we were there, the war broke out in Europe. The Fraziers wanted to go back to Shanghai. We all went back to Shanghai on a boat with room for 80 people, and we were 160. Everybody crammed into whatever ship they could catch. Supposedly, there were German raiders in the China Sea and it was blackout. It was not a nice trip back.

The parents of the little Italian-American girl engaged me as governess. I took it so I could have a roof over my head in a plush house. I had never done anything like that before and felt imprisoned. They were impossible people and very crude. The wife was very beautiful and remote. Her husband was rich and had race horses. There was lots of money but this didn't impress me. I didn't like the tone in the house. I lived there, but insisted that I could go out every night. There were lots of servants, so that was no problem. In the meantime, I had found other Viennese people and made my own circle of friends. One night, I couldn't get back into the house. The compound had high walls, and the caretaker lived in a little house at the entrance. It was midnight when I came home and he didn't hear me; he was a little deaf. I couldn't get in and had to go back to my friends. I decided, "This is it." I didn't go back to my governess job, just told them good-bye.

I had already talked to a girlfriend about opening a nursery school together. She was going to train me. I had no idea what to do. I liked children OK, and that was about it. She was in the process of getting a divorce and had a house we could use for the school. You didn't own a house in Shanghai. First of all, nobody had the money. Secondly, you could only rent. So I moved into my friend's house and lived in what was called the French Concession.

We opened the nursery school on January 1, 1940, with four children, one little table, and four little chairs. The next month, we had eight children, and so on. We lived there and had the school there. Downstairs was the living room/dining room and kitchen, and upstairs were two bedrooms. And then there was another staircase up to the servants' quarters. Servants were very inexpensive. It was no luxury to have a cookboy and an *amah* (nurse-maid), which we had.

We were very successful. And had fun. The school grew and grew. We were very quickly well known. We had all the British, Americans, Scandinavians, Italians, French, Swiss, you name it we had them—27 different nationalities through the years.

Pretty soon after we opened the school, Anne Marie, my friend and co-teacher, got polio. I had to close the school immediately. The parents had to make a decision whether to let their children continue. No doctor could tell me how polio is transmitted. The top pediatrician said to wash all the furniture with permanganate. I had a Viennese friend who offered me her house to use and continue the school. Many parents were frightened and didn't send their children back. But with a group of children, I was able to carry on. None of the children got polio. Eventually Anna Marie got better and she started helping. She was limping and wasn't the same anymore, but she had enormous energy to get well. We moved the school back into her house. It was tough—and that happened just when we started to really make a good go of it.

What happened to your school during wartime?

We had the school throughout the war, except we were not allowed to charge tuition in American dollars. Because inflation was so horrible, the money we took in became less and less. We made good money in the beginning, but it then sort of disintegrated. We still made a meager living, but it wasn't great. But we were enthusiastic and we were young enough.

Did you continue living with Anne Marie throughout this period?

Yes. In the meantime, I met Kurt. He had come with a friend from England because the British were interning every German and Austrian in England. They were sent to the Isle of Man or someplace and put in camps. Kurt and his friend wanted to escape this and didn't want to wait any longer for their quota number for the U.S. They had come via Canada to Shanghai, to continue waiting for their quota numbers and affidavits. A friend came to me one day and said, "I'm picking up two fellows from the boat. Let's take them to a nice Chinese restaurant and show them how to eat with chopsticks." That's how Kurt and I met!

We got married in '43. Anne Marie had a boyfriend and married soon afterward. Then we were two couples living in the house. We were living

Martha Schwarz and her husband, Kurt, Shanghai, China, 1943.

downstairs in a corner with a folding bed. We could not be sick because the school was in that same space. In the morning, the houseboy would come, put the bed together, and we were ready for school!

Kurt lived with me in the house already before we were married. That was very unusual at that time. Kurt had already been engaged in England to a girl. I think he would have been too decent to drop her. But a cable came telling him, "We don't know when this war is going to be over and I found somebody else, so good-bye." It was fine for us! Kurt was hoping for that. We continued living together and felt better. A month later, we got married. It's interesting how these things happen!

We had no family, only each other. But we had a very nice circle of friends by that time. We couldn't go out of town because it was Japanese occupied. We couldn't even go on a two-day honeymoon. We were imprisoned in the city. Kurt had all kinds of jobs. There are many rich stories I could tell.

The war years were very trying. The military occupation of Shanghai became threatening to our livelihood and home. We were constantly asked to prove that the nursery school was still in operation and was needed in the community. A Japanese general once came to the house and said he wanted it. Luckily, we never heard from him again. It was living from day to day with lots of anxiety and threats. Tom was born a week before the war ended. We were still in the hospital when Japan surrendered. The transition period from Japanese occupation forces to the takeover by Chinese civilians was difficult. Yet it went smoother than we all thought it would. The Japanese were disciplined and avoided confrontations with the very angry Chinese.

My uncle George, who had gotten my family to Versailles in 1938, had by this time settled successfully in Beverly Hills, California. He wrote that he had an apartment for us above his garage. So in 1947, we took a boat from Shanghai to San Francisco. The boat was an American military transport ship, not converted to a passenger boat. I was with 20 women and children in one cabin and Kurt was with 30 men in another cabin. The trip was not enjoyable! The advantage was that we had a dining room and were served by stewards and didn't have to go with a little bowl and pick up food. There were three of us to take care of two-year-old Tom. We had a friend on the same boat and the three of us would take turns because it was so strenuous to supervise him. There was always one person on duty. Tom was only OK when he was asleep. Otherwise, he was on the go, and there were many holes through which he could fall into the ocean.

It was a beautiful arrival going through the Golden Gate Bridge. It's something that one cannot forget. It was a beautiful, sunny day, August 20, 1947. We were picked up by an aunt of mine who just happened to be on a visit in San Francisco. We stayed in the Berkeley hills for three weeks. Little Tommy was very thin and the mother of our friend, Max Knight, was a very good cook. She made chicken soup and all kinds of goodies for him. He gained weight. Then we proceeded by train to Los Angeles and our new home in Beverly Hills.

From my memory of that house, your uncle must have been doing very well.

He did very well in Europe as director of Lever Bros. He and his wife left Paris when they saw what was happening.

I hated being in Beverly Hills because I didn't fit in. I was the poor relative, in the true sense of the word. We had no car. Kurt immediately rented an office, but it took time for business to get going. I remember times when we sat at the beach and said, "What are we going to do now?" He thought of going to library school and becoming a librarian. But he said, "I can't afford it because I have a family and I must make money. Who would pay for it?"

What was he doing in his office?

He continued in the rare book business—something that he always did. He had his Ph.D. in art history and was a very well-educated man. His father was originally a physician, but was interested in the history of medicine and wrote his dissertation on a very precious Wurzburg manuscript. He never practiced medicine and became a rare book dealer. (So Tom is third generation in the rare book business.) Kurt immediately started with the rare book business because this is what he knew. He knew already rare book people here by correspondence, from when he was in Vienna. He borrowed money and traveled. He had many business friends and got books on consignment.

When you came to Los Angeles, how did you express your hatred of Germany?

We *never* spoke German with Tom. That's why he never learned. We couldn't bring ourselves to speak German. Other parents did. I hated that German and we always spoke English.

Was that true already in Shanghai?

Yes. Kurt and I spoke English to each other. We both spoke English professionally and it came very natural. Maybe sometimes when we were with other Viennese we spoke German, but we didn't want to because we just hated everything German. To this day, I don't understand my friends in New York. They continue to speak German. They find that I am a snob when I want to speak English! So with them I speak German. When I'm with other Germans and Austrians here, I speak English. I have no desire to speak German.

When did you go back to Vienna for the first time, and how did that feel?

I went back in '61. (Kurt was there already in '51 on business.)

What was it like for you when you went?

Very emotional. I went back to my old house. It was full of bullet holes, and I wish I hadn't gone there. It was very disturbing. Kurt and I were there with both children, and we stayed for a week or two. I could hardly wait to get out of Vienna. I hated it. But I've been back since, again in '66, '75, and then the last time in '88. I don't think I'll go again. I bought some fabric and a replacement for a lamp. That was the reason I went back to Vienna last time! You can only get Augarten in Vienna.

When you were there, did you look up any people?

Yes, old friends. One who was not Jewish. And some Jews who had gone back—one who had lived in Manila, another who was in Shanghai and had gone back. He had lumberyards and was very well-to-do. His family got everything back and lived very well. I personally would never live in Vienna again.

Once you left Vienna, tell me what your feelings were about being Jewish.

It changed. I'm more Jewish than I was.

I don't mean now, but rather from the time in Vienna to the first years after immigration.

I always knew that I was Jewish. There was no doubt in my mind. But I was not a practicing Jew because I wasn't brought up that way. I had Christmas at home, not Chanukah.

Once you left Vienna, did you feel more Jewish?

Yes, absolutely. It became more and more pronounced.

What does that mean?

That I felt much closer to Judaism.

Once you had children, did you then celebrate some Jewish holidays?

No. Our children went to a school run by the Ethical Culture Society [an organization of Jews and Christians] because we wanted them to have some kind of religious education. Tom had Bible lessons because that's part of education, religion or no religion. I would do it differently today. I would give them a Jewish education and let them then decide what they want. But that's what we did. This was a joint decision between Kurt and me.

Were your first friends in Los Angeles mostly Jews?

My friends were all kinds of people. That was how it always was. I was accepted. Nobody ever said, "You are Jewish." **Marianne** and **Otto** were among the very first. Marianne called me. Somehow she got hold of our phone number. She called and said, "Was your maiden name Salzer?" And I said, "Yes." "Well, then it's you!" They were very nice to us. And through them, we met people in the *Gruppe*. Then, through Kurt's connections at

UCLA, we got to know some librarians, work colleagues, and people like that. They were mostly not Jewish.

You were latecomers to the Gruppe. *Did you go to* Gruppe *meetings regularly once you joined?*

No. Only once or twice.

How, then, did you get to know the people in the Gruppe?

Otto knew that **Fritz Frankel** and Kurt went to elementary school together and brought them together. They hadn't seen each other since elementary school. That was quite a few years! I met the **Sommers** through the Ethical Culture Society. I didn't know all the people in the *Gruppe*. We had no car and lived far from everybody else. It was very difficult. We were still struggling to establish ourselves here.

When you get together on New Year's Eve still now, when some of the old members get together, what does it feel like for you?

It feels comfortable.

When you are asked, "What are you?" or "What is your nationality?" do you easily answer, "I am an American"? Do you really feel that you are, or do you qualify it?

I usually say, "I'm an American, and I'll never lose my Viennese accent."

Do you feel 100 percent at home in Los Angeles?

Yes, even with the smog.

How long did it take to feel this way?

That's very hard to say. I hated living on Greenbrae Drive in Beverly Hills. As soon as I had a house of my own in 1957, then I felt I was my own person and had a real home. That was very important for me.

During your first years here, did you encounter any anti-Semitic incidents?

No. I was always aware that it exits, but personally nobody has ever said anything to me.

Before you left Vienna and also when you were in China, what ideas did you have about what America would be like?

There were some very funny things. In Shanghai, we couldn't afford coffee. It was too expensive on the black market. So we drank tea every morning. We were dreaming of having real good coffee every morning. And that's what we had when we came.

So America meant "coffee"?

America meant a place to get things that we couldn't get in the other countries.

Anything else that you imagined?

I was very apprehensive about living in my aunt's house. I knew her. It turned out to be worse than I thought it would be. But I liked my uncle very much, and as long as he was alive it was OK. At least, I was willing to swallow hard. But when he died, it became very difficult. Kurt, who was a much better person than I am, said to me, "You just have to wait." He pushed me through those difficult times. I would have rebelled much more. He had more decency, and he was more realistic about things.

America meant starting all over again. I wondered how it would be. And when I came, I was such a greenhorn. I remember I brought some petit point handbags and went to Bullocks [a department store] thinking I could sell them there!

You said earlier that in Vienna there was always laughter in your home . . .

Not always laughter, but there was a great sense of humor, particularly in my mother. On Sunday, everybody had guests. My father played bridge and my mother had somebody over. We were three children, and each one could have friends over. There was a buffet for everybody, which was much too rich and much too good. It was the cause of an obese family!

Martha and Kurt Schwarz, Los Angeles, 1984.

What I wanted to ask is whether you think that sense of humor and playfulness made it somehow easier for you to make some of the adjustments of immigration that were so traumatic for many people?

Absolutely. Everyone in my mother's family had a sense of humor. My uncle had a very great sense of humor. Tom has it, too. To some people, it might seem superficial or out of place, or they are offended by it. I find it very helpful.

Do you think that there's anything else about you, in your personality, that made the extreme adjustments of immigration possible?

Immigration was a challenge. I had to prove myself. When I wrote to my family that I had broken my engagement, I got letters saying, "Come back!" I wrote back that I was not returning to a burning Europe. A very strange correspondence developed because they wanted me to come back to Europe. I knew that would be *crazy*. Also, it was a challenge that I wanted. I often think about it.

Is there somebody, some incident, some words, or some object that was of special significance in sustaining you through the immigration years? You went all by yourself to Shanghai. Where did you get your strength and courage?

I have little things from my mother still, unimportant things that felt important. I have some cookbooks that have her name in them. I was very close to my mother. My friends from Vienna days talk about my mother and how they enjoyed her company. I remember that some of them brought her flowers, and that annoyed me no end. They would come to my house and bring my mother flowers instead of me! They liked her. It was a great compliment. Now I laugh when I think about it. She was very popular because she could tell good stories and then she pretended to be shocked if something was a little off color. We would say, "Let's go and shock mother," and we'd make up some silly story. We had a lot of fun in our house. There was a lot of humor, and for that I'm very thankful.

JOHN LESSER

JOHN LESSER

John Lesser was the last Jew to take—and pass—the law bar exam in Vienna. A few months later, he and his lawyer wife, Ruth, were out of the country. With permission, they flew to Switzerland; by train, it would have been more likely to have difficulty at the border. The wait for visas to the United States continued while the Swiss government pressured John and Ruth to leave the country. Under the guise of Ruth needing therapeutic baths in France, they received the requisite medical certificate and were able to move on. And eventually, on to the United States, where they had one son, Tom.

I got a doctorate of law in 1933 from the University of Vienna. I worked for the court, as was customary then, partly mandatory. You had to work for one year as sort of a court clerk. You took the state bar five years later. It's a very odd setup. I had known Ruth already at that time. She graduated in '34 with the same degree.

Were you students together?

John Lesser and his wife, Ruth, on their wedding day, Vienna, 1934.

No. The way we met might be quite interesting. I was in the second year of law school and Ruth was in the first year. The system was that you had to pass exams. You didn't have to go to lectures. She never did. But the time came, about three months before the first oral exam, which was pretty tough, that Ruth decided she needed help in preparation. She had a girlfriend who had gone to the same high school that I did. This girl told her that she knew me and perhaps I would want to help. So we had an appointment at the university and we met. I tutored her for about six weeks. I got paid pretty well. I needed that money.

We got married in 1934, after her graduation. Then, like me, she had to serve in court. The problem was to get a job with an attorney. We had to be in court for at least one year, but we could stay for another two years. Altogether, we had to have five years of practice. So, you had to be with another attorney for one or two of these five years. That was very difficult to get. Some people not only didn't get paid by the attorneys, but had to pay them to get a job as an assistant lawyer! Ruth did get a job before Hitler came. She worked with a lawyer in the twentieth district for six months, and I worked with an attorney in the first district for about three years.

You had to take the bar exam five years after completion of law school. You had to know lots of historical things, like church law and old German law, not the current law. In preparation, I went to a class. I studied and took my written exam at the end of March and the oral exam at the beginning of April 1938. Hitler was already in power. I had spent two years working all day long and studying at night. I can't say that I predicted what was coming. I feel that was very stupid of me. Anyway, I was the last Jew to take the bar exam. I could take it because I had already been issued a date for it. There were two of us taking it together. The other fellow came in with a "Heil Hitler." I just stood there. The two examiners were actually quite pleasant.

I passed the exam very well. That gave me the right to be a criminal lawyer. But in order to be a lawyer in civil cases, you had to remain with your lawyer for an additional two years. I was able to practice law with him for one month, until the beginning of May. During that time, I went once to the appeals court in the name of my senior lawyer. But after the first week of May, Jews were not allowed to practice anymore. From that time on, Ruth and I tried to get out of the country. I went to consulates every day.

So it was the loss of your positions that mobilized you to seek a way out of the country?

Now we knew what we were facing. We tried to get visas and couldn't. Not to anywhere. It was dangerous to walk on the streets of Vienna because they picked up Jewish boys. They closed off the street and took the Jews away. Nobody in their families knew what had happened or where they were. I was lucky it seems. We lived in a good district, where we had our own apartment. But to go from consulate to consulate, I had to go downtown and stand in lines. Finally, my father-in-law, who was a Polish citizen and had deposited some money in Switzerland, got us permission to go there.

Where was he at the time?

He was in Vienna, but as a Polish citizen he had no problems at that time. They didn't bother with aliens, only with those who were citizens of Austria. In August, we finally got tickets and left by plane. We didn't want to go by train because some people who did were picked up at the border and sent back.

Was what you were doing entirely legal?

Oh yes. We took our 10 or 20 shillings, all that was allowed, and our luggage and left. We had a very tearful good-bye with my parents, who took us to Schottenring, where we picked up the bus to the airport. My parents remained, alone. I was one of three sons. My oldest brother had died about four months before Hitler came of a disease that would be completely curable today. He was a doctor of law in Paris and was visiting at home when he got a streptococcal infection. His death left my parents in very bad shape. My second brother was a medical doctor, and he left Vienna before me. He had a connection with the British Consulate and got a visa to go as a teacher to Scotland. He taught at the university there. Later on, he got a position at USC here in Los Angeles—of all things, in pharmacology. Once he got permission to practice here, he became a surgeon and quite famous. So I was the last of the sons to leave and my parents were alone. It was very tough. That was August 1938.

We stayed in Switzerland, but the Swiss were very unpleasant. They pestered the life out of us to leave the country, although we had a deposit of about $4,000. They gave us at first two months, then another two weeks. As a rule, as long as you had money, they left you alone for a while. But they kept asking us to leave. We applied for American visas. I was on the Polish quota and Ruth was on the German one. (My family had immigrated to Austria in 1914. Ruth's parents, although Polish, had been studying at the university in Berlin when she was born.) So we were on different quotas. I didn't want to leave her alone and I didn't want to go by myself. When your visa came through, if you didn't use it in about four months you lost it. My father, despite the danger, was meanwhile running to the American Consulate in Vienna, trying to help us.

I found a school friend in Zurich. I told him my problems with the Swiss. I knew that sometimes they even sent people back. This friend had an idea. He said that there was a French consul in Laussane who was extremely nice. He thought that man might get us permission to go to France while waiting for the visas. I went to see him by myself. He was very pleasant. He asked, "How is your wife? Does she need baths in Aix les Bains?" That's a health resort in France that has all sorts of therapeutic baths!

I understood his suggestion. A cousin of Ruth's, a doctor, was in Switzerland, and he gave her a certificate that she needed these baths. That's how we got visas to France! We left Switzerland after four months and went to France. Thanks to money from my father-in-law, we didn't starve. We didn't have everything we wanted, but we had an apartment and spent the winter in Aix les Bains. Then I got my visa to the United States. Ruth didn't. We were wiring to my parents and my father tried everything. It didn't come. We were in Paris when it finally came. I had to go back to Chambery every two weeks to get permission to stay a bit longer. Then that was over. We got on a boat in Le Havre and were seasick the whole way—for 10 days. We were on the *Champlain,* a big boat that was sunk later on. It was January '39. We knew it would be a rough trip, but one didn't worry about such things. We had to get out! We arrived in New York at the end of the month. When we arrived, Albert Einstein was there waiting for some family of his. He was wearing sandals and was dressed very casually.

How had you gotten your affidavits?

We got those through a distant cousin of my father's who was in Los Angeles. My brother was already there and talked to him.

Did your parents remain in Vienna?

They went first to Finland. My mother's brother was chief rabbi in Finland, Dr. Federbusch. He was a scholar and wrote many Hebrew books. Despite his position, he couldn't get Ruth and me into Finland. But later, in 1939, he was able to bring my parents there. Ruth's parents were in Paris. They had an apartment there and didn't want to leave. We Jews think we're very smart! We're not always very smart. Sometimes we're very dumb! I don't consider myself generally as a very dumb person. But I was sitting for two years studying every night for a bar examination when Hitler was already in Germany, and saying, "It won't happen here." Stupidity exists!

It seems like denial to me.

It is *stupid.* But *nobody* expected it. Even in '39, nobody expected the Holocaust. We didn't know how far those people would go. We still thought they were human beings. Schuschnigg didn't know either, until Hitler slapped him in his face by taking over the Austrian government.

What happened when you got to New York?

It was the end of January 1939. We got a room without a bath, because we didn't have any money. My father-in-law knew somebody in New Jersey, just across the Hudson, who had a wax refining plant. I got a small office job there. That went on for about a year. My brother was here in Los Angeles, living alone. He pestered me every day. He said we shouldn't stay in New York, that it's so beautiful in California, that something would work out. We decided to visit first. After that visit, we decided to move. We took a train and came to Santa Monica. I remember we were all at the beach during the Pearl Harbor attack. I tried to find some work. That man who gave us the affidavits had markets here. I talked to him and he was actually very nice. But he wanted me to work in a market by starting as a boy who puts things on the shelf. I refused to do that. We still had some means to survive. We had a small apartment for $37 a month and some money that Ruth's father sent. That man had a friend who had a bottling company and needed somebody in the office. I took that job and earned $20 a week by keeping track of inventory.

Eventually, I sent tickets for my parents and they came here from Finland via Cuba. In Cuba, they waited for visas to the United States. I eventually got also Dr. Federbusch here, again through Cuba. I give my father all the credit in the world for what happened to me from then on. He was a very smart fellow, very devoted to me. I had a splendid idea at that time which

I think was partly his idea. We were talking about all sorts of things. He spoke a very broken English. But he made his real estate license and was quite successful as a broker. He helped me get started in my business.

I took out all the licenses that were available! That was in 1940. I got a real estate license, which was very simple. Then I wanted to get the general contractor's license. I found out that what you had to do was to look at a plan and figure out the lumber to use. I didn't know anything about this. I talked to some friends about this problem, including a lawyer. This man referred me to an architect he knew, **Fritz Frankel.** So I called him up. He said right away, "Let's sit down together." He turned out to be one of the finest guys I've met in my life. I don't say that easily of anybody. He is a very unusual human being.

After about 10 lessons, I passed the test and took out the B1 license. I made my whole financial career by building and acquiring real estate. I also took out an insurance license. That didn't require experience. If you passed the test, you got the license. So I had all those licenses.

Again, my father helped me, and he said, "Why don't you buy an apartment building?" I responded that I had no money. He said, "We'll figure out something." He found a building for us and it was the first of many that we bought. It's a four-story brick building in Beverly Hills. The seller was a very famous, Jewish, film producer. He was a very well-known man in the community here, in Jewish circles. The building had a lot of vacancies and the man wanted to sell it. We wanted to buy it. My father-in-law, meanwhile, had gotten to America and he had some money. But the man didn't want to sell to us. He said, "I think it's a lemon and I don't want to sell it to you because you're refugees." But, we talked him into it and we bought the building. We had to invest $15,000. My father insisted that my father-in-law would put up the whole $15,000 and that I eventually pay him back one third of that for my portion. I managed the building and, within three or four years, paid him back the $5,000. So, that's how it all started. We sold that building just after Ruth died in 1986, for $1.5 million.

Did you ever want to practice law again?

I did, but the state of California wouldn't even recognize my high school diploma! In addition, I didn't think that the position of lawyer in the United States was on the same level as in Europe. Here, it is a business position. I felt I could be a businessman without having an American law degree.

This is a more personal question. What about you, your personality, your style, made it possible for you to get through the difficulties you encountered during those transition years when you came here?

206

Necessity. Just doing what had to be done. Ruth was very helpful in that respect. I had a modest life in Vienna. She didn't. But she accepted whatever came. We didn't starve. We had what we needed. In the beginning, before I started work, we spent days in movie theaters, just to get acquainted with the American language!

What was it like being an enemy alien during the war years?

I never had any problem. I was drafted, but wasn't taken because of a prior injury. In 1943, I played tennis and a ball hit my eye. I was taken to the hospital and had 10 days of high fever that they gave me in order to absorb the blood in my eye. It was typhoid fever. I was pretty good for a while, but about a year later I developed a detachment of the retina and had surgery. When I went before the draft board, the doctor wouldn't take me. Otherwise they probably would have taken me into the war.

What were your feelings then, about being an Austrian?

I wasn't a patriot of Austria. I always felt the Austrians were worse than the Germans. I had no feelings for them. I had feelings for Vienna which is very beautiful. But the people who lived there didn't mean anything to me. I had enough of anti-Semitism at the university. I was the head of the *Juristenverein,* a Zionist group at the university, for many years. I met with top people like Cardinal Initzer. Later, he developed into a miserable anti-Semite. I was very active. We were beaten up quite often at the university. That was even before Hitler. I belonged to a Zionist fraternity too. Most Jewish fellows belonged to the Social Democrats. I refused to do that.

During your first years here, how did you express your hatred of the Germans? Did you boycott German goods or avoid Germans if you came into contact with them?

I didn't meet any. As far as goods are concerned, I still boycott them. I won't go out and buy any foreign products, German especially. I would never buy a Japanese car and I asked my son not to buy one. He said he doesn't want to have so many repairs. I told him I don't care even if I have repairs. I'm grateful to this country and I'll do anything that I can to help this country.

Would you have gone to a concert if there were a German conductor?

I wasn't crazy to go to a concert of Mr. Karajan. But otherwise, you can't hold it against every one of them. That goes too far.

Once you got to the States, did you speak only English or did you mix languages?

With Tom, we spoke only English. He doesn't understand German. With Ruth, sometimes I spoke German, but we tried to speak English.

Did you want Tom to learn German?

No. There was no reason for it. If we had some secrets, we could speak in German!

What was it like for you the first time you returned to Vienna?

I still liked the city. I went to see the apartment that we built and they let us look at it. I went to the cemetery because my brother is buried there. But I had no feeling for the country. I never had it when I lived there.

If somebody asks you, "What nationality are you?" do you say unequivocally, "American"? If so, when did you begin to feel that way?

Immediately, when I got my citizenship.

At what point did you feel really at home in this country?

I think since I arrived here. I know that there's probably anti-Semitism in this country too, but I never felt it.

You never had any direct experience with it?

No, not major experiences. Maybe somebody made a remark or so, but those things enter one ear and go out the other. I don't pay any attention to those things. People that are tired sometimes don't know what they are saying. But generally, I didn't have any bad experiences. I think this country was very good to me and I appreciate it. I had non-Jews as partners. Never had any problems.

Once you left your roots, so to speak, what was your attitude about being Jewish?

I was Jewish all my life. That's why I never felt that I was an Austrian. I spoke the language, but never felt at home there. I enjoyed the city, the theaters, and the opera. I enjoyed to live there. It was very pleasant living there. But the people were just miserable, as far as I could see.

Did you assume that you would remain there all your life?

Maybe I had too, but it wasn't easy. Sometimes a forceful exit is a blessing! I'm sure that I succeeded much more in this country than I would ever have there. I would probably have been a small lawyer there, not because I wasn't capable, but because of the anti-Semitism in courts and among potential clients. Gentiles just didn't take a Jewish lawyer. A big company wouldn't take a Jewish lawyer either. So I never had any special feeling about Austria. I was born there, and that's it. I was very strongly Jewish from the beginning of my life, although not religious. I was very active in Jewish affairs.

When you got here, did you join a synagogue?

No. I joined for a while later, but not as an active member because I was never religious. I joined Rabbi Sonderling's [**Gerty Frankel**'s uncle's] synagogue. I like him. I met with him very often privately. We studied together. He was a very learned man and I enjoyed it. He knew that I knew what I was talking about. I studied Bible and Talmud all my life. But I never was religious. My parents remained 90 percent kosher, but I never was.

I'm interested in your connection to the Gruppe. *What did it mean for you to be part of the* Gruppe? *What was the* Gruppe *like?*

I got into the *Gruppe* and enjoyed it very much. I enjoyed the interchange of opinions. I, like everyone else, delivered lectures several times and partici-pated in a lot of discussion, mainly because I'm pretty conservative in my political ideas. I had very strong discussions, but no fighting, with Eisgrau. He was completely opposite in his opinions from me. I'm sure that I didn't convince him, and he didn't convince me! And sometimes with **Bauer,** who was pretty much on the other side, too. I was the one in the *Gruppe* that was more to the right than the others. I enjoyed the discussions because I was used to doing that in Vienna where I was the head of a group in which we had lots of discussions between the Leftist Jews and the national Jews who were very interested in Palestine.

Although the Gruppe, *per se, doesn't exist anymore, how is it still important to you? Do you have a special feeling about these people?*

John and Ruth Lesser, Los Angeles, 1983.

I don't know exactly when they stopped meeting. Maybe they continued even after we didn't come anymore. We went for at least 10 years. When the **Frankels** lived on Rimpau, we used to meet with the them almost every day, for a while. I don't know why it broke up. Fritz doesn't know either. Maybe it was something between the women. There are a few people for whom I have special feelings—Frankels, **Wolmans** (even if I don't see them very often). We were very close with the **Bauers,** who flew with us quite often in our plane when Ruth and I were pilots.

Before you got to the United States, you must have had some ideas about what this country would be like. In what ways was it similar and what ways unlike your expectations?

I had no ideas about this country. I didn't even know where Hollywood was! We were never taught any geography or history of this country. To me, it was just the only country I could get into. I had never met anybody who had been here. It was *the* country that wanted me—well, allowed me, to come in.

Are you anything like the person you expected to be?

No. I was much more serious when I was young. I was a very serious student. At the moment, I feel completely different about life. It should be enjoyed, day by day.

When did this transition occur?

Perhaps when we started flying. We really thought it was a great pleasure every weekend to go to the airport and to go off to see something. We were both nature lovers (I still am) and liked to walk around in it. I spent my youth studying and not enjoying life. I guess the study was my enjoyment. And I went to theaters and operas for enjoyment in the evenings. But I didn't really have the means to do that. Mostly I studied. I don't say I was forced to do that. I liked to do it. But in this respect I changed. My outlook on life is completely different.

Do you think this was Ruth's influence?

Tragedy brings you to that change. After Ruth died [in 1986], I didn't complain or cry. I wasn't a burden to anybody, including my son. I just decided I had to continue. I'm leading a very nice life now. Much better than I thought I would do and better than other people thought I would do.

Did you talk to Tom at all about the immigration years?

Not in detail, but generally.

Do you remember when you began to tell him a little about your past?

Maybe when he was 20 or 25 years old, if he wanted some information like what I did over there. But it had nothing to do with emotions, just facts.

Perhaps you didn't choose to come forward with the emotions?

He wouldn't have understood. Some things cannot be explained. For example, you get into a situation where you know that your life is at stake and you decide either to give up and wait until you are killed, or you take the risk and go into the city and try to get a visa. If you don't get it, you come home and you're surprised that you're alive the next day. We saw Nazis coming into our house twice. I got rid of them, somehow. It was a matter of luck. We were very nice with the manager of the building and she said she wouldn't let anybody hurt us. Things just happen. We had a building there and we had an apartment. They wanted to force us to throw a Jew out. I had a small car which they took away. I adjusted to all that.

It sounds like you took each piece, step by step, and did whatever you had to.

That's what I did all my life. That's what I'm doing now.

How do you feel about having questions like these asked of you?

I feel fine. I'll be glad to answer any questions. No secrets. My life is open.

ANNIE AND JOSEPH "SEPP" LAMPL

Competitive sport was central to the lives of Annie and Sepp Lampl. Both trained at the Jewish Sports Club in Vienna: she, primarily a swimmer; he, a champion fencer. Annie was barely out of high school, still carrying the dream of going to America for a honeymoon, at the time of the Anschluss. *Sepp, already an engineer, was prepared and able to leave almost immediately. Annie's departure came later, and while America was no honeymoon, for Sepp it was the place in which he was able to fulfill his dream of working in the aircraft industry. They had two sons, John and Lanny.*

ANNIE: I was going to high school, but that was not my major interest. I was very involved in sports. Both my sister and I were members of the Hakoah, the only sports club in Vienna that produced young people who had national success, some even international success. There were any number of Jewish sports people trained there who were Olympic champions. In 1932

Lanny Lampl, Annie and Sepp's son, conducted most of this interview.

there was a wrestler who won in the Los Angeles games. There was a fencer, now in the United States, who won in 1938. There were quite a few Jewish athletes representing Austria in the Olympic games prior to Hitler.

Sport was something that made it possible for me to be involved outside the home. My home was not a happy place. My mother was sick as long as I can remember, in and out of hospitals during those years. My father was hardly ever there. He was away on business being a representative of one of the largest lumber exporting companies in Austria, traveling around all the Mediterranean, including Palestine, selling Austrian lumber. So my sister and I were pretty much on our own with our family cook/governess, with whom we were very good friends. Three times a week, I went to swimming training for two or three hours; summer, winter, and in-between. I competed in many swimming competitions and got several medals. I also did some track and field, and once won the 100-meter run across Vienna. I was the first to win among young people under 18. Our social activities were exclusively centered around sports. I met Sepp there, my sister met her first husband there. Sports was really the life we led. That was our major, major interest. In the winter we went skiing. If it wasn't with the ski classes offered by the school system, we went skiing with the same group of youngsters from the sport club to various places in the Alps for Christmas and Easter.

When at 13 and 14 my sister and I decided to join a sport club, we thought where we could go. There were only three very prominent clubs in Vienna. One was a Nazi club, so that was out. The Vienna Athletic Club was a very snobbish club for the upper classes. Although we were from the upper-middle class, having been brought up in a Social Democratic environment, that was out for us. The only one left was Hakoah, which was a Jewish club. My sister and I wondered how we could get around that because we really didn't know anything about being Jewish. But it turned out that religion was not an issue in the club. There were even some non-Jewish people there for the same reasons we joined. What mattered was to be good sportspeople with high moral standards. So we joined and both stayed there for the remaining four or five years we lived in Austria. The nicest thing is that the friendships we made in that club have lasted to this very day.

I was trying to figure out what I wanted to do. I had no idea. My mother died in January of 1938. That was very difficult. I really had a hard time because the relationship with my father was a poor one. I worked part-time in his office, a job I really despised. His secretary, who eventually, after my mother's death, became his wife, was a woman who disliked me and my sister as much as we disliked and mistrusted her. So it was a very, very difficult time. The person whom I trusted most, my governess, had gone to England. I corresponded with her. I was a very lonely, young, shy person, really not knowing what to do.

I knew Sepp at that time. We were very good friends. When Sepp proposed to me the year before, I was still in high school and I felt I was much too young to get married. Besides, he wanted to go to Palestine. There was no way I wanted to go there. I saw no reason to get married, go with Sepp, and not give myself any chance to meet possibly other people.

In those days Hitler was not taken so seriously. While I knew that my father and uncle were in danger because of their Social Democratic affiliations, my uncle especially because of his prominence in the party in the field of education, I was so ignorant and naive that I was quite fearless.

RUTH: *Are you saying that you realized your father and uncle were in danger for political reasons, not religious?*

ANNIE: Absolutely. Much more political than religious. My sister and I were very concerned to get my father out. We were able to arrange for him to leave for London in June of 1938. My father had a friend in the lumber business who belonged to the Nazi Party, though was not a Nazi at heart. He was really a good friend. We asked him to help my father, and he said, "Sure." So my father left on an airplane, which few people did at that time. That man who on the surface was supposedly a Nazi was a true friend of my father and helped him to get out. I think that's important to emphasize. Many Jewish people condemn all the Germans, regardless, and they are very offended if non-Jews condemn all the Jews, regardless. I have very little use for that.

My sister had a boyfriend who was in Colombia, but she did not want to go there directly for a variety of reasons. She chose to go to England as a domestic, which was a fairly easy thing to do. My father, already in London, was able to arrange that for her. She left early in September of '38. I had no intention to do that. My aim was to get to Los Angeles directly, one way or another. By that time, Sepp was there. I had told him the year before, "If we ever get married and we ever go on a honeymoon, the only place I want to go is America!" Little did I know the circumstances! The dream for America came from listening to my grandfather, who had been in America for at least 10 years. He was one of the first—if not the first—Singer Sewing Machine representatives in Europe.

LANNY: *How did you manage to get an affidavit?*

ANNIE: That was a very difficult thing. I had looked through my father's hundreds and hundreds of calling cards that he collected through his extensive travels. I was only interested to find Americans among his many cards, and there were quite a few. There was a police chief in New York, college professors from various places. Among them was a couple in Oakland, California.

I wrote to all of them. None answered except the woman in Oakland, Mrs. Daube, who wrote that she remembered my father very well, that her husband had died in the meantime, but she was very happy to send all the necessary papers to get me over. She did, immediately.

I was informed in September that my affidavit had arrived and that I would possibly get my visa at the end of the month; I should call back. I began preparations to leave. We all had to pay *Reichsflucht Steuer* [tax for fleeing the country] in order to get a passport. My father had deposited the amount of money necessary for me to leave. Then I came to the man who had taken over my father's office and asked for money for the trip from Vienna to Los Angeles. He replied that he wasn't interested that I leave, only that I *verrecken*. This very ugly, crude word is like the English word "croak." So I turned to my future parents-in-law, with whom I lived at the time, to pay for the trip. The Lampl parents at that time still had some money because Papa Lampl was still employed at the international company that he had been with for about 30 years. They were able to help me purchase a ticket from Antwerp directly to Los Angeles. I couldn't see myself going to New York first and begging for money. Not having been affiliated with any Jewish organization, I felt it would be too difficult to ask for help at HIAS. So I chose deliberately to go on a German boat through the Panama Canal, all the way to Los Angeles.

As I had been told to do, I called several times to find out if my visa was ready and was always told, "next week." After the third week, I was told, "Sorry, your papers got lost. You'll have to write your sponsor and ask for full duplication of all papers." I could do nothing but do so. Fortunately, Mrs. Daube was a wonderful, competent woman who immediately got everything together once again and sent them to me. But mail only went by boat then, so it took another six weeks until I finally got my new papers.

Years and years later, I met somebody of the American Consulate in Los Angeles and I told him how incompetent that American Consulate in Vienna had been. He asked my name. I told him, "Annie Wagner." He laughed and said that passport had been given to a German girl who had come to America as a spy! Papers from people with common names—Wagner, Schwartz, Schmidt, Weiss, Schneider, Müller—men and women alike, who also had average physical descriptions, were taken for Nazi spies. So, a German woman came to this country on my papers! They told me that there were 20 to 30 people like that.

I was still in Vienna at *Kristallnacht,* which was terrible for us. Papa Lampl's brother, who was a physician, shot himself when he came home to his office and home and saw everything totally demolished. Having a Catholic wife, he felt that with his death he could save her life and that she could at least go on living and get some reparations. I think she eventually did. She remained in Vienna and died there many years later.

LANNY: *It must have been a difficult time, waiting for your departure, Sepp having left already.*

ANNIE: Yes, Sepp had left. We corresponded, of course. One of the funny things in these times was that in every letter he wrote, and he wrote maybe once a week, "Please Annie, learn to cook, learn to clean. We'll never be able to have someone do these things for us." I had never done such things in all my life! I never washed a pair of stockings, never even boiled the water for coffee! I always felt there was nothing much to learn. If the young women from the country who were the cooks and maids could do this, I with my background and education and, hopefully, intelligence could too. I would have no problems. I was very confident, and that was that. I felt that as long as I could read some books and get some directions, I would do fine. And I think I did.

By the end of November I finally got my papers, and a couple of weeks later I was able to get out. It was a most pleasant trip. The very first night, the captain asked the steward in the dining room to see to it that I sat at his table. I sat at his right, one of 12 passengers on this freighter! So I had a very safe and interesting trip to Los Angeles. I arrived in San Pedro, with a swastika flag flying on the boat, on January 20, 1939.

LANNY: *Sepp, what was your life like prior to the immigration?*

SEPP: I had joined Hakoah and was fencing there before I met Annie. In 1935, I was chosen as one of the representatives to the Maccabi Games in Palestine. It was a fantastic experience to participate at such an event. I was lucky enough to make a fifth place in sabre. I contributed two points for the Austrian Maccabi team, which was the winner of the games that year. When I was there, one of the fencing managers asked me to stay in Palestine, even illegally. He said they would help me get a job and education there. But I wanted to return to Vienna, finish my studies, and then make up my mind where I would go.

I finished my studies and was an engineer. There was a depression in the country. I felt it wasn't worthwhile to struggle in Vienna. Work possibilities were very limited. I was resolved to emigrate. I worked in Italy for six months in 1937. While it was very pleasant and I enjoyed it, it wasn't such that I could stay there for my whole life. I returned to Vienna, but still wanted to get out of the country. Two nights before Hitler came into Austria, I was ready to go. But when I talked to Annie's father, he thought we should sleep on it. The next day it was too late to get out without special visas. I applied for visas to the U.S. and Australia. Fortunately for me, I was born in Italy, and the Italian quota to America was wide open. I got a number immediately and could get a visa.

RUTH: *How did it happen that you were born in Italy?*

SEPP: My father was a corporation lawyer in Italy for a while. He was a director of an international company that had offices in every capital of Europe, and he was in many of these. We were in Italy for a year or two, until World War I broke out. Then we all returned to Vienna. My father had to go into the war and came out as a captain. My brothers were born in Vienna.

My brother Hans and I got our affidavits from a family in Los Angeles. This German family had been helped to emigrate by relatives of ours, so they were obliged to help us. When they had been in Vienna earlier that year, Hans had become enamored with the daughter and he was eager to see her again. Hans was very fortunate. Despite his Austrian birth, he got out of Vienna with me. If you were over 21 and had a sibling or spouse under 21, you could take him or her along. My interest in coming to Los Angles was the aerospace industry.

We got out in July of 1938 and took a boat to New York. My other brother was already in Palestine since 1933, when he went there to study architecture. My parents remained in Vienna and got out later, through Belgium and France. We got them to the U.S. in 1941.

LANNY: *Where did your boat leave from?*

SEPP: It left from Le Havre, France. We went to New York, where we stayed for 8 or 10 days, got a train ticket with the courtesy of HIAS, and went to Los Angeles. Unfortunately, the family there was broke. They couldn't help us in any respect. We thought they would help us get started in our professional lives. Luckily, our Czech aunt had sent some money to them for us. We got some small jobs. And two or three months later, I got an engineering job at a small firm that made postal meters. Fairly soon, this company got interested in the aircraft industry, and within two years I was chief engineer of this little company. I was too essential for them to let me go to war, so I always had a deferment. We made all sorts of aircraft accessories, among them bomb racks for very sophisticated airplanes that were made in very high quantities. We had a real good probability of pulling through the war and having continuous employment.

LANNY: *So, after a fairly short time, you were able to get a job in your profession.*

ANNIE: At first, he had a very tough time. He could not get a job in the beginning, because he was considered an enemy alien. So in order to survive, he had to accept a job in the desert town of Mojave.

SEPP: As a hotel clerk. But when Annie came I moved back to Los Angeles, and I was lucky enough to immediately get the engineering job. At that time, any place that you worked, if you lived through the first two or three months and showed that you could, as they called it, "cut the mustard," you were in and you didn't have to show what kind of education you had or what papers you could substantiate that education with. You just had to show that you could do the work.

LANNY: *Tell me what it was like being an enemy alien.*

SEPP: The only problem was that it was very tough to get into the airplane business. That I was a Jew and a victim of the Germans was irrelevant. As an Austrian, I was an enemy alien and couldn't be hired by any of the big firms. You had to be an American citizen. But in 1940 or '41, I got a security clearance from both the airforce and navy departments because I was in an essential industry. That I was a Jew didn't make this clearance any easier. If I had been a German or Austrian gentile, I would also have gotten a clearance. Nobody asked about religion.

Overall, there was no animosity toward foreigners. I think everybody, at least so far as I was concerned, was very helpful and very friendly. I could immediately speak enough English because I was lucky enough to have learned English in Vienna. There was no language barrier, no problem of being understood or in understanding what I asked about.

LANNY: *How about for you, Annie?*

ANNIE: One very funny incident, speaking about language. When I arrived in San Pedro, I had to go through immigration. I could speak some English. The immigration officer had nothing to do because nobody else arrived, so he made fun of me and scared me. He asked me all kinds of questions. Some of them I didn't even know the answers to. He just wanted to make conversation to kill time. I will never forget what impressed me the most. He was an official, and I was used to European officials. He sat there leaning back in his chair with his feet on his desk. I had never ever seen that before in my life! I was in there for at least an hour. Sepp was outside, certain that something was wrong with my papers and they would send me straight back. But everything was all right. When it was all through, the official got up and said, "OK now, don't ever do it again." To this day, I have absolutely no idea what he meant by that!

Another funny thing happened when we got to the apartment that Sepp and Hans shared, a one-bedroom apartment. They turned on the radio and someone was singing, "Annie doesn't live here anymore." That was a popular song at the time. For me the strangest thing was that although it would have been perfectly OK with me to sleep on the sofa or even on the floor, the friends that Sepp and Hans had made said that was absolutely impossible. There was no way that a young woman could sleep in the same room with those two guys. I couldn't see much wrong with it, because we were used to sharing rooms in alpine huts in Austria. Boys and girls always stayed together. I don't think there was any sexual interaction. So, these friends whisked me off to a relative of theirs who lived in a very nice, big house. I had to stay there until Sepp and I got married. The friends arranged for us to get married a week later.

I had made a list of special demands which I had written to Sepp before coming. I would only get married under certain conditions. Number one was that *I* had to have a job. I didn't care what I was doing as long as I had a job. Another demand was that Sepp had to have a job. He didn't anymore, since he had come in from Mojave to meet me. There were quite many demands. Somehow he must have met them all, because we did get married a week after my arrival.

The next day [after the wedding] we went on the train to Oakland, where the woman who had given me the affidavit of support had reserved a suite in the best hotel in Oakland. That, of course, I felt very comfortable with because as children we were accustomed to go to the best hotels and have the best rooms. The next morning, we went to see Mrs. Daube. She was already then an elderly lady, in bed with a little silk cap. She looked at me when we walked into the room and started laughing. I felt absolutely terrible. I'd put on a very simple, very nice dress with a hat and gloves. What in the world had I done wrong? I said in a very apologetic way, "Is there anything that I did that wasn't appropriate?" She said, "No, not at all. I just expected a little, short, dark-haired girl, and here you are, tall, slender and fair, nothing that I ever expected you to be!"

After the weekend, we returned to L.A. I went to work and Sepp continued to look for a job. I had arrived in Los Angeles two Fridays before. I interviewed for a job in a factory on Saturday. Monday morning, I started working in a Jewish-owned hat factory. What became very painful to me was to see how not I but Mexicans and black people were treated—really very badly. Having come from Hitler Austria, it was a very painful observation. They obviously were not treated like the white American women. The other thing I observed was that several of the women in this factory who worked very, very hard did not work to support themselves. They were working to wear beautiful clothes and jewelry! They were dressed to the hilt and they worked exclusively for that purpose.

LANNY: *What about that struck you as being strange or different?*

ANNIE: I would never imagine that anybody would work under those circumstances. They worked very, very hard all day long to get a certain quota of hats finished, just to wear beautiful clothes and jewelry! We were so poor that the $12 or $14 a week we made was essential for rent and food. Somehow we managed. And somehow, when I had to cook and clean, I was able to do it. I found out how to live very economically. I don't think we ever starved. We had parties and we had company and we did fine.

LANNY: *What was your attitude then about being Jewish? Did it change as a result of Nazi persecution?*

ANNIE: I've never had much identification with anything Jewish because both my parents were already brought up without any religion. From my aunt on my mother's side in Budapest, I learned that some of her family was actually Christian, because that was politically and economically an important thing to do. They had not been in any way religious. The same was true of my father's family. Some of them weren't Jewish at all. Yet my father did give money for Jewish causes. In Vienna, my link to Jews was really only through the sport club. When I was asked by some of my clients [Annie is a psychotherapist] not so long ago how I have such high moral standards without religion, I said, "Maybe socialism was our religion." The standards there were very, very high. For a child, these were very important.

LANNY: *So I take it you didn't join a synagogue here or participate in any Jewish community activities.*

ANNIE: True. But here as in Vienna, we feel that we are connected to the Jews. That didn't at all change.

LANNY: *Where did you first live?*

ANNIE: We found a tiny house on North Normandy and this friend, Herbert Kline, Hans, Sepp, and I lived together. The Lampl parents were still in Vienna and asked us what we wanted in terms of furniture from their really luxurious apartment. Sepp and I discussed it and realized that their huge, fancy furniture would only fit into an equally elegant house, which we knew we could never in our lives afford. So I, having always loved Bieder-mayer furniture, asked them to please send us just the furniture of Sepp's room, which was really very beautiful, real antique Biedermayer. By June of 1939, the furniture arrived and we got our own apartment.

221

SEPP: By then, I had resumed my passion of fencing. When I first came to Los Angeles, among Annie's "demands" was that I keep on fencing. Since I didn't know anybody who was active in any sports, I opened up the telephone book and found the L.A. Athletic Club. I called up on the phone and was connected with the fencing coach, a very nice, old Dutch man. He asked me to come over and fence with them. After I did that for one night, he said he wanted me at the club. He said, "I know you don't have any money, so we'll give you a training card and you don't have to pay anything for it. When you have a job and can afford it, we'll give you a low-paying membership. But you have to promise that whenever there's a competition that you qualify for, you will fence for the club." That was certainly no problem! For the next 25–30 years, I fenced in all the competitions. In the nationals, I was ranked seventh in the U.S. and was on one of the Olympic squads.

LANNY: *Did you encounter any anti-Semitic incidents in the club or elsewhere in America?*

ANNIE: I don't remember any.

SEPP: Not personally, but at a gathering of friends I was asked, "How come they took you into the Los Angeles Athletic Club? They don't accept Jews." Nobody had ever told me anything about that, and I was accepted as one of the fencers. There were one or two other prominent fencers at the club that I knew were Jewish. But perhaps there was a *numerus clausus* for Jews, just like for Negroes.

ANNIE: We also knew some other members of the Los Angeles Athletic Club who were not fencers and were Jewish. It was a rather prestigious club to be a member of and how they got to be members, I don't know. It was a bit of a snobbish club. I'm not so sure they were anti-Jewish. They were probably anti-anybody different. But there were exceptions, like a Japanese man who later on even became a coach there.

RUTH: *At that time, did you know what was happening to Jews in Austria or Germany?*

SEPP: We didn't hear much about it. Nothing about the Holocaust.

ANNIE: We knew absolutely nothing. It all came out after the war. I don't think any one of us knew what was going on. Nobody knew what was going on. What we knew was that many people like **Fritz [Frankel]** had been in concentration camps. We knew that by the time we left, some had not gotten out yet, but what happened to them I still don't know.

RUTH: *Once you did hear what had happened, how did you feel that you had gotten out?*

SEPP: We felt lucky.

ANNIE: I never felt what some people felt, the guilt of the survivor. If for no other reason, once I got here I helped a lot of people come to this country. When I first came I felt that I was lucky to have gotten out. The people who gave our parents affidavits were very rich hotel owners and also the owners of Thrifty Drug Stores. They were friends of Hans. I got umpteen affidavits from them for many friends. They had a large hotel downtown and whenever I would walk into the hotel there was a son-in-law who would say, "Oh, the girl with the refugee business is coming." He shouted all the way across the lobby. I was so embarrassed. For years I was known as the girl with the refugee business. They were big Jews, very well to do, the Boruns. They had been in L.A. since the turn of the century.

LANNY: *During that time, did you express any hatred of Germany, perhaps by avoiding German products?*

SEPP: Oh yes, we avoided all German products. Only recently, I broke down and bought a German electric razor.

ANNIE: I think I avoided German products. I knew I would never want to buy a German car, which is true till this day. I don't avoid German small products, but to invest thousands of dollars in something large, for some strange reason, I'm still not willing to do.

LANNY: *Did you speak German or English with each other and with other German-speaking immigrants?*

ANNIE: Yes, we did speak German in those days together, and also two years later, in '41, when Sepp's parents came after their odyssey of being captured and in detention camps in France.

LANNY: *How were they able to leave Vienna?*

ANNIE: They had gone to Belgium from Vienna. When in 1941 the Germans overran Belgium, they were taken to southern France into two different detention camps, unknown to each other. They had agreed that if they ever got separated, they would write to a friend in Switzerland, the neutral country. They did, and their old friend sent letters to each of them telling the whereabouts of the other. We were working on getting them affidavits of support through a friend in Los Angeles who had lots of well-to-do relatives and friends. We were able to send affidavits to them in Marseilles. And we were able, with difficulty, to scrape together enough money for their boat tickets. Eventually, they met each other in Marseilles and left on one of the last transports leaving for the U.S. But then they were captured in Martinique.

SEPP: The Dutch captured that French boat and pulled it into Trinidad. We had to pay some more to get them from there.

ANNIE: We had to borrow money in order to get them to New York. In New York, they had lots of friends already, who took care of them.

SEPP: Then they came on a bus. We had an apartment that could accommodate the whole family. That's where John was born in 1942.

ANNIE: I never particularly wanted children. But the fact that we were able to get the parents out and there was a chance to get my father out, who was in England, was so encouraging, that when Sepp really pressured me to have children, I said, "OK." As long as we had all three parents out, I was ready to have a child.

LANNY: *Speaking now of John and me, did you try teaching German to us?*

ANNIE: I don't think we tried to teach you because I felt that while we lived with the parents and spoke German, somehow you would pick it up. I think you did as small children and I think to this day you probably understand a lot more than you're even aware of. With John, it was very difficult. As a three-year-old going to nursery school, he was very much aware that German was not a "desirable" language in those days. The Germans were the enemies, the Nazis. As a result, German was not a language that one spoke, period. I'm astonished about his awareness that this was not a language to use. Later on, he did learn it and we all used the language more.

LANNY: *Were most of your first friends here Jewish and/or immigrants?*

ANNIE: Viennese, sure. But our first and best friend, to this day, is a non-Jewish person.

SEPP: We had American friends very soon after we got here. We mixed well. We found friends among the people that we worked with. We found friends at the sports club and are still close with some of them.

ANNIE: A very close friend, Jimmy Marmor, gave us his lifelong earnings of $500 before joining the U.S. military. I knew him very well already from the sports club in Vienna, sort of like an older brother. This was in 1942, just after John was born. If it hadn't been for those $500, we could have never bought the house on Windsor.

SEPP: Whatever savings we had, whatever savings friends of ours loaned us, we put into the down payment for that house. That was one of the most important purchases that we ever did. It enabled us to have several families under one roof: my parents, Annie's father, my brother, and for a while, a distant cousin. It made us financially secure, so to speak, that we had a house that everybody could live in.

LANNY: *When did you first meet people in the* Gruppe?

ANNIE: In 1944, and I'm not sure how, we met **Gerty Frankel.** John was two years old and Miriam was one. They were both in tailor tots, small pushcarts for little children. Through Gerty, we met **Otto, Marianne,** and Ruth.

LANNY: *Did you live near each other?*

ANNIE: We lived very near each other, in walking distance. We saw each other several times a week and the children played together at Queen Anne Playground. And then we began to go to *Gruppe* meetings. We got together with all these friends. Our major purpose at the time was to support orphan children somewhere in the world. We pitched together enough money to support a child, I believe from Greece, with whom some of the members corresponded for many years.

LANNY: *What happened at the* Gruppe *meetings?*

ANNIE: We met in each other's homes. Very rarely at our house. It was a group of Viennese who met quite regularly. It was very enjoyable, and of course we exchanged ideas from child raising to jobs and vacations, as young people do. They were little dinner parties or afternoon gatherings. A big thing was birthday parties for the children.

225

SEPP: Some of the people made up reports of current events or things they were interested in. There was lively interest in certain areas that were discussed.

LANNY: *What significance, if any, does the* Gruppe *have for you today?*

SEPP: Just a social significance. It was just to socialize with certain people that were of the same upbringing. They all came from central Europe, had a similar education, similar interests. It was a type of social getting together that was of interest to us at the time.

ANNIE: I wish you wouldn't say us. It's very different for me! **Gerty** and **Marianne** both are very good personal friends. Gerty helped me enormously during later years when I had lost my sight and went back to school, which I had wanted to do ever since I stepped on American soil. Gerty was interested in what I was doing and eventually she also became a counselor at the Southern California Counseling Center, where I had done my internship and was working. Marianne, with her interest in psychology, has always had a special closeness to me because we share many ideas. With these two friends I share a lot of interests, so there is a close personal friendship which goes way beyond the social connections one usually has with people. My relationships with them are very different than with others of the *Gruppe*.

LANNY: *Was America anything like you expected it to be?*

ANNIE: I don't think I had any expectations at all. I was very open, as I hope I am still today. When I go into a new venture, I try not to have any expectations. I have expectations of myself maybe, but not of what the situation is going to be. I guess I've been very fortunate to have always had that feeling to be just really open.

LANNY: *How about for you, Sepp?*

SEPP: I didn't have any preconceived ideas or specific expectations. I just took it as it came, day by day. Looking backward, I think I was very lucky and very happy about being in this country and enjoying life and the opportunities it gave me.

RUTH: *Do you feel "at home" in Los Angeles? If so, when did you begin to feel so? Also, do you comfortably identify yourselves as Americans?*

ANNIE: I make a difference between where I'm at home and where I'm being an American. I believe I felt really at home when we moved to this house in 1954. Prior to that, Sepp and I, from the day we got married, never lived without friends and relatives. Already when a very young child in Austria I was dreaming of living on top of a hill, like the robber barons, though I didn't have any idea where I wanted to live. When I came to L.A. and saw the hills, I knew I wanted to live in those hills. I feel that this is my home in the hills. That it happens to be in America is secondary. I'm not sure I would feel the same in a place like Colombia, where my sister lives. But I'd probably feel the same in Canada or maybe in Switzerland.

I am an American citizen. I would never say, "I am an American." I feel much more that I am an Austrian. My background, my whole way of thinking, and all that is much more Austrian than American—to this day.

SEPP: I feel that I couldn't live in any European state anymore because I feel that Europeans are much more narrow-minded than here. So I feel that I am American now by choice. I feel very much at home.

RUTH: *Is there someone, an incident, phrase, or object that was of special significance in sustaining you through the immigration years?*

SEPP: I can't really say that. Whatever happened, I tried to grab the opportunity of whatever came my way.

RUTH: *What can you tell me about yourselves that you think enabled you to cope with the many transitions of immigration?*

ANNIE: I was fearless in many different ways. I never felt, like many others under severe circumstances, that anything like this could happen to me. That's of course, denial. It never occurred to me that the Nazis could grab me, that anything could happen to me, really. I was very fortunate that nothing ever did. I think whenever you go into any kind of difficult situation with some assurance and being fearless, it is helpful. It is not being fearless, but rather acknowledging that being afraid is OK.

RUTH: *Anything else?*

ANNIE: My father was the kind of person who was very adaptable, and I think he had the aim not only to teach and preach social democracy but really live it. For that I am very grateful. I learned from his example.

Also, both my sister and I were brought up not to rely on a man for sure but really to rely on ourselves. And when I came here, and Sepp and I

Annie and "Sepp" Lampl,
Los Angeles, 1940.

married, I insisted that I have a job and support him while he looked for a
job that was appropriate for his education. I saw nothing wrong in that. I
firmly believe now, as then, that a woman has to be absolutely self-sufficient.
I was not brought up to be a good housewife and mother! That's the last
thing on earth my father had in mind. We were brought up to be self-
sufficient women, period. Both my sister and I are.

Another thing—I was brought up to do the best I can. I try to do that
whether it's scrubbing my kitchen floor or writing an academic paper. That
general idea has certainly helped me. It didn't matter what I was doing as
long as I was doing it well. I get impatient with people who do slipshod
work, whatever it is. That is one thing that I am very grateful for from my
father and certainly my governess. Also significant is that I have somehow
known who I was. For that, I have again to thank these two people. I have
always had some feeling of self—whatever that was and no matter how
criticized I've been for that. Sometimes that sense was of being very insecure
and sometimes OK. I think those two things about me helped me. They
would have helped no matter where I was and what circumstances may have
happened. Certainly having become blind has put a damper on my life, but
it hasn't kept me from living.

For me, one of the most influential things about my mother was that when
she became ill in her early 30s with Parkinson's, she gave up. Not having a
good relationship with my father made the situation much worse. When I
started losing my sight, I was determined that I would not let this get to
me, that I would go on and lead a very different life, that I would go on as
best I could, in spite of the physical impairment, rather than let it devastate

me. In some way, having my mother as a negative role model was very helpful. Until this day, I think that negative role models are just as valuable as positive ones.

RUTH: *Sepp, what about you? What about you made it possible to adapt to so many new conditions? I think you are one of the few in the* Gruppe *who was directly able to use their European education. Would you say that it was your professional background that provided your bridge for the immigration process?*

SEPP: As far as I was concerned, I came to the United States and finally got into my chosen profession, and stayed here ever since. I had my ups and downs, but in general I stayed with that profession until half a year ago. . . . I found that my education was very broad and I could fit into any place, into any specialty. I was very happy about that and knew that would help me a great deal.

RUTH: *When did you first return to Vienna and what did that feel like for you?*

ANNIE: We went in the spring of 1961. It was strange to be back in a place that I knew very well and had no real connection to anymore—except when I visited my mother's grave. I felt maybe like a lover feels with an old love, that you know it very well, but have no connection with it anymore, not really. I felt a world of difference between myself and everything around me. But I had no bad feelings.

SEPP: I felt that I knew it very well, that I knew my way around. I enjoyed just being there for a short while and seeing the sights, maybe going to the theater, seeing some of my old friends.

RUTH: *How has it felt for you to do these interviews?*

SEPP: It's all right. It's interesting to keep a record of some of the things that happened, and how we got connected to people of the same *Stambaum* [ancestry]. It's a good record and I hope it will help our successors to know what happened to us, what gave us the idea of coming here and doing what we did.

ANNIE: It barely scratches the surface. What made or didn't make any of us are really things of great depth, as were the ups and downs that we all have suffered and gone through. I see what we've done like a map, a surface map. What's underneath is partly too private and partly would be much too long-winded for anybody to listen to.

HEDY WOLF

Hedy Wolf

Hedy Wolf was just making headway as a gymnastics teacher when all Jewish teachers in Germany were categorically dismissed—except from Jewish schools. In one of these Jewish schools, she met Ernest, her husband-to-be. When Ernest was offered a position as principal of a school in Sweden, they accepted. The wait for immigration visas to the United States took three years. By then, the Atlantic was mined and they had to travel eastward, via Russia, Japan, and the Pacific Ocean. They had one daughter, Miriam.

Before those hard years started, I was very happy. Finally, after many years, I was allowed to learn what I really wanted to. My parents wanted me to study music and I tried that out, but it wasn't for me to sit for my whole life, to sit in a chair and teach children how to play the piano. I got a breakdown because they just wouldn't let me learn something else which I wanted so badly. I wanted to study gymnastics. My father was a wonderful man, but he said, "That's no profession." Finally I got through to it, but it took a breakdown.

I had been in Berlin to study music with the best teachers. But I never liked large cities. I still don't like them. I couldn't see the sky. I just died there! I said I'd never go back into a big city. I wanted to go to Stuttgart. It was closer to home and in my home state. Somebody helped me, and finally I went to Stuttgart in 1930. It was very German and I loved it there. For the first year I studied gymnastics in a school that was not very good, so I left it. My parents thought I was very difficult that I gave up again. Thankfully, I then found an excellent school where I learned so much.

I was very happy. I was there for about two-and-a-half years. I always liked boys—in a nice way. At that time you were just friends. You went on hikes, went into those old cities around Stuttgart and could explore. I always had company going places where I wouldn't have gone alone. We went to the Schwäbische Alb, a lovely mountainous region in the middle of Württemberg. After those two years, it was already getting close toward Hitler. I finished my studies in November 1932 and was prepared to teach gymnastics to adults and children. With another girl and my teacher, I had a plan to open gymnastic schools all over Württemberg. We had it all figured out, and it would have worked out beautifully.

I taught maybe for two or three months at the beginning of '33 and had wonderful success. I taught privately and in schools and clubs. But then, except in the Jewish school, I was kicked out of everything. I still have the letters that advised me that no Jewish teachers could teach in regular schools and that clubs had to let you go. So, except in the Jewish schools, everything was closed to me. It had looked so promising. Well anyway, that was the beginning of '33, the beginning of Hitler years.

I had a friend in Stuttgart and we wanted to marry some day. He was a student of engineering. He wasn't Jewish. When action against Jews started up, I thought to myself, I can't do that to him. I told him that there wouldn't be any future for him with me, that I couldn't drag him into such an insecure future. We ended our relationship. That wasn't easy, obviously. By the way, I heard from him later on, but we never saw each other again.

So I had enough of Germany. I couldn't stand it anymore. What should I do there? I wanted to learn English to be able to come to America maybe someday.

Before going on, I have to tell you a very strange story from long before then. When I was 15, my parents sent me to Geneva to school. I had vacation often and living in southern Germany, that wasn't too far away. At the end of one of those vacations, going back to Geneva on the train, there was a young fellow sitting across from me. He started talking with me, but I wasn't interested. He left. Across from me also there was an older man. He came over to me and said he observed me and was glad I didn't start talking to that other man. He sat with me until Geneva and asked me what I was doing and so forth. He also said, "If you ever come to England, be sure to visit us." He gave me a little card with his address. I was a young girl and didn't pay any attention to that card. Months later when I went home on vacation again, I showed it to my father. He looked at it and said, "Do you know who that was? That was a member of Parliament!" He was a very nice man of the Labor Party. I saved the card. That was in the '20s.

So when many years later I thought about learning English, I remembered that man. I thought, "Gee whiz, I'm going to try. I want to go to England. I want to learn English. I'm going to write to his family." And I did. They invited me immediately to come and stay with them and to teach their two daughters to speak German. I went!

This was at the end of '33. But it didn't work out so well. I was very spoiled. Because I had an older brother who was mentally retarded, we always had a governess. I never had to do anything as a child. Everything was done for me. I didn't have to make my bed, I didn't have to tie my shoes, so to speak. I was very dependent without knowing it. It hurt me all my life. So it didn't work out so well in London. It was a lovely family. They were wonderful. I fitted there, too, but I didn't know what to do with those children. So I looked for another job and then went from job to job. Nothing worked out because I couldn't cook, I couldn't take care of children, and I was very lonesome in such a large city. I had some friends, but that didn't help. I had another breakdown then, a very severe one. All I could do was to go home.

I returned to that little town, Laupheim, where I was born. There was a large Jewish community. Many of my old friends were there again. They had been kicked out of their jobs or schools elsewhere. That was the way it was. I was there for a year or so. It was very desperate. Jews weren't allowed to work. The Nazis wanted us to do *nothing*. You can kill people that way and they tried hard. It was just terrible. There I was, old enough to make my own living. I was in my late 20s and living with my parents. There was nothing I could do. A friend of ours in that little town brought me to a Jewish boarding school nearby, in Herrlingen. It was a wonderful school and became quite famous later on. I got a position there, one or two days a week. The rest of the time I taught Jewish children in Laupheim. It wasn't much work, but was something.

In Herrlingen I met my husband-to-be, who was teaching there, also having been kicked out of his intended career. From there, we left Germany when Ernest got a position at a similar boarding school in Sweden. That was good for him but not for me, because I had no position there. I was just the wife of my husband. They wanted me to do this and that. I gave gym lessons for an hour in the morning, and during the rest of the day I had to do whatever there was to be done, like typing. I didn't fit there. I don't fit into a community where you are always together with people, especially children. I wasn't used to it. I grew up without brothers or sisters. I liked to be alone. It was very unsatisfactory for me, but we lived there for as long as we had to, until we got our papers to move to America.

When you first applied for a visa and affidavit to the United States, were you still in Germany?

We had applied of course, but we had to wait. That's why we went to Sweden. It took three years before we could come.

From whom did you get the affidavits?

My mother's brother. My mother, by the way, had already immigrated and was living in New York.

Did this uncle live in Los Angeles?

Yes. Our journey to the U.S. was an interesting one. We were in Sweden and it was late 1940. The Atlantic was mined so we couldn't go to New York. I was very happy about this. We had to go via the Pacific Ocean via Russia, and arrived in San Francisco. My uncle and his family met us and brought us to Los Angeles.

Where did you live?

After staying with our relatives, we rented a back room on Santa Monica Boulevard toward downtown, where we had to share the toilet and the bathroom with other people. I remember the first money I earned. I was so proud that I could bring $5 to the Bank of America! It was a lot of money at that time.

We met many other people who came from Europe who had the same background and the same future and the same worries and the same thoughts. It started alright. Getting used to a foreign country is never easy, but we were young and we had our lives ahead of us. So we didn't worry too much and it worked out.

How did you find your first jobs?

Through Jewish organizations. I worked all the time, first as a maid. Then, somebody helped me to get a position in a doctor's office. I liked that quite well. I wasn't a nurse and had to do all the dirty work, but it was a very efficient and well-known gynecologist's office. After about two years, the doctor said to me, "I won't raise your salary. You should go back to your old profession. You should become a teacher again." She was a wonderful woman, very understanding. She was Jewish herself and she didn't like for me to just sit in that office. She said, "You go back and become a gym teacher. That's what you are made for."

But that didn't work out so quickly. First, I went to a commercial school and then worked at an insurance company for several years until Ernest found a college job and we moved here to San Diego. In the meantime, Miri was born in 1946, in Los Angeles.

We moved in 1947. I had to learn to drive. A lucky thing happened. (Things like that happened to me quite often in life.) I spoke with my driving teacher about an elderly lady who had her lesson before me. He told me that she had such a hard time. I said, "She probably doesn't coordinate so well." He asked, "How come you talk about coordination?" I said to him, "I'm actually a physical fitness teacher." He told his boss about me. And that man called the next day and asked whether I wanted a job. That's how I got a job in adult education in a local high school! I can't believe it, I was there for 30 years at that same position. It was very hard at first. Nobody did exercises at that time. I taught at one school after another in the same district, little by little, and ended up with a huge job. Not too well paid but that didn't matter. Between Ernest and me, we did quite well.

Did that lucky break come the first year you were in San Diego?

No, it was three years later. First I did all sorts of things. I wanted to stay home. I believed in bringing a child up yourself, not having help. I took other children in, just to earn a little money.

In your immigration you had to make many adaptations. Is there something about you, your personality, that helped you do this?

I don't think so. If I had been alone, I wouldn't have been so successful. As I said, I was spoiled. I would have made it in my profession eventually, but not so well with what I had to do at the start. It helped me a great deal that I was married.

When you came, you were considered an enemy alien because you were German. What did that mean? What constraints did that put on you?

We were pretty lucky. They didn't put us behind wires like they did the Japanese. Of course it affected me because we weren't really Germans anymore. The Germans kicked us out, so how could we all of a sudden again be German? It was a very weird, not to be understood situation. The constraints were mainly that you couldn't travel farther than a certain number of miles from home to your place of work. Ernest had a position in Glendale. He was at a military academy, teaching. He lived there. I had the position in the doctor's office in downtown, Los Angeles. That far I could travel. So at that time, we lived in different places. I took the bus to go to see him. For several weeks, every Friday afternoon or Saturday morning, I had to go to the consul general and ask for permission to travel to my husband. He was a very nice young man. At first he gave a permit to me each week. Later on, since he understood the situation real well, he laughed and gave me a permanent permit so I wouldn't have to come each week. I remember this very well because not so many nice things happened!

Why were those permits required? Were they trying to keep track of you? What did it matter where you were?

You always had to be in your own home at night. I could not stay overnight with Ernest.

How did you feel at that time about being a German?

I wasn't German anymore. I wasn't an American either. We were without a country. What bothered me was that I did not *belong*, that I had no passport.

During the last 50 years, if somebody asked you, "What are you?" was there a time when you were able to say, "I'm American," and really feel it?

I was very happy to say it. I liked to say it. On those holidays when we lived in our own house, like the Fourth of July, I hung a flag out because I wasn't allowed in Germany to use a flag. Not that I care about the flag, but all these privileges or whatever you want to call them, these symbols were taken away from us. But here I could do it again and I did it. It was a small gesture, but I could do it. I *belonged*. I was like everybody else. Nobody asked me what I was.

Was there a point at which you felt really at home in this country?

Yes, as much as it can be under our circumstances.

How long did this take?

It was long ago, but it's always with reservations. It's never *quite* belonging. There's anti-Semitism everywhere. I think wherever we go, we seem different to other people. That's our fate. I personally don't feel different, but we are made to feel different. People are different toward us after they know that we're Jewish. But I found wonderful friends here. I always had many—I hate to say it this way—"gentile" friends. It didn't make any difference who they were. I just liked them. It's not hard for me to get acquainted with people if I feel that they have similar thoughts and meaning in life. Then we become very good friends. And I have many.

You've brought up several things I'd like to pursue. In Germany, did you have many friends who were not Jews?

Yes. Mostly they were not Jews. In that connection, I'll tell you something. When I was studying, I always met people. The school was close to Stuttgart and there were often young fellows sitting across from me in the train. Some invited me to come to Tübingen where the university was, to a dance. I told them I couldn't come because I was Jewish. I always was a conscious Jew. I never negated it in any way. It's my nature. I just say the way things are. My father was like that too.

When you came to Los Angeles, who were your first friends? People with whom you could feel an emotional connection?

There was the *Gruppe* mainly. The people of the *Gruppe* were our main friends as long as we lived in Los Angeles.

What was the Gruppe *for you? Why did you get together?*

It was companionship, understanding, home atmosphere, friends, all which you need in a foreign country.

Did you also see Gruppe *people outside of the meetings?*

Yes, of course. Children were born at that time. It meant a lot. I actually didn't want to move away from Los Angeles. We lived then in Westwood, which was real nice. I liked it there. I don't like big cities, but Los Angeles wasn't a big city. It was open, not like Berlin. I think way back once in a while, not often. It is terrible that that had to happen to us. Germany is a beautiful country. I loved it. I *loved* it. I had those wonderful friends which I had to give up. I loved it there.

Were you able to reestablish any of your old friendships?

Oh yes. Somebody in that little town of Laupheim got my address here, and they all started writing to me. Very good friends. I visited them three times when we were in Europe.

What was it like the first time you went back?

I can't describe it. I never could. To come to that little town where you lived your formative years, the main years of your life, and to come back under such circumstances. It can't be described. In German, the word *Wehmut* is close. It's a very sad and longing feeling, tinged with joy and sadness, with remembrance.

Were there many Jews in the town when you grew up?

There was a large, well-known, well-established Jewish community of two or three hundred. The town had only about 6,000 people. Everybody knew each other. My grandfather and father were born there. My father was beloved by the whole town, by Jews and non-Jews. I was the third generation. We *belonged* there. I would have left the town because it was too small, but I belonged there.

Were there any Jews in Laupheim when you returned?

No, there were none left. They're all in Israel, here, or dead. I went back there in 1963 for the first time. I went by myself. Those people in my town were so wonderful. They cried. Everybody was genuinely loving and sorry about what we had to go through. They really meant it with their hearts.

Had some of them been active Nazis?

Yes. They told me so, one of them especially. He was a school friend and he became a ranger in southern Germany in the forest. After the war, he became a very good friend of mine. He told me that until the end of his life he'd be sorry for what he did to us. I saw him during each of my three visits and we kept on writing.

Did you believe his sincerity?

Yes, I certainly do believe it. Why would he continue to write to me? Because I had so many friends, I had deep feelings. It really got to me, all these years. The friendships existed beyond Hitler. Should I have been so shortsighted and not gone beyond? You can't do that! A human being is a human being, and if they feel differently now, so they feel differently after what had happened. I felt differently, too, and I let it happen that I had those friends still. And they were wonderful to me. Their lives had changed. So they went with Hitler? Maybe if I had not been Jewish and put under pressure, I might have done the same. What do I know? Would I have had the strength not to go along with them? We had long conversations. They were all real.

Returning to the first years in Los Angeles, how did you express your hatred of Germany? Did you boycott products?

No. Many people did. Of course I hated Germany at the beginning. I felt once in a while like a traitor. People wouldn't buy a Volkswagen, even sit in one. But it was a good car, so we bought one. I didn't feel good about it. A lot about Germany still bothers me. But still I went there. Some people wouldn't look at it anymore. Anyway, I don't *belong* in Germany anymore. On the other hand, that Hitler was *one* man—such a weird human being who brought all that on. Why should I bow to him? We had to change our lives. That was a matter of survival. But now, it's the past. It's history and we survived it. So I don't give it much thought. I rather live in the now. What happened isn't important anymore at this time of my life. Life goes on, and every human being has its destiny.

Did you speak German or English once you came to Los Angeles?

We spoke English. I learned it in England.

Did you make a conscious effort to speak only English?

Not especially. We just spoke like we do now, mostly English. It didn't matter. We both knew English.

When Miri was born did you want her to learn German?

We spoke English to her. But we wanted her to know German, too. There was a conflict. Should it be German, or why not speak French to her? We both knew French. We asked a psychologist whether we should start a second language with her. He was of the opinion that it would confuse her. So we didn't try until later. We did again when she started school, when she was seven or eight years old. But Miri didn't want to know German because of all that history behind it. She knew of course why we were here. She was very sensitive and not too stable. We stopped pushing her. She knows German a little bit anyway. But we didn't teach it to her anymore and we didn't speak to her anymore in German. Now she loves French and hates German!

When you first came, what was your attitude about being Jewish? Did you feel more Jewish or less Jewish than before?

Probably more. I wasn't ever very Jewish. I was a Jew, I mean positively. When I was in Stuttgart and in training to become a gym teacher, I lived with a lovely family, not Jewish. There were several other young people rooming there. There was one other Jewish girl. She didn't want to be Jewish. That made me so angry. I remember once at dinner I said, "Come on, you are Jewish." I couldn't take her attitude! I was Jewish, but not religiously. I'm born that way and that's the way I am.

Were there any Jewish traditions in your home?

In that small town, oh yes. All the holidays were observed. Not strictly at home, but we had all the holidays and we didn't go to school on the High Holidays. In such a small town you were 10 times Jewish! In the street, kids cussed us out! "*Jud . . .*" [Jew!] It was everywhere! So we called back, "*Christ . . .*" [Gentile!] At that time you could still do that. Oh yes, they were nasty to us! They threw rocks after us. Everybody knew who did it. Anti-Semitism was and is everywhere. I don't think it will ever die out.

Did you ever experience an anti-Semitic incident in this country?

Not directly, but I feel it. I know it's here. It's the way it is in the world. It just exists, no matter what you do. Neo-Nazism is spreading in this country, too.

It's interesting that even though you feel this way, you've had many close friends who weren't Jewish.

Yes, and in these relationships we had very interesting conversations that hopefully helped others understand us as Jews better. In the community [a retirement community] where we now live, there are maybe 10 Jews and we are closer to them than maybe anybody else. But with the others I am close, too. I am lucky with people.

You're the first person with whom I've discussed these things who has really said to me, "A person is a person—regardless." Also, you distinguish between a German and a Nazi. Many of your fellow immigrants seem less inclined to do that. That you could go back to Germany and still remember how you felt about those people as human beings and reestablish connections is unusual.

But they were wonderful to me! When I left, they sent me books. That's honesty. It's from way back.

While in Germany, you must have had some ideas about life in America. Did it turn out to be anything like you expected?

In the little town I was born in, there were quite a few "old" Jews who had immigrated to America and became very successful. One was the founder of Universal Film Studios; Lämmle was his name. He came back often in summer. We called him King Charles and his entourage. He gave many affidavits to people in my town. I knew America would be better than the old country. We looked forward to coming here and making a life for ourselves.

Is there some person, an incident, a phrase, or some object that was of special significance in sustaining you through those very difficult immigration years?

All I can think of was that I was married to Ernest and he was a strong person. He went forward and he arranged everything. All I had to do was follow him. I was very happy.

Did you talk much about the immigration years with Ernest, Miriam, or others?

No. Just silence. Who wants to bring that back? If people asked questions, I'd answer. But otherwise I wouldn't bring it up. We were too busy thinking of other things.

ERNEST WOLF

Ernest M. Wolf

Ernest Wolf had just completed his Ph.D. in French when the doors to academia were closed to Jews in Germany. For the next six years, he taught prospective Jewish emigrants the languages they might need—English, Spanish, French, Hebrew. Thanks to his teaching skills, Ernest and his new wife, Hedy, were able to leave Germany when Ernest became the principal of a boarding school in Sweden. The school was also a center for young people who were learning agricultural skills for immigration to Palestine. Ernest and Hedy learned too, hoping to be among those admitted to Palestine.

I finished my studies in 1934, one year after Hitler came to power. I was in Bonn to earn my Ph.D. Jews were not allowed to become professors or teachers anymore. So I went back to my hometown, Dortmund, and taught English, French, and Spanish to prospective emigrants. That was everybody, practically, in the classes the Jewish community had developed for such purposes. After I had done that for a year, I got a position at the Jüdische Landschulheim Herrlingen in southern Germany. It was a boarding school.

I taught there from '35 to '37. That's where I met Hedy, and we married. During those two years, I taught mostly foreign languages, including modern Hebrew, which I had acquired partly though the Zionist movement, partly through my profession as a linguist. At the school you were away from the rest of the population. It was a very close-knit school, and you lived there a completely Zionist- and Jewish-oriented life.

It was clearly becoming more and more dangerous for Jews in Germany. The principal of the school in Germany recommended me to the principal of a similar school in southern Sweden, another boarding school for Jewish children. In '37 we moved from Germany to Sweden. The school of which I was the principal, a school for Jewish refugee children, was also a cultural center for training young people for immigration to Palestine. We taught them modern Hebrew and Jewish history and civilization. We didn't teach them how to work on the land. For that, they were distributed with farmers in the area. It was near Lund in southern Sweden. Hedy and I wanted to prepare for the possibility of going to Palestine, so we too went on *hachsharah*, which consisted of work on farmland and learning about agriculture. So during the last year we did that.

I should explain why we did not go to Palestine. We wanted to go very much. At that time, you could not go without a certificate of immigration from the British. We didn't get one. Hedy's mother had a relative in Los Angeles who was rich and very generous. He gave lots of affidavits. So we had also applied for immigration visas to the U.S. as early as we could from Sweden, in 1937. Those came first. We left as soon as we got them. It was strange because practically all the students we had at the school and the young people on *hachsharah* went to Palestine. We were like the duck whose ducklings swim away. We didn't go and we sent all the others! This has always seemed very ironical to us. But that's how it worked out.

Do you have any idea why your papers for Palestine didn't come through?

Yes. The certificates were given to people who were in immediate danger of life. We were not, in Sweden. Also, they were given to children. There was a youth *aliyah*. Students of ours came under that category. Among people on *hachsharah*, there was what was called the *aliyah bet* [the illegal immigration]. They went without certificates. Somehow, we were never contacted by the *aliyah bet*. I don't know why not. So, we had to go to the U.S. because we didn't get the certificates for legal immigration to Palestine.

In 1940, there was a special deal under Roosevelt. Ten thousand Jewish refugees were admitted to the U.S. over the quota. We were among those 10,000 admitted under "special status." We were processed faster than others.

Ernest and Hedy Wolf, Sweden, 1940.

We weren't regarded as Germans, just as Jews. I don't know how they counted beyond which quota. Whether French, German, or whatever, it didn't matter at that time.

The war had broken out in Europe during '39. We couldn't go via the Atlantic Ocean anymore. The only route open to America was by way of Russia and Japan. We had to go from Sweden by way of Russia on the Trans-Siberian Railway to Vladivostok. From there we took a Japanese ship to Japan. Then we took another ship to the United States by way of Hawaii. At that time, November 1940, there were the first stirrings of the war reaching America. There was a kind of false alarm. Ships from Japan were not easy to get anymore. Many were cancelled. I happened to have a cousin living in Yokohama who was in the travel business at American Express, and he got us two berths on a ship that left the day after we arrived in Japan. So when we left, there were all the people that had come with us from Russia standing on the dock. We felt like traitors. We were going and they had to wait. Fortunately, the ships were not stopped and others left later. So we didn't really gain much.

We arrived in San Francisco. Relatives of Hedy were expecting us at the dock. They drove us down to Los Angeles. For the first two or three months, we stayed with them in their house. Later, we got small apartments.

Were you able to use your European education?

Not immediately. When we arrived in Los Angeles, I tried to use the agricultural experience first. I became a gardener. No, first I was a plumber's helper. But then I became a maintenance gardener, on my own. After about three years of that, I began thinking more about getting back into my profession. I had my Ph.D. So I took courses at UCLA toward a teaching credential, which I did then get after two or three years. Then I started teaching, first high school and junior college in Los Angeles and Santa Monica. That's the way I got back into my profession. Then I accepted the position here at San Diego State College in 1947.

What do you think about you as a person, in terms of your character or personality, made it possible for you to make so many adaptations to a new life once you got to Los Angeles?

How should I explain that? You *have* to adapt. You have to do the best you can in each position you are in. You have to adapt to circumstances. This is part of being alive. If you don't adapt, you die, like a species. It wasn't easy, but since I spoke the language it was not too bad. I carried on in more or less the way I used to do. I remember when I was a gardener, immediately I made a file of all the plants with their botanical names. I approached it from my academic point of view. I never lost that. In the first months, when I was the plumber's helper, I had to learn American slang. This was very different from the British English we were taught in German schools! But adaptation is the law of life and if you have some brains, you adapt.

What was it like during those first years, being an enemy alien? Did you have to adjust your life in certain ways?

There were some restrictions. Enemy aliens could not go more than five miles from their place of residence. It didn't apply if you had a job somewhere else. You could go there. I had a teaching job in Glendale for a while. Hedy was restricted in visiting me. She had to apply for permission each time.

Was it just that the police wanted to know where people were and to monitor them?

There was a spy scare. All the Japanese were removed to camps. The authorities regarded us as enemy aliens because we were of German descent. The first five years until our naturalization we were actually not Americans.

How did you feel at that time about being German?

It was a very uncomfortable feeling. We felt it was very unfair to regard us as Germans since the Germans had driven *us* out! We thought that the American authorities were very dense to treat German Jews as enemy aliens. It didn't make sense. But that's the bureaucratic mind.

How in those years did you express your hatred of Germany? Did you boycott German products?

It was hatred of Nazis, not of Germany. We did not boycott German products. In fact, about 12 years later, when we acquired a new car, we bought a Volkswagen. Many of our friends didn't approve of that.

Of course we were very much up in arms against the Nazis. I remember I started writing articles in my field. The first article I wrote was about Nazi taint and ideology among German professors at universities here. Some textbooks published here showed strong Nazi leanings. That article was rejected by the journal I sent it to because they felt it was too aggressive, too negative.

My feelings were against Nazis, not Germans. We made many German friends here—not Jews.

How long after the war was this?

About 10 years after we came. Also, although my field was French and Romance languages, actually I taught German mostly because the college needed a German professor. So through that, too, I had contact with non-Jewish Germans. We're still seeing some of them.

If you had come into contact with Germans while you were still in Los Angeles, would you have avoided them?

I don't think so because, as I said, I made the distinction between Nazis and Germans. Not all Germans were Nazis, though they were not active in resisting. I tried to judge people as persons. We later met people that had been in the SS, but they turned around and were sorry. Others were not. With those who were not, I didn't make contact for long. But the others I took as persons. I tried to not judge people in aggregate, like all Germans are bad, or all Jews are good. Some Germans are bad, some Germans are good.

When was the first time you went back to Germany? What did it feel like to go back to your hometown?

After we had been in San Diego for a while, I started to organize and lead study tours to Europe. The first time I brought students to Dortmund was in 1955. It felt terrible. I couldn't believe that people could be so self-satisfied and carry on the old ways as if nothing had happened. For me, it was like visiting a huge cemetery. That's what I told one of my friends. He asked why I didn't move back to Germany. "I can't live in a cemetery." This was a non-Jewish person, but he could understand.

So your first visit back was in a professional context, leading your students. That must have been especially strange. It was a traumatic personal voyage, and you had students to whom you had to relate in an academic way.

It was an emotional trip, but still I could tell them from experience about recent history. Since I had lived through it, I could make it vivid for them. As we know, Germany later developed toward a stable democracy. But there remains a residue of emotional rejection of what happened during those dreadful years. Now the whole business has become a vast industry—Holocaust and so on. Technically, we are not Holocaust survivors because we weren't in concentration camps. We're Hitler refugees. But I don't know why they make this distinction.

Did you speak English fluently before you came here?

I taught it.

When you spoke with Hedy, what language did you use, and when Miriam was born, how did you deal with the two languages?

Hedy and I spoke English with each other. We just slipped into it, I think. We tried to teach German to Miriam, just as a language, because we felt it would somehow help her. But she didn't take very much to it.

With Miriam, did you teach it as a foreign language, or did you just talk to her?

Like a foreign language. In fact, one of our non-Jewish German friends had a daughter who was a little older than Miriam and we hired her for some time to teach Miriam. Miriam was about 10 then.

What about when she was younger, two or three?

We tried to speak German to her and answer only in German when she talked to us. I'll never forget, when she was four or five years old, she planted herself in front of me with her hands on her hips and said, "Daddy, I was born speaking English and I want to stay that way!" She rejected German. It seems that her generation has rejected Germans and the German language more than we did. Now she can speak it but doesn't like to.

I'm interested in what your attitude was during those early years in Los Angeles about being a Jew. Did the war accentuate your Jewishness or push you away from it?

I was very active. I became a teacher in Sunday schools very soon. I was a member of the University Synagogue, which has moved, in the meantime, to Westwood. There is a plaque on which my name as cofounder is listed. So yes, I was quite active. The experiences of the Nazi time made me much more conscious of being Jewish. Afterward, I wrote an article about Martin Buber for American journals and kept up on Jewish things. That continued. I was involved in the Zionist organization. I founded the Hillel councillorship here on the San Diego campus.

In those early years, did you encounter any anti-Semitic incidents, either personally or by observation?

I can't remember any particular incident. In fact, I can only marvel that there were none. Everybody tried to help us. I tried consciously not to blame any of my nonsuccesses on anti-Semitism, because if you do that, you absolve yourself from any blame and throw it on someone else. That's very immature. So there may have been anti-Semitism, but I tried not to exaggerate. There was a colleague in my department, here at San Diego State who opposed me very much. He may have had anti-Semitic motives. At least other colleagues thought so. I attributed the issue to be one of a clash of personalities. No, I experienced no direct attacks and I don't think any discrimination. On the contrary. Of course what they say behind my back, I don't know.

Who were you first friends when you came to L.A., and how did your social network begin to grow?

I don't remember how we met the *Gruppe*. I think we first met the **Iken-bergs** through a local Zionist group. I met Fred once through this affiliation already in Germany. I think that was the first connection here. I also knew

Rudy Brook, but I don't think he joined the *Gruppe* until sometime later. He had been employed at the Jewish Landschulheim in Sweden where I was principal. He came over before us and worked as a gardener. When I was a gardener here, I worked for a short time with him.

What would you say was the purpose of the Gruppe*? What was the* Gruppe *like? What happened at meetings?*

The *Gruppe* was human and social contact. They were just social occasions. We talked about our worries and experiences. It was a mixture of social and ideological matters. With the **Ikenbergs,** it was also Zionism—how to try to fit into the American Zionist and Jewish structure, organizations, and community. We had long discussions about whether we should form a separate group of German Jewish Zionists or integrate into the existing Zionist organizations here. We tried to keep separate, but this was a great mistake, I think. We should have immediately tried to join the others and become active within the structure. But it was so different from what we were used to. Here it was mostly fund raising and religion. In Germany, it was more practical work of preparation for immigration.

Did you see any of the people outside of meetings as well?

Yes. The *Gruppe* didn't meet regularly. It was not an organization. It was an informal social unit. It didn't have schedules, a constitution, or anything like that! Sometimes we met people singly, sometimes we visited them, sometimes they visited us, sometimes there were invitations with several of them. It was very informal.

If somebody says to you, "What are you?" do you say, "I am an American," and feel it unequivocally?

No, I can't say that. I'm an American because I live in this country and it has been good to me. I made a career, published books and other things, but I don't think I can ever feel like an American who was *born* here. I have too much baggage carrying with me. I'm a European American, not 100 percent American. I can't feel like that.

Were there family traditions you experienced as a child, Jewish or not, that you brought with you and established in your family here?

No. My family did not do such things because my father died in the First World War, fighting on the German side. My mother had three boys to bring up and a store to run. She didn't have much time. Later she remarried. The second husband was pleasant enough, but it didn't make for a strong family to develop. So there was nothing that I could carry over here.

Was your Jewishness something that you found on your own?

That was something that I acquired on my own through my involvement with the Zionist movement.

Did your brothers become as Jewish as you did?

One brother, my twin, immigrated to Palestine. But he was no great Zionist. It was because of circumstances. The other brother, a few years older, went to South America. Later he came to this country and lived in San Francisco. For a year or two he came to San Diego because he had a nervous breakdown, and I brought him down here into a home. Then he went back to Germany, to a home there. About half a year afterward, he died there. So there were no family traditions I could carry on here because really the family was not very close-knit.

Was America anything like you imagined it would be, either when growing up or just prior to your immigration? In what ways is it similar or different from expectations?

That's a big question that's hard to answer. I was impressed of course by the tremendous size and vastness of this country and by the great tolerance for other people, at least if they're white. I was impressed too by the beauty of the landscape in the western states. When we became a little more affluent, we traveled and camped in these areas. We discovered the Indians who are still here and I became very interested in them. As a child, my only acquaintance with America was through the *Lederstrumpf Geschichten* (*Leatherstocking Tales*), in which James Fenimore Cooper told about Indians and the conquest of the frontier. That was well known all over the world. We played Indians, like cops and robbers.

German children played cowboys and Indians?

Oh yes. Very intensely. Since then, I've had an interest in Indians. We traveled through the part of America where the *Leatherstocking Tales* took place. Maybe that book subconsciously accounts for my great interest in Indians now.

Returning to my question, was America anything like you expected?

No. I didn't expect such great clashes of differences between the espoused and actual values that people follow. But you have to take the bad with the good. You have to adapt. After all, it was the only country that took Jews in, except Palestine and South America. Anyway, we came here as refugees and we were accepted, were not subjected to discrimination, and could exercise our professions. We have every reason to be grateful and not too critical of this country.

Did you talk to Miriam about your immigration years? Did she ask questions?

No, I tried not to dwell too much on the past. Hedy does much more of that. Hedy told her. I thought one should look forward, not backward. It would hinder you psychologically. So I never talked much about it to Miriam.

Did you keep it out of your own mind?

No, of course not. But I didn't dwell upon it with others.

Epilogue

In this collection of oral histories, the contributors are an unusually homogeneous group who lived through the same limited period of history. Beyond that, as the *Gruppe,* they really did share a common past. Yet while they may speak of the same or similar events, the experiences and perceptions of these events are as dissimilar as the individuals themselves. Some differences may be attributed to the vagaries of memory, but only some. I find it particularly fascinating to read the histories of spouses, one directly after the other, to get two views, often quite disparate, of what was primarily a shared life. Additionally, because all participants responded to the same basic questions, their voices join together to create a powerful and richly textured panorama of a shared history.

I have spent many hours with members of the *Gruppe,* with them directly and with their recorded words. My impression is that these people seem amazingly "normal." True, they did not experience cataclysmic affronts and tortures as camp survivors or suffer annihilation of their immediate families. Those men who were in concentration camps were so before death was a commonplace phenomenon. And among the *Gruppe,* "only" a single parent of five and the siblings of two were killed. While most lost varying numbers of aunts, uncles, and cousins, some lost none. Generally, family trees of Holocaust survivors (as differentiated from Hitler refugees) are drastically more grim. Nevertheless, *Gruppe* members went through extraordinary upheaval, fear, and loss. I expected to find more evidence of damage.

Instead, I found that the contributors told their stories without bitterness or anger, many with a sense of adventure and even humor. They did not portray themselves as heroes or victims but as ordinary people doing what they could to survive and taking one step at a time in a climate of increasing threats to their existence. At critical junctures, they took their lives in hand, made and acted on decisions, and, as most emphasized, had good luck. Continuing this pattern, they adapted to yet again new conditions in the United States. Thus, despite having lost family, home, friends, profession, and status, some of them could describe their first years here as the best of their lives, a period lived intensely and simply.

I found myself wondering if there was some universal motif that kept these people moving ahead against such adversity. When asked directly what helped them cross over from a world of persecution to one of promise, all readily acknowledged that their partner was essential in their ability to survive. If I look at the histories, it becomes clear that despite all the misery that other human beings inflicted on them, there were many instances of compassion and assistance from other people. Time and time again, individuals and organizations, both in Europe and the United States, provided help. And although many attributed their opportunities to "luck," there was often a caring person behind that luck. In Los Angeles, individuals of the *Gruppe* supported one another, again affirming the significance of connection among people. Human relationship lay at the core of survival.

In *Against All Odds*, William Helmreich suggests that there are 10 general traits, or qualities, present in those survivors who were able to lead positive and useful lives following the war. Although his study sample was of survivors, the same characteristics are clear among the *Gruppe* refugees: (1) flexibility, (2) assertiveness, (3) tenacity, (4) courage, (5) optimism, (6) intelligence, (7) distancing ability, (8) group consciousness, (9) assimilation of the knowledge that they survived, and (10) a sense of meaningfulness in life.[1]

I would agree with Helmreich that possessing these characteristics also enabled the *Gruppe* members to put their new lives into place in an amazingly short time. Starting from scratch, they struggled gallantly for the first years, found new ways to apply their skills, educational, or professional training, established families, and became U.S. citizens as quickly as possible. By the end of the first decade, most were professionally well established. Although none of the qualified lawyers ever practiced law again, they, like the rest, acknowledged that as Jews, even without Hitler in Germany or Austria, the likelihood of employment in any profession would have been slim. In Los Angeles, most in the *Gruppe* attained a high level of achievement and financial success. At the time these interviews were collected, all were in their late 70s or early 80s and some were still working in their professions.

Making a new home and establishing a family was critical for all in the *Gruppe*. Within the first few years, five of the 11 couples had one child; the rest had two. This low birth rate was true also among the other couples in the original *Gruppe*. I suspect most couples did not have larger families because of what in those days was their advanced age for parenting and financial concern. None of the couples in the *Gruppe* divorced each other, which concurs with established documentation of a very low divorce rate among survivors. Of the 14 individuals interviewed directly, 11 remain alive as of this writing.

Of the 17 *Gruppe* children, all but two married and nearly all had two children. Two of the children married each other. I am one of those who did not marry and have a family; for me, this book has become a means of passing on my heritage. Almost all children remained in California, and nearly all attained a master's, doctorate, or law degree (surprise, no M.D.s!). They have intermarried and divorced at rates comparable to those of their Jewish peers.

When I distributed this collection of interviews to the *Gruppe,* I was amazed at the dispassionate response. I had anticipated excitement, enthusiasm, or at least appreciation. One *Gruppe* member explained. Emigration and immigration were periods of intensity, living on the edge, taking risks, feeling great hope. Participants had been in the prime of their lives, full of youthful energy and anticipation. In hindsight, those bygone days were for many the emotionally richest of their lives—lives now coming to an end. Their own words, their own lives, were becoming history.

Note

1. William B. Helmreich, *Against All Odds* (New York: Simon & Schuster, 1992), 267–68.

Appendix A:

Timeline of Some Key Events during the Third Reich

1933 January   Adolf Hitler appointed Reich chancellor.

March   Dachau, first concentration camp in Germany, established.

April   Jewish stores boycotted. Jews dismissed from civil service (teachers included).

May   Jews dismissed from universities and the press. Books by Jews and by opponents of Nazism burned in public.

July   Nazi Party proclaimed by law the one and only legal political party in Germany.

October   Withdrawal of Germany from the League of Nations.

1935 May   Jews barred from restaurants, shops, public benches.

September   Basic anti-Jewish legislation passed at Nuremberg.

1937 November   Germany and Japan sign a political and military treaty.

1938 March   *Anschluss:* Austria is annexed to the Third Reich.

September   Munich Conference: Britain and France agree to the German annexation of part of Czechoslovakia.

October   "Aryanization" of property of German Jews begins. Jews of Polish citizenship expelled from Germany.

November   Herschel Grynszpan assassinates Ernst vom Rath of the German Embassy in Paris. *Kristallnacht:* anti-Jewish riots in Germany and Austria—30,000 Jews arrested, 191 synagogues destroyed, 7,500 shops looted. Jewish children forbidden in public schools.

December   *Aliya Bet* established in Palestine.

1939 March   Germany occupies the rest of Czechoslovakia.

September   Germany invades Poland: beginning of World War II. The Reich issues a decree to establish ghettos in occupied Poland. Britain and France declare war on Germany. Red Army invades eastern Poland.

1940	April	Germany occupies Denmark and southern Norway. Heinrich Himmler issues directive to establish Auschwitz.
	May	Germany undertakes massive invasion of Holland, Belgium, and France.
	October	Nazis establish Warsaw ghetto, require all Jews to move into ghetto within six weeks.
1941	April	Germany invades Yugoslavia and Greece.
	May	Hermann Goering bans emigration of Jews from all occupied territories.
	June	Germany attacks the Soviet Union.
	July	Hermann Goering appoints Reinhard Heydrich to implement the Final Solution.
	October	Theresienstadt ("model" concentration camp) established in Czechoslovakia. Deportations begin to ghettos in conquered territories.
	December	Japanese attack Pearl Harbor. Germany and Italy declare war on the United States.
1942	January	Wannsee Conference: details of plan to exterminate 11 million European Jews drafted.
	March	Extermination begins, first at Sobibor.
1945	May	Germany surrenders: end of the Third Reich.

Appendix B:

European Landmarks of the *Gruppe*

Appendix C:

Immigration Routes of the *Gruppe*

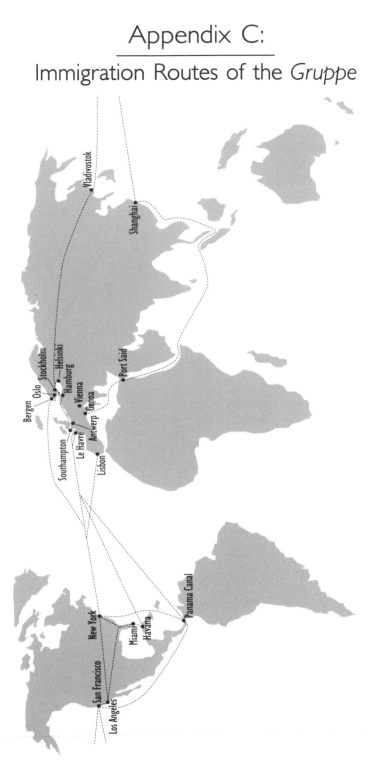

Appendix D:
Gruppe Connections

1. 1928 Dance parties at Margit Loeffler's house
   1940 Margit brought Frank to Wolmans
2. 1915 Through mutual playmate who lived in Marianne's building
3. 1926 Attended same high school
   1947 Mutual friend saw Martha walking in street, called Marianne
4. 1920 Attended same school from grade two
5. 1930 Gretl was girlfriend of Otto's friend, Karl Schloss
6. 1933 Through Gretl
   1938 Attempted to leave Austria together
   1940 Lived in same L.A. apartment building
7. 1925 Attended same high school, different grades
   1941 Through Viennese name dropping between Fritz & John Lesser
8. 1944 ?
9. 1940 Mutual friend referred John to Fritz as coach in preparation for contractor license

10. 1918 Attended same elementary school
11. 1928 Dance classes & parties at Margit Loeffler's house
12. 1940 Worked at Los Angeles Period Furniture Co.
13. 1910 Same hometown. Families knew each other through Zionist leanings
    1924 Formed Jewish club in hometown
    1941 Welcomed Dreyfuss couple to L.A.
14. 1927 On train en route to Zionist fraternity convention
15. 1930 Through Zionist work in Germany
    1940 At L.A. Zionist group meeting
16. 1941 Citizenship classes at Hollywood High School
17. 1938 Worked at Landschulheim in Sweden
    1941 Worked briefly together as gardeners

* Deceased prior to interview collection; included here because were essential link in Gruppe formation

Glossary

Abitur (German).   Final exam of university-preparatory high school in Germany.

aliyah (Hebrew).   Immigration to Palestine or Israel.

Anschluss.   Annexation of Austria to Third Reich, March 12, 1938.

Gestapo.   German state secret police during the Nazi regime.

hachsharah (Hebrew).   Agricultural training facility to prepare Jews for immigration to Palestine's kibbutzim.

Haganah.   Underground Jewish defense organization in Palestine.

Havdalah.   Ceremony to mark the end of the Sabbath.

Heurigen.   Festival of the new wine in Austria.

HIAS   (Hebrew Immigrant Assistance Society). Relief agency that provides resettlement services to Jews immigrating to America. Maintains offices worldwide.

Hochschule (German).   University, college.

judenrein (German).   Free of Jews; literally, "cleansed."

Judensteuer (German).   Tax paid on items Jews took out of Germany.

Kaddish (Hebrew).   Mourner's prayer for those who have died.

Kiddush (Hebrew).   Blessing recited over wine on festivals.

Kristallnacht.   "Night of broken glass." Nazi-sanctioned riots throughout Germany and Austria, November 9–10, 1938. Synagogues and other Jewish buildings burned, businesses looted, 30,000 Jews arrested.

Kultusgemeinde.   The Jewish community council, officially created by the national government, authorized to handle all Jewish affairs and to oversee the operation of all Jewish institutions. A portion of each Jew's income tax was directed toward this umbrella organization.

Magen David (Hebrew).   Star of David, symbol of Judaism.

Matura (German).   Final exam of university-preparatory high school in Austria.

Pesach.   Passover. Jewish festival commemorating the exodus of Jews from Egypt; marked by the Seder ritual and eating of matzo.

pogrom.   Systematic massacre and murderous attacks on Jews.

SA.   *Sturmabteilung,* storm troopers, Brownshirts. The militia of the Nazi Party.

Schikse (German).   Gentile.

Shabbat.   Sabbath.

SS.   *Schutzstaffeln,* Blackshirts. Elite military unit of Nazi party that served as Hitler's bodyguards; later staffed the concentration camps.

tallis, talleisim (Yiddish).   Prayer shawl.

Torah.   The five books of Moses (first five books of the Old Testament) handwritten in Hebrew on a parchment scroll.

Zionism.   Movement with the goal of making Palestine the Jewish homeland, first convened by Theodor Herzl in 1897 in Basel, Switzerland.

Selected Bibliography

Berenbaum, Michael. *The World Must Know: The History of the Holocaust as Told in the United States Holocaust Memorial Museum*. Boston: Little Brown and Company, 1993.

Berkley, George E. *Vienna and Its Jews: The Tragedy of Success 1880s–1980s*. Cambridge: Abt Books, 1988.

Dawidowicz, Lucy S. *The War against the Jews 1933–1945*. New York: Bantam Books, 1975.

Gay, Ruth. *The Jews of Germany: A Historical Portrait*. New Haven: Yale University Press, 1992.

Gribetz, Judah. *The Timetables of Jewish History*. New York: Touchstone, 1993.

Hass, Aaron. *In the Shadow of the Holocaust*. Ithaca: Cornell University Press, 1990.

Heibut, Anthony. *Exiled in Paradise: German Refugee Artists and the Intellectuals in America from the 1930s to Present*. New York: Viking Press, 1983.

Helmreich, William B. *Against All Odds: Holocaust Survivors and the Successful Lives They Made in America*. New York: Simon & Schuster, 1992.

Hilberg, Raul. *The Destruction of the European Jews*. Chicago: Quadrangle Books, 1961.

Hoffer, Gerda. *The Utitz Legacy: A Personalized History of Central European Jewry*. Jerusalem: Posner & Sons, 1988.

Lewin, Rhoda, ed. *Witness to the Holocaust*. Boston: Twayne Publishers, 1990.

Libo, Kenneth, and Irving Howe. *We Lived There Too*. New York: St. Martin's/ Marek, 1984.

Miller, Judith. *One, by One, by One: Facing the Holocaust*. New York: Touchstone, 1990.

Neumeyer, Kathleen. "A Promised Land," *Los Angeles*, June 1985, 170–203.

Phillips, Bruce. "Los Angeles Jewry: A Demographic Portrait," *American Jewish Yearbook, 1986*, 126–95.

Sachar, Howard M. *A History of the Jews in America*. New York: Alfred A. Knopf, 1992.

Sandberg, Neil C. *Jewish Life in Los Angeles*. Lanham, Md.: University Press of America, 1986.

Spaulding, E. Wilder. *The First Invaders: The Story of the Austrian Impact upon America*. Vienna: Österreichischer Bundesverlag für Unterricht, Wissenschaft und Kunst, 1968.

Varon, Benno Weiser. *Professions of a Lucky Jew*. New York: Cornwall Books, 1992.

Vorspan, Max, and Lloyd P. Gartner. *History of the Jews of Los Angeles*. Philadelphia: Jewish Publishing Society of America, 1970.

Wyman, David S. *The Abandonment of the Jews: America and the Holocaust 1941–1945*. New York: Pantheon Books, 1984.

Index

affidavits. *See* visas

Aliyah, 116, 117, 120, 244

Anschluss, 3–4, 37, 79, 135; Ann Ikenberg on, 96–97; Fritz Frankel on, 79; Gerty Frankel on, 51–52, 53; Marianne Wolman on, xxi, 3–4; Otto Wolman on, 28–29; resistance to, 29

anti-Semitism: Annie and Sepp Lampl on, 222; Ann Ikenberg on, 107, 113; in Austria, 45, 87, 107, 178; employment and, xx, xxi, 26, 155, 165, 179; English language phrases and, 71; Ernest Wolf on, 249; Ernie Sommer on, 155; Frank Bauer on, 178, 179; Fritz Frankel on, 87, 91; Gerty Frankel on, 71, 74; in Germany, 107, 120; Hedy Wolf on, 236–37, 240; housing and, 21, 46; Irene and Paul Dreyfuss and, 120, 121; John Lesser on, 207, 208, 209; in Los Angeles, 21, 46–47, 71, 91, 107, 121, 155, 179, 208, 222, 236–37; Marianne Wolman on, 3–4, 21; Martha Schwarz on, 185, 197; Otto Wolman on, 26, 27, 45, 46–47; U.S. reluctance to admit Jewish refugees and, xxviii; universities in Austria and Germany and, 27, 46, 78, 207, 249; in Vienna, 3–4, 6, 27, 107, 178, 185, 207, 209

arrests of Jews: Ann Ikenberg on, xxiii, 97–98; of Ernie Sommer, 150; of Frank Bauer, xxvi, 170; of Fred Ikenberg, 98–99; of Fritz Frankel, 79–80; John Lesser on, xxvi, 203; *Kristallnacht* and, xxii, xxiii, 7, 34, 90, 98, 105, 106, 149–50, 178, 187; Otto Wolman on, 29,

30; of Paul Dreyfuss, 117–18; of Rudy Brook, 124

Auschwitz concentration camp, 117, 160

Australia, xxvi, 12

Austria: activities of Nazis in, xx–xxi, 172; *Anschluss* in, xxi, 3–4, 28–29, 37, 51–52, 79, 135; anti-Semitism in, 45, 87, 107, 178; attempts to escape or flee from, xxvi, 32, 67; Gerty Frankel's feelings about, after immigration, 70; Jewish athletes in, 213–14; Jewish population of, before Hitler, xxii; Jewish population of, with emigration, xxiv, xxvi; *Kristallnacht* in, xxii, 7, 34, 90, 178, 187, 216; Marianne Wolman's feelings about, after immigration, 22; Otto Wolman's feelings about, after immigration, 44, 45; persecution of Jews in, xxi–xxii, 29–31; return of immigrants to, 24, 49, 74, 91, 181–82, 194–95, 208, 229; signing a document about not returning to, xxv, 6, 22; U.S. quota for immigrants from, xxviii; World War I and changes in, xx; *see also* emigration

Austrian Jews: conditions for, before Hitler's rise, xix, 27; economic conditions and employment of, 26, 27; persecution and dismantling of community of, xxi–xxii, 29, 30; population of, before Hitler's rise, xxii; Zionism and, 26–27, 45, 90; *see also* emigration

awareness among American Jews of fate of European Jews, xxviii, 67–68, 69, 106, 130–31, 158, 222–23, 223–24

Bauer, Bob, 20, 111, 169, 176, 182
Bauer, Frank, 109, 169–83; anti-Semitism and, 178, 179; arrest of, xxvi, 170; conversion back to Judaism of, 178, 179; educational background of, 170; employment of, 170, 175; expectations of life after immigration, 181; family background of, 169; on feeling like an American, 180–81; feeling of being at home in Los Angeles, 181; feelings about Germans, after immigration, 177; formation of the *Gruppe* and, 19, 20, 108, 110; friendships of, 73, 177, 180; getting affidavits and visas, 170–71, 173–74; *Gruppe* and, 180–81, 209, 263; housing used by, 175–76; internment at Dachau of, xxvi, 171, 172; Jewish heritage of, 177–79; journey to Los Angeles, 175; journey to New York, 174; life in Los Angeles after immigration, 175–76; life in Vienna before emigration, 169–70; Lutheran background of, 177, 178, 179; marriage of, 173, 179; photographs of, 169, 175, 183; return to Vienna, after immigration, 181–82; stay in New York, 174–75; on sustaining individuals during immigration years, 183; talking about the immigration experience, 182; use of German and English languages, 176
Bauer, Magda, 19, 73, 108, 109, 169, 183; employment of, 175, getting Frank's visa and, 171, 172; marriage of, 173, 179; photographs of, 175, 183
Bauer, Harry, 5, 6, 14
Belgium: Jewish immigration to, 116–17, 218, 223; Nazi invasion of, 37, 117
Berlin, Eva and Rudy Brook's life in, 124
Blau-Weiss youth movement, 26, 162
Bloomsbury House. See Refugee Relief Committee, Bloomsbury House
Brand, Judge Edward R., 101
Brook, Rudy and Eva, 121, 123–28; change of name by, 127; employment of, 125–26; family background of, 123–24; feelings about German things, after immigration, 127; *Gruppe* and, 20, 110, 121, 128, 163, 250, 263; housing used by, 125; Irene Dreyfusss's work with, 118; life in Berlin before immigration, 124; life in Los Angeles after immigration, 125–27; marriage of, 124;

photographs of, 123, 126; Rudy's experience in jail, 124; pension from Germany for, 104; religious observance by, 127; stay in New York, 125; talking about the immigration experience, 128; Zionist activities and, 124, 127
Brook, Tom, 123, 125, 127
Brook, Vincent, 121, 123, 127
Buchenwald concentration camp: Fritz Frankel's internment in, 58, 80–81, 90, 222; *Kristallnacht* and incarceration in, xxii, 150; Yom Kippur in, 90

Canada, 12, 191
Chamberlain, Neville, 33
children of members of the *Gruppe*, 20, 43, 110, 111, 121, 225, 254–55; German-language use and, 21–22, 143, 160, 176, 194, 224, 239–40, 248–49; immigration experience of parents discussed with, 74–75, 91–92, 114, 128, 144–45, 182, 211, 241, 252; meaning of *Gruppe* to, 122; Quakers and assistance to, 135, 151–52, 160, 176, 194, 224, 239–40; using a nurse for, 111
China: Jewish immigration to, xxvi, 29, 188; Martha Schwarz's journey to, 189
Christian Socialist party (Austria), 78
citizenship: Ann Ikenberg on, 109; John Lesser on, 208; Marianne Wolman on, 22
Cohn, Rabbi Franklin, 110, 120
concentration camps, 150; communication with families from, 172; emigration and release of inmates from, xxiv, 59–60, 80, 99, 171; knowledge of, 30, 67, 69, 106, 222–23; *Kristallnacht* and incarceration in, xxii, 149–50; see also specific camps
Congress, and admission of Jewish refugees, xxviii
Council of Jewish Women, 136, 137, 139, 140, 153, 154, 173
Cuba, 205; Ernie Sommer's stay in, 150–51, 152; Theja Sommer's stay in, 137–39, 144, 149
Czechoslovakia, 16; emigration by Jewish population of, xxvi; escape of Austrian Jews to, 30, 56; immigrants from, 18, 188; Nazi invasion of, xxii, 11, 31–32, 33, 37, 135

Dachau concentration camp: Frank Bauer's internment in, xxvi, 171, 172; Fritz

Frankel's internment in, 29, 51, 55, 58, 77, 79–81, 222; *Kristallnacht* and incarceration in, xxii; roundup of Jews for, 55, 98, 79, 170

Depression: in Austria and Germany, xx, 26, 169; conditions in Los Angeles and, xxx; finding employment and, 14, 42, 48, 61; U.S. reluctance to admit Jewish refugees and, xxviii

Dresden, Germany: *Kristallnacht* in, 149–50; Theja Sommer's stay in, 131, 132, 134

Dreyfuss, Heiner, 116, 120

Dreyfuss, Irene and Paul, 115–22; anti-Semitism and, 120, 121; attitudes about being Jewish, 120; educational background of, 116; employment of, 116–17, 118; feelings about Germans, after immigration, 119–20; foreignness of America for Paul, 119; friendships of, 162–63; getting affidavits and visas, 110, 117–18; *Gruppe* and, 110, 120–21, 140–41, 263; initial meeting and marriage of, 116; journey to Los Angeles, 118; life in Los Angeles after immigration, 118–19; life in Switzerland, 115, 119, 120, 121; Paul's arrest and, 117, 118; photographs of, 115, 122; stay in Italy, 116–17; synagogue membership of, 120, 121; use of German and English languages, 119; Zionism and, 94, 120

Dreyfuss, Judy. *See* Navon, Judy Dreyfuss

Dreyfuss, Michael, xxvii, 115

Düsseldorf, Ann and Fred Ikenberg's escape from, 97–98

economic factors: employment in Vienna and, 26, 27, 45, 169–70; finding employment and, 14, 42, 48, 61, 147; German legislation and official persecution of Jews and, xx; immigrants in Los Angeles and, xxx; Nazi policies on emigration and, xxiv, xxv, 28; rise of Nazis in Austria and, xxi; U.S. reluctance to admit Jewish refugees and, xxviii

education: for a better position, 42–43, 64–65, 103; preparing for immigration through, 35, 58, 79

educational background of immigrants: Annie Lampl, 217; Ann Ikenberg, 94; Ernest Wolf, 243, 246; Ernie Sommers, 147, 148; Frank Bauer, 170; Fritz

Frankel, 77; Gerty Frankel, 64–65; Hedy Wolf, 231–32; John Lesser, 201–2; Marianne Wolman, 5, 15; Martha Schwarz, 186; Otto Wolman, 25, 35, 41, 42–43; Paul Dreyfuss, 116

Einstein, Albert, 204

Eisgrau, Siegfried, 19–20, 72, 108, 109, 110

Ellis Island, 135, 144

emigration: as reaction to rise of Nazis, xxiii, xxiv; attempts to escape or flee as, xxvi, 30, 67; bureaucratic barriers to, xxiv–xxv, 171, 187–88; changes in German and Austrian Jewish population from, xxiii–xxiv; destinations in, xxvii, xxix, 28, 29–30, 31; employment offers from Jews outside the Reich to facilitate, 6, 34–35, 56, 59, 82, 173; "escort" used in, xxvi, 32–33; flight tax on, xxiv, 99; from Austria before the German invasion, 27; *Gruppe* and, xxiv–xxv; *Kristallnacht* as impetus for, xxiii; to Palestine, xxvi, xxvii, 26–27, 28, 31, 45–46, 116, 120, 122, 238; personal agony of decision in, xxiv; release from concentration camps for, xxiv, 80, 99, 171; studies preparing for, 35, 58, 79, 243; transport of personal property in, xxv, 56–57, 99–100, 175, 188

employment: Annie and Sepp Lampl on, 217, 218–19, 220–21, 227; Ann Ikenberg on, 101–2; anti-Semitism and, xx, xxi, 26, 155, 165, 179; economic conditions and, 14, 42, 45, 48; education for a better position and, 42–43, 64–65, 103; in England, 6, 8–11, 31, 34, 59, 60, 82; Ernest Wolf on, 233, 235, 236, 243–44, 246; Ernie Sommer on, 131–32, 148, 149, 153, 154–55; finding employment and, 14, 40–41, 42, 61–62, 64, 101, 102–3, 153, 220; Fritz Frankel on, 60, 65, 77–78, 79, 82, 83, 84; Gerty Frankel on, 53–54, 56, 57, 59, 60, 61–62, 64–65, 83; in Germany, 94–95, 130–31, 132, 148, 232, 243–44; Hedy Wolf on, 233, 234–25, 236; 25–27, 28, 53–54, 56, 57, 64–65, 77, 78, 79, 170, 202; John Lesser on, 202, 205, 206; in Los Angeles, xxx, 15, 18–19, 40–43, 64–65, 83, 84, 101–2, 154–55, 205, 206, 220–21, 234–35, 236, 246; Marianne Wolman on, xxx, 6, 8–11, 15,

employment (cont.)
16, 17–18, 18–19; Martha Schwarz on,
186, 189, 190–91; movie industry and,
xxx, 101; in New York, 61–62, 83; Otto
Wolman on, 25–27, 28, 40–43;
persecution of Jews and loss of, 53–54,
96, 203; in Santa Barbara, 16, 17–18; in
Shanghai, 189, 190–91; in Sweden, 125,
233, 244; Theja Sommer on, 130–31,
132, in Vienna, 3–4
enemy aliens: Austrian immigrants treated
as, 176, 207, 218, 219; German
immigrants treated as, 108–9, 118, 156,
235–36, 246; Japanese immigrants treated
as, 108, 246
England. See Great Britain
English language: Ann Ikenberg on use of,
112; anti-Semitic phrases in, 71; Ernie
Sommer on, 160–61; Frank Bauer on,
176; Gerty Frankel on use of, 70–71;
Hedy Wolf on, 232, 233, 239, 248; Irene
and Paul Dreyfuss on use of, 119; John
Lesser on, 207, 208; Marianne Wolman
on use of, 9, 20; Martha Schwarz on use
of, 194; Otto Wolman on use of, 39, 43;
preparing for immigration by learning,
79; Sepp Lampl on, 219; teaching, to
German and Austrian children, 9; Theja
Sommer on, 160
Esslau, Gretl, 19, 102, 108, 110, 163, 263
Esslau, Herman, 19, 32, 33, 38–39, 108,
110, 111, 163, 263
Ethical Culture Society, 195, 196
Europe, Jews in. See Austrian Jews; German
Jews; Jews in Europe

family traditions: Ernest Wolf on, 250–51;
Gerty Frankel on, 74
Federation of Zionist Pioneering
Organizations, 124
Finland: Frank Bauer's emigration to, 171,
171, 173; Jewish immigration to, 205;
Russian invasion of, 173, 174
Fischer, Bert and Lilo, 20, 110
Fligelman, Julius, 103
France: detention camps in, 223–24;
Jewish immigration to, xxvi, 218; John
Lesser's stay in, 204; Martha Schwarz's
stay in, 188, 189; Nazi occupation of, 16,
37
Frankel, Daniel, 51, 74
Frankel, Fritz, 57, 77–92; on adaptations
necessary for immigration, 84–85; on the
Anschluss, 78, 79–80; on anti-Semitism,
87; arrest of, 79–80; assistance to John
Lesser from, 206; attitude about being
Jewish, 85, 90; concentration camp
internment of, 29, 51, 55, 58, 77, 79–81,
222; decision to move to California,
62–63; desire to leave Vienna, 78–79;
educational background of, 77;
employment of, 60, 65, 77–78, 79, 82,
83, 84; experience of anti-Semitism in Los
Angeles, 91; feelings about Austria, after
immigration, 85; feelings about Germans,
after immigration, 86–87; friendships of,
87–88, 196; getting affidavits and visas,
59–60, 80, 81–82; Gruppe and, 20, 73,
88–90, 110, 210, 263; housing in Los
Angeles, 83, 84; journey to Los Angeles,
83; journey to New York, 82–83; life in
Los Angeles after immigration, 82–86;
life in Vienna before emigration, 77–82;
marriage to Gerty, 63, 83; photographs
of, 77, 84; reaction to interview by, 92;
religious observance by, 88–89, 90, 179;
return to Vienna, after immigration,
91–92; stay in London, 60, 82; stay in
Middleton, New York, 61, 83; talking
about the immigration experience, 91–92;
treatment of, as an immigrant, 85–86;
Zionism and, 90
Frankel, Gerty, 51–75, 81, 209; on
adaptations necessary for immigration,
66–67; on the Anschluss, 51–52, decision
to move to California, 62–63; educational
background of, 64 65; employment of,
53–54, 56, 57, 59, 60, 61–62, 64–65,
83; expectations of life after immigration,
74; experience of anti-Semitism in Los
Angeles, 71; feelings about Austria, after
immigration, 70; feelings about Germans,
after immigration, 70; friendships of,
72–73, 226; Gestapo harassment of,
54–55; getting affidavits and visas,
52–53, 56, 58, 59, 60, 61; Gruppe and,
20, 72–73, 88, 110, 210, 225, 263;
housing in Los Angeles, 63; housing in
Vienna, 54, 55, 56, 57–58; journey to
London, 60–61, 65; journey to Los
Angeles, 63, 83; journey to New York,
61; knowledge of the fate of Jews through
letters, 68–70; knowledge of World War
II events, 67–68; on leaving Vienna,

65–66; life in Los Angeles after immigration, 63–65; life in Vienna before emigration, 51–60; living off savings, 58; marriage to Fritz, 63, 83; mother's illness and hospitalization, 53, 55–56; 53; photographs of, 51, 84; on procuring documents for emigration, xxiv–xxv, 59; reaction to interview by, 75; return to Vienna, after immigration, 74; shipping personal property from Vienna, 56–57; stay in London, 60–61; stay in New York, 61–62, 83; talking about the immigration experience, 74–75; treatment of, as an immigrant, 71; use of English language, 70–71; volunteer work of, 57, 58; Zionism and, 65, 70

Frankel, Karl, 59, 60, 82, 84

Frankel, Miriam. *See* Rogson, Miriam Frankel

Frankel, Willi, 108, 110

friendships: Annie and Sepp Lampl on, 224–25; Ann Ikenberg on, 104, 105–6; Ernest Wolf on, 247, 249–50; Ernie Sommer on, 162–63; with former Nazis, 238; Frank Bauer on, 177, 180; Fritz Frankel on, 87–88; Gerty Frankel on, 72–73; Hedy Wolf on, 237, 238–39, 240–41; immigrants to Los Angeles and, xxx–xxxi, 118; Irene and Paul Dreyfuss and, 118–19, 120, 122; John Lesser on, 210; Marianne Wolman on, 6, 19, 22–23; Theja Sommer on, 132, 136, 137–38; with non-Jews, 22–23, 45, 87–88, 104, 105–6, 120, 132, 177, 194, 196, 214, 224–25, 237, 240–41, 247; with other Jews, 6, 23, 137–38, 177, 195–96; *see also Gruppe*

Gaspar, Bela, and Gaspar Color Co., 110, 116–17, 118, 119, 121

German Jews: arrests of, xxii, xxiii, xxvi, 30; conditions for, before Hitler's rise, xix; legislation and official persecution of, xx; population of, before Hitler's rise, xxii; restitution from Germany for, 104; World War I and, xix–xx, xxiv, 95; Zionist movement and, xxvii, 106; *see also* emigration; persecution of Jews

German language: Annie Lampl on, 223, 224; Ann Ikenberg on use of, 112; children of immigrants and use of, 143, 160, 176, 194, 224, 239–40; Ernest Wolf on, 248–49; Ernie Sommer on, 160; Eva and Rudy Brook and use of, 127; Frank Bauer on, 176; *Gruppe* and use of, 141; Hedy Wolf on, 239–40; Irene and Paul Dreyfuss on use of, 119; John Lesser on, 208; Marianne Wolman on use of, 20, 21–22; Martha Schwarz on use of, 194; Otto Wolman on use of, 49; Theja Sommer on use of, 143

Germany: Ann Ikenberg's feelings about, after immigration, 112; Ann Ikenberg's life in, before emigration, 93–100; Ann Ikenberg's return to, after immigration, 113; anti-Semitism in, 107, 120; Ernest Wolf's feelings about, after immigration, 247; Ernest Wolf's life in, before emigration, 243–44; Ernest Wolf's return to, after immigration, 248; Ernie Sommer's feelings about, after immigration, 156–57, 158; Ernie Sommer's return to, after immigration, 158–60; escape of Austrian Jews to, 30, 32–33; Eva and Rudy Brook's feelings about, after immigration, 127–28; Frank Bauer's feelings about, after immigration, 177; Gerty Frankel's feelings about, after immigration, 70; Hedy Wolf's feelings about, after immigration, 236, 239; Hedy Wolf's life in, before emigration, 231–32; Hedy Wolf's return to, after immigration, 238; Irene and Paul Dreyfuss's feelings about, after immigration, 119–20; Jewish life before Hitler's assumption of power in, xix; Jewish population of, before Hitler, xxii; Jewish population of, with emigration, xxiii–xxiv, xxvi; *Kristallnacht* in, xxii–xxiii, 97–98, 105, 106, 145–50; legislation and official persecution of Jews in, xx; Marianne Wolman's feelings about, after immigration, 22; Martha Schwarz's feelings about, after immigration, 194; Munich Pact with, 33; Nuremberg Race Laws of 1935 in, xx; Otto Wolman's feelings about, after immigration, 44, 45; restitution to German Jews by, 104; return of immigrants to, 113, 158–60, 238, 248; Theja Sommer's feelings about, after immigration, 142, 156–57, 158; Theja Sommer's life in, before emigration, 131–32, 134; U.S. quota for immigrants from, xxviii, 5; World War I and, xix–xx,

Germany (*cont.*)
xxiv; Zionist organizations in, 93, 94–95, 124; *see also* emigration
Gershwin, Peggy, 125–26
Gestapo, xxvi, 56, 59, 82, 999, 100, 105, 150; Ann Ikenberg's harassment by, 97–98; Frank Bauer's deportation to Dachau, 170–71; Fred Ikenberg's arrest by, 98; Fritz Frankel's deportation to Dachau and, 77, 79–80; removal of Jews from their homes by, 29, 30, 54, 55, 211; roundups of Jews by, 55, 98, 171; Zionist organizations and, 95–96; *see also* arrests of Jews; SA (Brownshirts); SS (Blackshirts)
Glauber, Trudy, 136, 143–44
Goebbels, Paul Joseph, 96
Goering, Hermann, 95, 97, 98
Goldenblank, Sybil Sommer, 129, 132, 133, 135, 136, 138, 139, 143, 144, 151, 152, 160
Granach, Alexander, 110
Great Britain: getting a visa to, 4, 5, 34, 56, 59; Jewish immigration to, xxvi, 31, 35–36, 191, 215; Palestine and, xxvii
Greene, Mrs., 6–7, 8, 35
Griffiths, James, 7
Gruppe: Annie and Sepp Lampl and, 225–26; Ann Ikenberg and, 19, 108–10, 111–12; characteristics of, xix, 43, 72, 88, 141, 163–64, 254; children of members of, 20, 21–22, 43, 51, 111, 122, 254–55; connections among, 263, differences between Viennese and German Jews in, 141, 163–64; emigration and, xxiv–xxv; Ernest Wolf and, 249–50; Ernie Sommer and, 163–64; Eva and Rudy Brook and, 128; formation of, 19–20, 43, 108–9; Frank Bauer on, 180–81; friendships within, 110, 119, 180; Fritz Frankel on, 88–90; Gerty Frankel on, 72–73; guest speakers for, 110, 120, 125; Hedy Wolf on, 237; immigration routes taken by, xxix; Irene and Paul Dreyfuss and, 120–21; John Lesser on, 209–10; Marianne Wolman and, 19–21, 72; meetings of, 72, 110–111, 225–26; Otto Wolman on, 43; projects undertaken by, 72; reactions to receiving visas among, xxviii–xxix; as representative of refugees fleeing Hitler, xix; support among members of, 234; Theja Sommer and,

140–41; wait during the immigration process and, xxviii; Zionism and, 110, 111, 249, 250
Grynszpan, Herschel, xxii, 97
Gurs concentration camp, Dreyfuss interment at, 117, 118

Hakoah, 45, 213, 214, 217
Hamburg: Ernie Sommer's life in, 148–49
Havana: Ernie Sommer's stay in, 150–51, 152; Theja Sommer's stay in, 137–39
Hebrew Immigrant Assistance Society (HIAS), xxix, 82, 83, 152, 174, 216, 218
Hechalutz, 124
Heibut, Anthony, xix
Helmreich, William, 254
Herzl, Theodor, 90, 93
HIAS (Hebrew Immigrant Assistance Society), xxix, 82, 83, 152, 174, 216, 218
Hillel organizations, 249
Hitler, Adolf, 95; annexation of Sudetenland by, xxii, 31, 33; *Anschluss* and, xxi, 53, 78, 79, 205; appointment as chancellor, xx; invasion of Czechoslovakia by, xxii, 11; official persecution of Jews and, xx
Holland: Nazi invasion of, 37; Theja Sommer's life in, 129–30, 132
housing: Annie and Sepp Lampl on, 219–20, 221, 224, 225; Ann Ikenberg on, 101; anti-Semitism and, 21, 46; in England, 6, 11, 36–37; Ernest Wolf on, 245; Ernie Sommer on, 152, 154; finding, 18; Fritz Frankel on, 83, 84; Gerty Frankel on, 54, 55, 56, 57–58, 63; Hedy Wolf on, 234; in Cuba, 138, 152; John Lesser on, 205; in Los Angeles, xxx, xxxi, 15, 18, 40, 63, 83, 84, 101, 141, 154, 193, 196, 205, 219–20, 221, 224, 225, 234, 245; Marianne Wolman on, 6, 11, 13, 14, 15, 18, 21; Martha Schwarz on, 190, 191–92, 193, 196; in New York, 13, 14, 38–39, 100, 136; Otto Wolman on, 36–37, 38–39, 40, 45; persecution of Jews and loss of, 54, 55, 56; in Shanghai, 190, 191–92; subletting part of an apartment for, 57–58; Theja Sommer on, 136, 138, 141; in Vienna, 54, 55, 56, 57–58
Hungary: escape of Austrian Jews to, 30; immigrants from, 18, 188

Ikenberg, Ann ("Annchen"), 93–114; on adaptations necessary for immigration, 114; on the *Anschluss*, 96–97; on anti-Semitism, 107, 113; on arrest of Jews, xxiii, 97–98; on bureaucracy of emigration, xxiv, 99, 100; educational background of, 94; employment of, 101–2; escape from Düsseldorf, 97–98; family background of, 93; feelings about Germans, after immigration, 112; formation of the *Gruppe* and, 19, 108–10; friendships with gentiles, 104, 105–6; Gestapo harassment of, 97–98; getting affidavits and visas, 96, 99; *Gruppe* and, 111–12, 249, 250, 263; housing used by, 101; Jewish identity and refusal to change names, 103; journey to Los Angeles, 100–101; knowledge of the fate of Jews, 106; on *Kristallnacht*, xxiii, 97–98, 105, 106; life in Germany before emigration, 93–100, 118; life in Los Angeles after immigration, 101–4; on meeting Fred, 94–95; pension from Germany for, 105; photographs of, 93, 102; reaction to interview by, 114; religious observance in Germany, 112–13; religious observance in Los Angeles, 112; restitution from Germany for, 104; return to Germany, after immigration, 113; shipping personal property from Germany, 99–100; stays in New York, 96–97, 100; talking about the immigration experience, 114; visit to Palestine, 96; use of English and German languages, 112; work with Zionist organizations, 95–96, 105, 107

Ikenberg, Danny, 20, 93, 105, 111

Ikenberg, Fred, xxiii, 93, 118; arrest of, 98–99; educational background of, 94–95, 104; employment of, 95, 103, 104–5; experience of anti-Semitism by, 113; finding employment, 101, 102–3; *Gruppe* and, 19, 249, 250; initial meeting and early relationship with Ann, 94–95; pension from Germany for, 104, 105; photograph of, 102; work with Zionist organizations, 95–96, 105, 107

Ikenberg, Ruth, 93, 105

immigration: adaptations needed for new life after, 66–67, 84–85, 114, 141–42, 143, 156, 198, 206–7, 227–28, 229, 235, 246, 252, 253–54; destinations in, xxvii, xxix; differences between earlier groups and, xix; expectations of American life after, 47–48, 74, 143–44, 165–66, 181, 197, 210, 226, 241, 251–52; German and Austrian orphans and, 8–11; problems encountered in, xxv–xxvi; process for seeking affidavits and visas for, xxvi–xxviii; quotas in, xxvi; reactions to receiving visas in, xxviii–xxix; routes taken during, xxxix, 261; studies to prepare for, 35, 58, 79; talent of individuals in, xix; U.S. visa requirements for, xxvii–xxviii; wait for visas in, xxviii, 152–53; willingness of immigrants to talk about their experience of, 74–75, 91–92, 114, 128, 144–45, 182, 211, 241, 252

Immigration Act of 1924 (United States), xxviii

intermarriage, xxix, xxii, 255

interview experience: Annie and Sepp Lampl on, 229; Ann Ikenberg on, 114; Ernie Sommer on, 167; Fritz Frankel on, 92; Gerty Frankel on, 75; John Lesser on, 212; Otto Wolman on, 49–50; Theja Sommer on, 144

isolationism, and reluctance to admit Jewish refugees, xxviii

Israel, 116, 120, 122, 238

Italy: Irene and Paul Dreyfuss's stay in, 116–17; Otto Wolman's employment in, 26; Sepp Lampl's stay in, 217–18

Japanese aliens, deportation of, 108, 246

Jewish identity: Ann Ikenberg on changing names and, 103; Ernest Wolf on, 251; Eva and Rudy Brook's change of name and, 127; Frank Bauer on, 177–79; Fritz Frankel on, 85, 90; Irene and Paul Dreyfuss and, 120; John Lesser on, 208–9; Martha Schwarz on, 195; Otto Wolman on, 43–44; Theja Sommer on, 141, 142

Jewish businesses: *Anschluss* and, xxi, 28, 34; Nazi taking of, 30–31, 54, 131; plundering of, 97; restitution from Germany for loss of, 104

Jewish population: emigration and changes in, xxiii–xxiv, xxvi; in Germany and Austria before Hitler, xxii; in Los Angeles, xxix, xxx; in Vienna before Hitler, xxii

Jews in Europe: awareness among American Jews of fate of, xxviii, 67–68, 69, 106,

Jews in Europe (*cont.*)
130–31, 158, 222–23, 223–24;
emigration of, as a reaction to
persecution, xxiv; racial identity as basis
for persecution of, xx; *see also* Austrian
Jews; German Jews
journeys of immigrants. *See* travels of
immigrants

Kempner, Robert, 104
Kirshbaum, Debbie, 129, 144
Knee, Steffy, 30–31, 36
Koch, Ilse, 81
Kristallnacht, 90, 187; aftermath of, xxiii,
34; Annie Lampl on, 216; Ann Ikenberg
on, xxiii, 97–98, 105, 106; in Austria,
xxii, 7, 34, 90, 178, 187, 216; awareness
of, in United States, xxviii; Ernie Sommer
on, xxii–xxiii, 149–50; Frank Bauer on,
178; in Germany, xxii–xxiii, 97–98, 105,
106, 145–50; Marianne Wolman on, 7;
Otto Wolman on, 34; precipitating event
for, xxii, 97
Kulturbund, 134
Kultusgemeinde: Fritz Frankel and, 77, 79;
Gerty Frankel and, 57, 58

Labor Zionists, 45, 46, 110
Lampl, Annie and Sepp, 213–30; on
adaptations necessary for immigration,
227–28, 229; educational background of,
217; employment of, 217, 218–19,
220–21, 226; expectations of life after
immigration, 226; experience of anti-
Semitism in Los Angeles, 222; feeling of
being at home in Los Angeles, 226–27;
feelings about Germans, after
immigration, 223; friendships of, 224–25;
getting affidavits and visas, 215–16, 217,
218, 223; *Gruppe* and, 110, 225–26,
263; housing used by, 219–20, 221, 224,
225; on immigrating to the United States,
xxvii, 215–16, 217–18; journey to Los
Angeles, 216, 217, 218; knowledge of the
fate of Jews, 222–23, 223–24;
Kristallnacht and, 216; life in Los Angeles
after immigration, 218–21; life in Vienna
before emigration, 213–16, 218;
photographs of, 213, 228; reaction to
interview by, 229; religious observance
by, 221; return to Vienna, after
immigration, 229; sports activities and,
213–14, 219, 222; sustaining individuals
during immigration years, 227; use of
English language by, 219; use of German
language by, 223, 224
Lampl, Hans, 218, 220, 221
Lampl, John, 213, 224
Lampl, Lanny, 213, 224
language use. *See* English language; German
language; Yiddish language
Latin America: Jewish immigration to, xxvi
Lesser, John, 201–12; on adaptations
necessary for immigration, 206–7; on
arrest of Jews, xxvi, 203; attitudes about
being Jewish, 208–9; educational
background of, 201–2; employment of,
202, 205, 206; expectations of life after
immigration, 210; experience of anti-
Semitism, 207, 208, 209; family
background of, 203–4; on feeling like an
American, 208; feelings about being
Austrian, 207, 208–9; feelings about
Germans, after immigration, 207;
friendships of, 210; on Gestapo
harassment, 203, 211; getting affidavits
and visas, 203, 204; *Gruppe* and, 110,
209–10, 263; housing used by, 205;
initial meeting and marriage to Ruth,
202; journey to Los Angeles, 205;
journey to New York, 203; life in Los
Angeles after immigration, 205–6, life in
Vienna before emigration, 201–2, 208–9;
photographs of, 201, 202, 210; reaction
to interview by, 212; religious observance
by, 209; return to Vienna, after
immigration, 208; stay in New York, 205;
stay in Switzerland, 203, 204; talking
about the immigration experience, 211;
use of English language by, 207, 208; use
of German language by, 208
Lesser, Ruth, 202, 207, 210, 211, 225, 263
Lesser, Tom, 111, 201, 208, 211
Links, Bill, 4–5, 14, 15, 16, 39
Loeffler, Mrs., 14, 18, 19
London, 215; employment of immigrants
in, 35, 36, 38, 59, 60, 232; experience of
World War II in, 11, 12, 35, 36; Fritz
Frankel's stay in, 82; Gerty Frankel's stay
in, 60–61; journeys of immigrants to, 6,
60–61, 65; Marianne Wolman's stay in,
6–12; Otto Wolman's stay in, 7–8, 10,
11, 34–38
Los Angeles: Annie and Sepp Lampl's life

in, 218–21, 226; Ann Ikenberg's life in, 101–4; anti-Semitism in, 21, 46–47, 71, 91, 121, 155, 179, 208, 236–37; Austrian Jews treated as enemy aliens in, 176, 207, 218, 219; as destination of immigrants, xxix; employment of immigrants in, 15, 18–19, 64–65, 83, 84, 101–2, 118, 125–26, 154–55, 175, 206, 218–19, 226, 234–25, 236, 246; Ernest Wolf's life in, xxxi, 245–46; Eva and Rudy Brook's life in, 125–27; on feeling at home living in, 23, 44–45, 142–43, 165, 181, 226–27, 236–37; Frank Bauer's life in, 175–76; Fritz Frankel's life in, 82–86; German Jews treated as enemy aliens in, 108–9, 118, 156, 235–36, 246; Gerty Frankel's life in, 63–65; Hedy Wolf's life in, xxx–xxxi, 234–35, 237; housing used by immigrants in, xxx, xxxi, 15, 18, 40, 63, 83, 84, 101, 125, 141, 154, 175–76, 193, 196, 205, 219–20, 221, 224, 225, 234, 245; Irene and Paul Dreyfuss's life in, 118–19, 121–22; Jewish life in, xxix–xxx; Jewish population of, xxix, xxx; John Lesser's life in, 205–6; journeys of immigrants to, 14, 23, 39, 63, 100–101, 118, 140, 175, 193, 205, 216, 217, 218, 234; Marianne Wolman's life in, 18–21, 23, 46; Martha Schwarz's life in, 193–97; Otto Wolman's life in, 40–43, 44–45; Theja Sommer's life in, 140–41, 142–43; treatment of immigrants to, 21, 46

Lutheran church, and Frank Bauer, 177, 178, 179

Mannheimer, Ernest, 12, 24
Meyer, Charles and Susan, 110
Meyer, Michael, 110
Miami: Ernie Sommer's stay in, 153–54; Theja Sommer's stay in, 139–40
Middleton, New York, Fritz Frankel's stay in, 61, 83
movie industry: Jewish immigrants and, xxx, 101, 241; Rudy Brook's employment and, 125–26
Munich Pact, 33

Navon, Judy Dreyfuss, 115, 118, 120, 122
Nazis: annexation of Sudetenland and, xxii, 31, 33; Hitler's appointment as chancellor and rise of, xx; invasion of Czechoslovakia by, xxii, 11, 31–32, 33, 135; Jewish businesses taken by, 30–31, 54, 131; Jewish emigration as reaction to, xxiii, xxiv, 28; Munich Pact and, 33; policies on emigration imposed by, xxiv

New York City: Ann Ikenberg's stay in, 96–97, 100; assistance for settling in, 174–75; as destination of immigrants, xxix; employment of immigrants in, 61–62, 83, 205; Eva and Rudy Brook's stay in, 125; Frank Bauer's stay in, 174–75; Gerty Frankel's stay in, 61–62, 83; housing used in, 13, 14, 38–39, 100, 136, 205; John Lesser's stay in, 205; journeys of immigrants to, 12–13, 16, 17, 37, 38, 61, 96, 100, 135–36, 174, 204, 218, 224, 261; Marianne Wolman's stay in, 12–14; Otto Wolman's stay in, 38–39

non-Jews: anti-Nazi sentiments of, 105; awareness of Nazi horrors among, 6–7, 67, 69; friendships of immigrants with, 22–23, 45, 87–88, 104, 105–6, 120, 177, 194, 196, 224–25, 237, 240–41, 247

Norway: Frank Bauer's travel through, 173–74; Nazi invasion of, 67
Nuremberg Race Laws (Germany), xx

Olympic games, 213–14, 222

Palestine: Ann and Fred Ikenberg's visit to, 93, 96; Annie and Sepp Lampl and, 214, 217; Ann Ikenberg's fundraising for, 95–96; discussions in the *Gruppe* regarding, 209; immigration of Jews to, xxvi, xxvii, 31, 45, 65, 99, 116, 120, 122, 215, 218, 238, 244, 251, 252; Otto Wolman's emigration to, 26–27, 45–46
Passover, 88–89
Pearl Harbor, 205
persecution of Jews: *Anschluss* and, xxi, 28–29; avoidance of Jewish children in school, 133; before the Nazi occupation, 27; dismantling of Jewish community in Austria and, xxi–xxii, 29–30; emigration as a response to, xxiv, 28; Hitler's appointment as chancellor and official policy of, xx; *Kristallnacht* and, xxii–xxiii; loss of employment and, 53–54, 96, 232, 233; loss of housing and, 54, 55, 56; loss of passport and, 131; plundering and taking of Jewish businesses and, 30–31,

persecution of Jews (*cont.*)
54, 97; prohibition on taking the bar
exam, 202–3; racial identity as basis for,
xx; removal of Jews from their homes by
Gestapo, 29, 30, 54, 55, 211; restrictions
on movement of Jews and, 132–133,
134; Rudy Brook's jailing and, 124; Theja
Sommer and, 131, 132–133, 134; use of
hospitals by Jews and, 55–56; *see also*
arrests of Jews
pogroms, 106; Ann Ikenberg on, 97
Poland: anti-Semitism in, 157; deportation
of Jews from, 37; Nazi invasion of, 11,
31, 37; World War I and, 25
Polish Jews, 106, 131, 203; in Germany,
deportation of, xxii; hiding of, 97; quotas
for, and immigration, 8, 12, 17, 25, 29,
138, 204
political parties, in Austria, 78
Providence, Rhode Island, 96; Gerty
Frankel's stay in, 61
public opinion, and admission of Jewish
refugees, xxviii

Quakers, and assistance to Jewish children,
135, 151–52
quotas in immigration, xxvi; experience of
immigrants regarding, xxviii, 5, 8, 12,
16–17, 25, 29, 52–53, 137, 138–39,
152, 204, 217; selling a number and,
138–39; U.S. policies and, xxviii, 5,
244–45

racism, immigrant's observation of, 14
Refugee Relief Committee, Bloomsbury
House: Gerty Frankel and, 60–61; Otto
Wolman and, 35, 36, 38
Reich: annexation of Sudetenland and, xxii,
31, 33; emigration and Jewish population
of, xxvi; Hitler's appointment as
chancellor of, xx; timeline of key events
during, 257–58
religious observance: Annie and Sepp
Lampl on, 221; Ann Ikenberg on,
112–13; Ernie Sommer on, 161; Eva
Brook and, 127; Frank Bauer's conversion
back to Judaism, 178, 179; Fritz Frankel
on, 88–89; Hedy Wolf on, 240; John
Lesser on, 209; life in Germany and,
112–13, 134; life in Los Angeles and, 23,
40, 112, 127, 179, 195; life in Vienna
and, 40, 47, 88–89; Marianne Wolman

on, 23; Martha Schwarz on, 195; Otto
Wolman on, 44, 47; Theja Sommer on,
134
restitution, 104
Rogson, Miriam Frankel, 20, 51, 73, 74,
111
Roosevelt, Franklin D., xxviii, 67, 69, 100,
117, 244
Russia, 138; emigration of Austrian Jews to,
27, 67; immigration of Jews from, 41,
102, 179; invasion of Finland by, 173,
174; Nazi invasion of, 11

SA (Brownshirts): Gerty Frankel's
harassment by, 54–55; *see also* Gestapo
Sachsenhauser concentration camp, xxii
San Diego: Ernest Wolf's stay in, 246, 249;
Hedy Wolf's stay in, 235
San Diego State College, 246, 249
Santa Barbara: Marianne Wolman's stay in,
16–18; Otto Wolman's stay in, 39–40
Schuschnigg, Kurt von, xxi, 52, 205
Schwarz, Kurt, 187, 191, 192, 193–94,
198, 263
Schwarz, Martha, 185–99; on adaptations
necessary for immigration, 198; departure
from Vienna, 187–88; educational
background of, 186; employment of, 186,
189, 190–91; expectations of life after
immigration, 197; experience of anti-
Semitism by, 185, 197; family
background of, 185–86; feeling of being
at home in Los Angeles, 196; on feeling
like an American, 196; feelings about
Germans, after immigration, 194;
friendships of, 190, 192, 194–95,
195–96; Gestapo harassment of, 187;
Gruppe and, 110, 263; housing used by,
190, 191–92, 193, 196; Jewish identity
of, 195; journey to Los Angeles, 193;
journey to Shanghai, 189; life in Los
Angeles after immigration, 193–97; life in
Vienna before emigration, 185–87,
197–98; marriage of, 191; photographs
of, 185, 192, 198; religious observance
by, 195; return to Vienna, after
immigration, 194–95; stay in France,
187, 189; stay in Shanghai, 189–93, 194,
199; sustaining individuals during
immigration years, 199; use of German
and English languages, 194
Schwarz, Patricia, 185

Schwarz, Tom, 185, 192, 193, 194
Shanghai: Jewish immigration to, xxvi, 29; Martha Schwarz's stay in, 188, 189–93, 194, 199
social conditions: in Austria, after World War I, xx; in Germany, before Hitler's assumption of power, xix; in Los Angeles, xxix–xxx
Social Democratic party (Austria), 78, 207, 214, 215
social life: outside the *Gruppe*, 72–73; *see also* friendships
Socialism, 185; Annie Lampl on, 221; Ann Ikenberg on, 105–6; Austrian Jews and, 27; Otto Wolman on, 45, 46
Soest, Germany, 159–60
Sommer, Ernie, 147–67; on adaptations necessary for immigration, 156; arrest of, as a student, 147–48; arrest of, by the Gestapo, 150; decision to leave Germany, 134–35, 148; educational background of, 147, 148; employment of, 131–32, 148, 149, 153, 154–55; expectations of life after immigration, 165–66; experience of anti-Semitism by, 155, 165; on feeling like an American, 164; feeling of being at home in Los Angeles, 165; feelings about Germans, after immigration, 156–57, 158; friendships of, 73, 118–19, 162–63, 196; getting an a affidavit and visas, 135, 137, 138, 149, 150, 151, 152–53; *Gruppe* and, 110, 163–64, 263; housing used by, 152, 154; on importance of Theja to, 166; initial meeting and marriage to Theja, 130, 131, 148; journey to Cuba, 150–51, 152; journey to Los Angeles, 154; knowledge of the fate of Jews in Germany, 158; on *Kristallnacht*, xxii–xxiii, 149–50; life in Germany, 131–32, 148–49; life in Los Angeles, 140, 154–55; photographs of, 133, 147, 166; reaction to interview by, 167; religious observance by, 161; return to Germany, after immigration, 158–60; stay in Cuba, 152; stay in Holland, 148; stay in Miami, 153–54; use of English language by, 160–61; use of German language by, 160; Zionism and, 162
Sommer, Sybil. *See* Goldenblank, Sybil Sommer
Sommer, Theja, 129–45; on adaptations necessary for immigration, 141–42, 143;

attempt to sell her quota number, 138–39; daughter's illness and, 139–40; decision to leave Germany, 134–35, 148; employment of, 130–31, 132; Ernie Sommer on importance of, 166; expectations of life after immigration, 143–44; on feeling like an American, 142; feeling of being at home in Los Angeles, 142–43; feelings about Germans, after immigration, 142, 156–57, 158; friendships of, 73, 118–19, 132, 136, 137–38, 196; getting an affidavit and visas, 135, 136–37, 150, 152–53; *Gruppe* and, 110, 140–41, 263; housing used by, 136, 138, 141; initial meeting and marriage to Ernie, 130, 131, 148; Jewish identity of, 141, 142; journey to Los Angeles, 140; journey to New York, 135–36; knowledge of the fate of Jews in Germany, 130–31, 158; life in Germany, 131–32, 134; life in Los Angeles, 140–41, 142–43; photographs of, 129, 133, 166; reaction to interview by, 145; religious observance by, 134; restrictions on movement of Jews and, 132–133, 134; stay in Cuba, 137–39, 149; stay in Holland, 129–30, 132; stay in Miami, 139–40; talking about the immigration experience, 144–45; use of English language by, 160; use of German language by, 143; Zionism and, 162
Sommer, Vita and Geo, 108, 110
Sonderling, Rabbi Jacob, 62, 209
South America, Jewish immigration to, 251, 252
sports clubs, and Annie and Sepp Lampl, 213–14, 222
SS (Blackshirts): Marianne Wolman's harassment by, 5; Martha Schwarz's harassment by, 187; *see also* Gestapo
State Department, and admission of Jewish refugees, xxviii
Statue of Liberty, 13, 38, 136
Sudetenland, annexation of, xxii, 31, 33
Sweden: Ernest Wolf's stay in, 244; Rudy Brook's stay in, 125, 250
Switzerland: attempts of Austrian Jews to escape to, xxvi; Irene and Paul Dreyfuss's life in, 115, 119, 120, 121; John Lesser's stay in, 203, 204
synagogue membership: Annie Lampl on, 221; Ann Ikenberg on, 112; Ernie

synagogue membership (*cont.*)
Sommer on, 161; Frank Bauer on, 178;
Irene and Paul Dreyfuss and, 120, 121;
John Lesser on, 209; Marianne Wolman
on, 23

Theresienstadt concentration camp, 68, 160
travels of immigrants: Annie and Sepp
Lampl on, 216, 217, 218; Ann Ikenberg
on, 100–101; Council of Jewish Women
and, 136, 137, 139, 140, 153, 154, 173;
to Cuba, 138, 149, 150–51, 152; Fritz
Frankel on, 82–83; Gerty Frankel on,
60–61, 63, 65; Hedy Wolf on, 234; Irene
and Paul Dreyfuss and, 118; John Lesser
on, 203, 205; to London, 6, 60–61, 65;
to Los Angeles, 14–15, 23, 40, 63,
100–101, 118, 140, 193, 205, 216, 217,
218, 234; Marianne Wolman on, 6,
12–13, 14–15, 23, 37; Martha Schwarz
on, 189, 193; to Miami, 139, 153; to
New York, 12–13, 16, 17, 37, 38, 61,
82–83, 96, 136, 174, 204, 218, 224;
Otto Wolman on, 37, 38; routes taken
during, 261; to Shanghai, 189; Theja
Sommer on, 136, 138

United States: awareness by *Gruppe* of
fate of European Jews in, xxviii, 67–68,
69, 106, 130–31, 168, 222–23, 223–24;
as destination of immigrants, xxvii, xxix,
148; immigration quotas in, xxviii;
immigration requirements of, xxvii–xxviii;
Jewish immigration to, xxvi; process for
seeking visa for, xxvi–xxviii, xxviii;
reluctance to admit Jewish refugees to,
xxviii
universities: anti-Semitism at, 27, 46, 207,
249; Nazi students at, 78, 247
University of California, Los Angeles
(UCLA), 15, 196, 246
University of Vienna, 5, 15, 201

Varon, Benno Weiser, xxi
Versailles, Martha Schwarz's stay in, 187,
189
Versailles Treaty, xx
Vienna: Annie and Sepp Lampl on life in,
before emigration, 213–16, 218; Annie
and Sepp Lampl's return to, after
immigration, 229; *Anschluss* in, xxi, 3–4,
28–29; anti-Semitism in, 3–4, 6, 45, 107,

178, 207, 209; attempts to escape or flee
from, xxvi, 30; economic conditions and
employment in, 26, 27, 45, 169–70;
employment of Jews in, 3–4, 25–27, 28,
53–54, 56, 57, 64–65, 170; Frank Bauer
on life in, before emigration, 169–70;
Frank Bauer's return to, after
immigration, 181–82; friendships with
Jews in, 6, 88, 23, 177; friendships with
non-Jews in, 22–23, 87–88, 177, 185,
214; Fritz Frankel on life in, before
emigration, 77–82; Gerty Frankel on life
in, before emigration, 51–60, 65–66;
Gerty Frankel's return to, after
immigration, 74; housing in, 55, 56,
57–58; Jewish population of, before
Hitler, xxii, 27, 65; John Lesser on life in,
before emigration, 201–2, 208–9; John
Lesser's return to, after immigration, 208;
Kristallnacht in, 34, 90, 178, 187, 216;
Marianne Wolman on life in, before
emigration, 3–4, 22; Marianne Wolman's
return to, after immigration, 24; Martha
Schwarz on life in, before emigration,
185–87, 197–98; Martha Schwarz's
return to, after immigration, 194–95;
Nazi taking of Jewish businesses in,
30–31, 54; Otto Wolman on life in,
before emigration, 25–34, 45; Otto
Wolman's return to, after immigration,
49; persecution of Jews in, xxi–xxii, 27,
29, 30, 53; return of immigrants to, 24,
49, 74, 91, 181–82, 194–95, 208, 229;
Zionist youth movement in, 26–27,
45–46, 207

visas: affidavits for, xxvii, 4–5, 16, 33–34,
52, 96, 117, 136–37, 173–74, 204,
215–16, 218, 223, 224, 234, 244–45;
Annie and Sepp Lampl on, 215–16, 217,
218; Ann Ikenberg on, 96, 99; arrest of
Jews while in line for, xxvi, 170; black-
market forgeries of, 80; Ernest Wolf on,
244–45; Fritz Frankel on, 59–60, 80,
81–82; Gerty Frankel on, 52–53, 58, 60,
61; Irene and Paul Dreyfuss on, 110,
117–18; John Lesser on, 203, 204;
Marianne Wolman on, 4–5, 11–12;
medical exam for, 99, 150; Otto Wolman
on, xxvii, 8, 12, 16–17, 25, 29–30,
33–34, 38; process for seeking,
xxvi–xxviii; procuring documents for,
xxiv–xxv, 59; quotas and, xxviii, 5, 8, 12,

visas (cont.)
52–53, 137, 138–39, 204, 217, 244–45; reactions to receiving, xxviii–xxix, 11–12, 37, 38, 60; "theft" of, 216; Theja Sommer on, 135, 136–37, 150, 152–53; time limits on, xxviii–xxix, 11–12, 53, 61; United States requirements for, xxvii–xxviii; wait for, xxviii, 11, 58, 152–53
vom Rath, Ernst, xxii, xxiii, 97

Washington, D.C., visits of immigrants to, 14, 100
Weinman, Gerda, 125
Wilde, Cornel, 126
Wohlmann, Regi, 26, 27
Wolf, Ernest, 108, 231, 243–52; on adaptations necessary for immigration, 246, 252; educational background of, 243, 246; employment of, 233, 235, 236, 243–44, 246; expectations of life after immigration, 251–52; experience of anti-Semitism by, 249; on family traditions, 250–51; feelings about Germany, after immigration, 247; on feeling like an American, 250; friendships of, 247, 249–50; getting an affidavit and visas, 244–45; Gruppe and, 108, 110, 249–50, 263; housing used by, 245; journey to Los Angeles, 245; life in Germany before emigration, 243–44; life in Los Angeles after immigration, xxxi, 245–46; meeting and marriage of, 244; photographs of, 243, 245; return to Germany, after immigration, 248; stay in Sweden, 244; talking about the immigration experience, 252; use of English by, 243, 248; use of German language by, 248–49; Zionism and, 244, 249, 250, 251
Wolf, Hedy, 221–41, 246; on adaptations necessary for immigration, 235; on anti-Semitism, 236–37, 240; educational background of, 231–32; employment of, 233, 234–25, 236; expectations of life after immigration, 241; feeling of being at home in Los Angeles, 236–37; feelings about Germany, after immigration, 236, 239; friendships of, 237, 238–39, 240–41; getting an affidavit and a visa, 234; Gruppe and, 237, 263; housing used by, 234; journey to Los Angeles, 234, 245; life in Germany before emigration, 231–32; life in Los Angeles

after immigration, xxx, 234–35, 237; meeting and marriage of, 244; photographs of, 231, 245; religious observance by, 240; return to Germany, after immigration, 238; sustaining individuals during immigration years, 241; talking about the immigration experience, 241; use of English language by, 232, 233, 239, 248; use of German language by, 239–40
Wolf, Miriam, 231, 235, 239, 248–49, 252
Wolffsohn, David, 93
Wolman, Marianne, 3–24; acceptance of, in the United States, 23; on the Anschluss, xxi, 3–4; decision to have a child, 20; educational background of, 5, 15; employment of, 3–4, 6, 8–11, 15, 16, 17–18, 18–19, 34; experience of anti-Semitism in Los Angeles, 21, 46; experience of air raids in London, 11, 12; feeling of being at home in Los Angeles, 23; feelings about Germany and Austria, after immigration, 22; friendships of, 6, 19, 22–23, 73, 163, 195, 210, 225, 226; Gestapo harassment of, 5–6; getting an affidavit and a visa, 4–5, 11–12; Gruppe and, 19–21, 72, 108, 263; helping others to leave Vienna, 7–8, 12, 16; housing used by, 6, 11, 13, 14, 15, 17–18, 176; initial stay in Los Angeles, 15–16; journey to London, 6; journey to Los Angeles, 14–15, 23, 40; journey to New York, 12–13, 37; on Kristallnacht, 7; life in Los Angeles after immigration, 18–21; life in Vienna before emigration, 3–4, 22; marriage to Otto Wolman, 18; Otto on importance of, 38, 39, 49–50; Otto's illness and recuperation and, 17–18, 35, 40; photographs of, 3, 48, 49; religious observance by, 23, 179; return to Vienna, after immigration, 24; reunion with Otto, 17, 40; on signing a document about not returning to Austria after emigration, xxv, 6, 22; stay in London, 6–12; stay in New York, 13–14; stay in Santa Barbara, 16–18; sustaining individuals during immigration years, 24; treatment of, as an immigrant, 21; use of English language, 9, 20; use of German language, 20, 21–22
Wolman, Otto, 25–50, 195; decision to leave Vienna, 29–30, 31–32; educational

Wolman, Otto (*cont.*)
background of, 25, 35, 41, 42–43;
emigration to Palestine by, 26–27,
45–46; employment of, 19, 25–27, 28,
35, 36, 38, 40–43; "escort" for
emigration used by, xxvi, 32–33;
expectations of life after immigration,
47–48; experience of anti-Semitism in Los
Angeles, 46–47; feeling of being at home
in Los Angeles, 44–45; feelings about
being Jewish, 43–44; feelings about
Germany and Austria, after immigration,
44, 45; getting affidavits and a visa, xxvii,
7, 8, 12, 16–17, 25, 29–30, 33–34, 38;
Gruppe and, 19, 20, 43, 108, 110, 163,
210, 225, 263; housing used by, 8, 10,
11, 17–18, 36–37, 40, 176; illness and
recuperation of, 17–18, 35, 40;
immigration of parents of, 36–37; on
importance of Marianne, 38, 39, 49–50;
on *Kristallnacht*, 34; journey to Los
Angeles, 40; journey to New York, 38;
life in Los Angeles after immigration,
40–43, 47; life in Vienna before
emigration, 25–34; Marianne on
importance of, 24; Marianne's journeys
and, 5, 6, 7, 12–13, 23, 34, 37; marriage
to Marianne, 18; photographs of, 25, 48,
49; reaction to interview by, 50; religious
observance in Los Angeles, 44; religious
observance in Vienna, 44, 47; return to
Vienna, after immigration, 50; reunion
with Marianne, 17, 40; stay in London,
7–8, 10, 11, 34–38; stay in New York,
38–39; stay in Santa Barbara, 17–18,
39–40; studies to prepare for
immigration, 35; sustaining individuals
during immigration years, 49–50; talking
about the immigration experience, 49–50;
treatment of, as an immigrant, 43; use of
English language, 39, 43; use of German
language, 49; Zionism and, 26–27,
45–46, 90
Wolman, Ruth, 3, 21–22
World War I, 25, 31, 96; Austria and, xx,
218; German Jews and, xix–xx, xxiv, 95,
251

Yiddish language, 141; Eva and Rudy Brook
and, 127
Yom Kippur, 90
Yugoslavia, escape of Austrian Jews to, 30

Zionism: Ann Ikenberg on, 95–96, 105,
107; Austrian Jews and, 26–27, 28, 45,
90; Ernest Wolf and, 244, 249, 250, 251;
Ernie Sommer and, 162; Fritz Frankel on,
90; German Jews and, xxvii, 106; Gerty
Frankel on, 65, 70; *Gruppe* and, 110,
111, 249, 250; immigrants to the United
States and, 46, 102; immigration to
Palestine and, 99, 116; Irene Dreyfuss
and, 122; John Lasser on, 207; Otto
Wolman on, 26–27, 45–46; Paul
Dreyfuss and, 94, 120; Rudy Brook and,
124, 127; Thea Sommer and, 162
Zionist Federation of Germany, 95, 96

The Author

Ruth E. Wolman is the daughter of Viennese refugees who settled in Los Angeles in 1939. She holds a B.A. in psychology from the University of California, Berkeley, and an M.A. in human development from Tufts University. Trained as a psychologist, she has also been a computer consultant and teacher. She is the editor of *Strength in Diversity,* a book on intercultural education, and has contributed to several journals and books on child development and education.